# Psychoanalytic Therapy with Infants and Parents

D0165396

*Psychoanalytic Therapy with Infants and Parents* provides a clear guide to clinical psychoanalytic work with distressed babies and unhappy parents, a numerous clinical group so often in need of urgent help. Although psychoanalytic work is primarily verbal, and infants have limited language, this form of treatment is receiving increased attention among therapists. Björn Salomonsson explores how such work can be possible and benefit infants, how to work with the parents (especially the mother) and how major psychoanalytic concepts such as primal repression, infantile sexuality and transference can be worked with and understood in these therapies.

Björn Salomonsson argues that attachment concepts, though important, cannot solely help explain everyday problems with breastfeeding, sleeping and weaning, or more recalcitrant interaction disorders. He shows how we also need psychoanalytic concepts to better understand, not only such 'baby worries', but also adult clients' non-verbal communications and interactions. Throughout, he uses extensive practice-based examples and also refers to his research, which provides evidence for the effectiveness of this practice.

*Psychoanalytic Therapy with Infants and Parents* provides a unique perspective on working psychoanalytically with parents and infants. This book will be essential reading for psychoanalysts and therapists working with children as well as adults.

**Björn Salomonsson** is a training and child psychoanalyst of the Swedish Psychoanalytical Association, a psychoanalyst in private practice and a consultant psychoanalyst at the Mama Mia Child Health Centre, Stockholm. He is also a researcher at the Department of Women's and Children's Health at the Karolinska Institutet, Stockholm.

# Psychoanalytic Therapy with Infants and Parents

## Practice, theory and results

Björn Salomonsson

Routledge
Taylor & Francis Group

LONDON AND NEW YORK

First published 2014
by Routledge
27 Church Road, Hove, East Sussex BN3 2FA

and by Routledge
711 Third Avenue, New York, NY 10017

*Routledge is an imprint of the Taylor & Francis Group, an informa business*

© 2014 Björn Salomonsson

*British Library Cataloguing in Publication Data*
A catalogue record for this book is available from the British Library

*Library of Congress Cataloging in Publication Data*
A catalog record for this book has been requested

ISBN: 978-0-415-71856-1 (hbk)
ISBN: 978-0-415-71857-8 (pbk)
ISBN: 978-1-315-84867-9 (ebk)

Typeset in Times New Roman
by RefineCatch Ltd, Bungay, Suffolk

Printed and bound in Great Britain by
TJ International Ltd, Padstow, Cornwall

# Table of contents

# List of figures

# List of tables

# Introduction

Here is the essence of this book in these first two paragraphs: sometimes, babies and parents have a hard time together. Parents may be anxious because the baby does not sleep, calm down or enjoy the breast – or because they cannot love the child or themselves or are too anxious to enjoy parenthood. If we venture to verbalize our imaginations about the baby's experience, we may write: 'Baby worries 'cos things are no good with Mum'. This book thus deals with "baby worries" in two senses of the term: when parents worry about their infants and when little ones have bad or worrying experiences. It thus takes for granted that babies have things on their minds. Psychoanalysts usually refer to them as "representations"; simply put, the term refers to a mental image that combines an idea with an affect. For example, if you think of "horse" you will notice that you are combining a concept with whatever feelings you attach to that animal. This book emphasizes that psychoanalytic theory has always thought that babies form representations about themselves and their parents. We can never prove their content but parent–infant therapy helps in us forming assumptions about them. To do this we also need to address the baby. We do not believe that he understands us literally but that he grasps our communication beyond the verbal levels. Our aim of such communications is to contain his anxieties and the parent's feelings of worry, worthlessness, guilt and anger.

If such dyads do not receive help early, the baby may develop recalcitrant character traits and symptoms. Baby worries may then go into hiding or, as we say, succumb to primal repression. Once we institute parent–infant therapy the baby sometimes develops a specific relationship with the analyst, which merits the name "transference". This book thus argues that classic psychoanalytic concepts are applicable to these therapies. Another example is infantile sexuality, which, as I will argue, may be involved in breastfeeding problems. The book's final point is that parent–infant therapies, just like other treatments, may be subjected to systematic quantitative and qualitative evaluations. Such trials do not only compare different therapy modes but may also indicate for which kind of babies and parents each mode is most efficacious. They may also teach us how to organize psychotherapy for families with baby worries.

The practice of parent–infant therapy is slowly spreading throughout the world. We see this in the increasing number of publications and of participants at international congresses, such as the WAIMH, World Association of Infant Mental Health. Newspapers and TV also show an increasing interest in the psychology of parenthood. A search on Google yields more than four million hits on "postnatal depression". YouTube contains clips of miraculous babies uploaded by proud parents as well as scientific recordings of parent–infant interactions from labs around the globe. No doubt, parent–infant mental health and its treatment is in the air.

This book conveys my experiences of working as a psychoanalyst with babies and parents. I have written it for therapists and analysts who are interested in – or just curious about – a psychoanalytic perspective on babies and parents. I also have another target group in mind; therapists working with whatever age and in whatever setting, for example, couples, groups and individuals. I have a special reason for inviting this group. Every therapist working with an adult patient sometimes gets the impression of talking to a child or even a baby. Beneath the grownup's rational explanations and elaborated theories, the therapist hears the voice of a humiliated child or a bereaved baby. Parent–infant work can give new perspectives on such therapies. Finally, the book addresses anyone who has pondered about the inner world of babies; whether in fascination, joy, puzzlement or worry.

Let us begin with an everyday vignette; we will soon discover that it deserves profound reflection. One-month-old Andy and his mother are in the kitchen. While she is busy he is lying next to her, seemingly happy and content. Suddenly he starts crying. Mum finishes her things and picks him up one minute later. While holding him she comforts him and asks him, "There, there, Andy, are you hungry?" She starts breastfeeding him. If the boy got what he wanted one would expect him to calm down immediately. But as every parent knows this may take a while. He continues crying and glaring at Mum, who responds by saying, "Now, now Andy, aren't you angry at your silly Mum who didn't pick you up at once!?"

Why doesn't Andrew calm down immediately? Why does his mother say he is angry and that he thinks she is silly? One might dismiss such questions as irrelevant and uninteresting. Babies have been kicking and crying since time immemorial without anyone ever knowing why. Alternatively, parents have explained such phenomena by claiming, "He's got a tummy-ache again" or, "He didn't get enough sleep last night". Accordingly, such everyday events would not be worthy of a clinician's reflections. To be true, parents who consult me rarely complain about such trivia, which the British poet William Blake (1994) termed "little pretty infant wiles"; rather, they contact me when things have got worse and worrying. Nevertheless, once you listen to their stories you often learn that the worries started one day as an everyday "infant wile", like the one with Andy and his Mum.

What goes on in Andy? This book will bring out evidence from consulting rooms and infant research labs that babies rapidly develop a complex mental life. They have astute capacities for observation, thought, emotion, intention and communication. I will argue that we may regard a baby as young as one month as an active participant in a psychotherapeutic process. We must immediately qualify this statement by adding the obvious; his emotional and cognitive abilities are restricted and he neither understands nor expresses himself in words. However, he is able to express his dawning mental life through a smile, a grimace, a jerk, an avoiding gaze, etc. He also perceives and experiences our non-verbal modes of communication such as how we hold, talk and listen to him. These abilities, which develop in constant interaction with his loved ones, make him a dawning *person*. He is about to develop a unique mind and he tries to communicate what he wishes, fears, enjoys and detests or, to put it more cautiously and simply, what makes him feel good or bad. He communicates this not only to his parents but sometimes also to a therapist who enters in a dialogue with him.

Taking the questions on Andy from another angle, one might retort that his mother just fancies things when speaking of anger and silliness. Parents have always been challenged to differentiate their fancies from correct observations and then arrive at reasonable conclusions; now the baby is *actually* cold, warm, sick or hungry. This is a taxing task. Every parent imputes onto the baby emotional motives, personality traits and future prospects or misgivings. In our dealings with infants, the line is thinly drawn between observations and imaginings. The latter sometimes seem stunning and strange, since they are rooted in the parent's unconscious. One aspect of the art of parenthood is to cool down and retract from such imaginings. Once the parent intuits that s/he is about to project her personal unconscious onto the child she will realize, "I guess my fantasies made me lose my head". This process of learning how to walk the tightrope between sober observations, fantastic projections and coming back to one's senses is a major challenge, especially for first-time parents.

Andy's mother seems to sit firmly in the saddle. Her tone is amused and relaxed with him and we would not be surprised if Andy soon calms down. The situation is different when a mother feels that her baby *never* calms down and is *always* screaming at her. We are then entering that special unhappiness among young parents called postnatal or – as it is increasingly called – perinatal depression. I will presently return to the doubtful heuristic value of this term. Let us for the moment leave this issue aside and merely certify; a parent's frame of mind is of importance for what she feels and observes about her child.

I have searched for a diagnostic system to pinpoint the conditions for which parents with babies seek professional help. For children and adults, we have the DSM-IVTR (DSM-IVTR, 2000) plus a psychoanalytic terminology covering emotions, conflicts, defences and object relations. For infants there exists "The diagnostic classification of mental health and developmental disorders of infancy and early childhood" (DC 0–3:R; ZERO-TO-THREE, 2005). Modelled on the DSM-IV, it describes baby disorders and the parent–infant relationship qualities. It may well be used for research and is especially valuable for slightly older infants than the ones I will focus on. The challenge with describing emotional disturbances during infancy is that they are volatile and involve two or more persons. As Winnicott expressed it, "There is no such thing as an infant. Whenever one finds an infant one finds maternal care, and without maternal care there would be no infant" (1975, p. xxxvii). His point was that the observable and the unconscious aspects of mother and baby were closely intermingled.

A mother's primary preoccupation (Winnicott, 1956) often results in her describing the problems in a vague or fluctuating way. I have therefore chosen a simple term, "baby worries", to cover any apprehension that a parent may have concerning her/his role *qua* parent, the baby's behaviour and one's contact with the little one. As said previously, the term can also be read as a statement by the baby, suggesting that *he* is worried as well. He indicates this by displaying some behaviour that alarms the parents, or by struggling with what seems like troublesome emotions. If we combine the idea that babies are mindful and communicative persons with our insight that parents sometimes observe babies through glasses coloured by their own emotional suffering, we may safely conclude that baby worries need to be taken seriously and professional assistance offered.

Does this imply that any whim of a worried mother needs to be treated professionally? Not at all; only that when she sends out such signals we need to listen carefully. The same is true if she denies any problems with her baby but we sense something else in our countertransference. If we intuit, in our transient identification with the child, that 'Baby worries, Baby no feel good', we should listen to the little one. To offer a consultation with a specially trained psychotherapist can be felt as supportive and helpful by the mother – especially if we cooperate closely and smoothly with her Child Health Centre nurse. During such a consultation, the mother can decide if she desires further treatment or if our encounter was enough to help her settle things.

This book describes my psychoanalytic work in private practice and as a consultant at the Mama Mia Child Health Centre in Stockholm. Parents who contact me at my office know about my interest in baby worries. They already have a hunch that some psychological problem is lurking behind their distress. I see these mothers (sometimes fathers) and babies in my ordinary consulting-room. Apart from the couch, which is mostly used for changing diapers, there are two chairs for adults and a little one for young children, with a little table of suitable height. There is also a box where a baby can grab a teddy-bear, a frog, a ball and some other toys.

The other cases were seen at the Mama Mia Child Health Centre, which is a privately run but fully subsidized unit in central Stockholm. Sweden has a long and proud history of high-quality health care for infants and young children. Child Health Centres (CHC, or "BVC" in Swedish) offer check-ups up to six years of age. Nurse calls follow a schedule; weekly the first month, monthly up to four months and every second month during the rest of the first year followed by check-ups at one-and-a-half, three, four and five years. They comprise weighing and measuring the baby, providing inoculations, nutritional advice and paediatric visits. In Stockholm, almost all mothers with newborns visit the CHC regularly.

Changes in urbanization, social mobility and family patterns have moved parents, geographically and emotionally, away from their families of origin. Thus, the CHC nurse has become central in helping parents with baby worries. Her developmental guidance (Lojkasek, Cohen & Muir, 1994) is the usual way of taking care of baby worries, via individual contacts and/or in parental groups (Mittag, 2009). She seeks to promote a secure attachment and to detect depression, often by using the Edinburgh Postnatal Depression Scale (EPDS; Cox, Holden & Sagovsky, 1987). If she finds that problems need further attention, she may offer an appointment with a paediatrician or a psychologist from the child psychiatric team. Some CHCs offer infant massage (Field, 2000) and Child Development Programmes (Hundeide, 2007).

The Mama Mia staff consists of nine nurses and two paediatricians. The nurses are trained in paediatric medicine and prevention and also have a keen interest in parental and infant psychology. I supervise them one hour weekly and then I meet parents and infants in psychoanalytically oriented brief consultations and lengthy therapies. My consulting room is next to one of the nurses' offices. It is a bit unusual to do therapy among baby-scales, stethoscopes and diapers, but it works surprisingly well. The vicinity between our offices makes it easier for mothers who feel ashamed, afraid or sceptical to cross the threshold to my room and start talking about their baby worries.

This volume issues mainly from cases where I used a technique that pays special attention to the infant: mother–infant psychoanalytic treatment (MIP; Norman, 2001, 2004). It often implies working in depth and at length. My idea is *not* to recommend MIP to every case of baby worries but to let it help us understand the internal worlds of baby and mother and how they interact. MIP is also a tool for approaching essential theoretical issues. Towards the end of the book, I will report on a randomized controlled trial evaluating MIP treatments. A second volume will focus on brief psychoanalytic consultations and nurse supervisions at the CHC.

Some details on the text: I will use inverted commas, "xxx", when quoting an author or a patient. When I wish to convey what a baby might be thinking, I will use apostrophes, 'yyy'. To be gender neutral, I sometimes refer to the therapist as s/he. In the long run this makes tedious reading, so I will mainly use "he" for the therapist, simply because I am a man. If I tend to call the parent "she" more often than "he", it is because I see many more mothers than fathers.

## I What goes on in a baby's mind? One-month-old Nic

Parent–infant psychotherapy confronts us with important theoretical and technical issues. Some apply already to a boy such as Andy. His mother obviously attributes thoughts and feelings to her crying son. Chapters 1 and 2 examine the logical and clinical grounds for such assumptions. The first chapter brings in Nicholas (Nic) who was two weeks old when he started psychoanalytic treatment with his mother Theresa (Tessie). She had a painful wound on one nipple. Though it healed quickly, he continued fretting at the breast. She felt hopeless in front of the gigantic changes implied in becoming a mother.

I got the idea that Nic harboured differential representations of his mother's breasts; with one there were no problems, but with the other one breastfeeding had been complicated by her pain. I assumed Nic also had two images of mother's mind, as it were: one benevolent and welcoming, the other rejecting and annoyed. He seemed to extend this dichotomy onto himself; bad Nic and good Nic. This may lead the reader to believing that I am repeating Kleinian clichés. However, the idea of infant representations was natural to Freud and, in fact, the entire psychoanalytic theory depends on this assumption. Chapter 1 compares his ideas of what goes on in a baby's mind with those of Daniel Stern, who warned against attributing any ideational content to the baby's affects. Chapter 1 ends at a seeming dead-end; we cannot know what goes on in the baby's mind – yet, as clinicians we run into an awkward and ineffective position if we just shrug our shoulders saying, "OK, the baby is screaming when he is looking at Mum but I have no clue what goes on inside him".

## 2 Primal representations: three-month-old Tina

Chapter 2 suggests a way out of the dead-end; we are entitled to assume that a baby produces and uses psychic representations – provided we clarify that we base our assumptions on a "qualified adultomorphic" view. We observe baby and mother carefully – and let our private experiences inspire our imaginations of what goes on inside the baby. We also check the validity of our fantasies and countertransference by comparing them with observations and the responses to interventions. The possibility of doing such continuous double checks, inwards and outwards, makes the psychoanalytic situation fruitful for studying infant representations.

Every parent uses adultomorphic views to understand the baby. Our therapies challenge us with grasping *how* this understanding comes about. It raises an even more profound philosophical question: how do we acquire knowledge at all? In a naïve mode of thinking, knowledge is a thing hiding inside the object. Our task is to dig it out, look at it and grasp its meaning. The word "insight" is a telling metaphor of this essentialist theory of mind. The science of semiotics looks at this process differently; we do not know about a *thing* but rather about the *sign* pertaining to it, and for which we have created a corresponding *interpretant*. Thus, we create knowledge by computing various mental signs. In other words, we do not reach certainty "by comparing *beliefs* with how things *are* . . . [but] by showing that these beliefs are required if our total body of beliefs is to be fully consistent and coherent" (Cooper, 1999, p. 8). If Andy's mother said, "I know what's on his mind; he's angry with me", we would shake our heads in disbelief. But if she said, "I guess he's angry. That fits with my other observations and his responses when have I talked and handled him similarly", we would be more inclined to believe her.

A semiotic psychoanalytic perspective implies that we regard the individual not as governed by internal drives but by *signs* fabricated in interaction with others. Chapter 2 introduces two French psychoanalytic concepts; the enigmatic message (Laplanche, 1999a) and the pictogram (Aulagnier, 2001). The latter leads me to suggest a term for what goes on in a baby's mind: *primal representations*. I will illustrate the concept with a three-month-old girl whose mother could not decide whether to call her Tina or Christina. This reflected her ambivalence. I was also led to conclude that *the girl's* primal representations of mother were ambivalent. I place primal representations somewhere between Stern's vitality affect and representation in the traditional psychoanalytic sense. During the first year of life, they will become welded together with the corresponding word representations. Paradoxically, this decreases our possibilities of helping the child in therapy. As he starts using language, representations become more rigid and less amenable to therapeutic influence.

## 3 Containment: maternal music and paternal words with three-month-old Frida

The term *containment* summarizes the analyst's work in trying to understand what goes on in the patient's mind and to communicate it to her. Bion (1962a) referred to a mother who perceives and "metabolizes" her child's anxieties – and to an analyst who handles the patient's psychic pain. He did not work with babies but his intuitions and experiences with psychotic patients engendered a theory of how two inner worlds interact: baby and mother and patient and analyst. Chapter 3 investigates how I contained a baby girl who was quite well but who got frantic on one occasion. Frida's mother Kate began therapy during pregnancy. One day Frida, now three months old, panicked between two analytic sessions. The day before, Kate had difficulties in acknowledging her anger with me. This blocked her ability to contain the girl. This, I hypothesized, resulted in the girl's panic, which I could now observe. This enabled me to contain her, while I also addressed the mother's understandable wrath and humiliation.

Chapter 3 argues why we need to talk to the baby about her anxieties and not only via the mother. The term "music of containment" refers to such non-verbal communication: gestures, tone of voice, sounds of words, facial expressions, bodily movements, dress, smells, etc. Stern (1985, p. 56) uses dance and music to portray the baby's affective life. Golse (2006) utilizes metaphors from the world of opera. Being an amateur clarinettist, interplay has always been important to me. Actually, "interplay" only covers half the story of making music. The other part is to "inter-listen" to one's fellow musicians' voices. Parent–infant therapy can be thought of as a trio, where each "musical phrase" may be a commentary to what the other(s) expressed.

In therapy, commentaries are framed in different "musical languages". The analyst is addressing the baby through words, an earnest tone of voice and a sincere look. The baby responds in another language, as when Frida screamed and avoided my eyes. Our interplay had a powerful impact on the mother; she realized that her anger with me had prevented her from containing Frida. Kate told me about this in words, anguished looks and blushing cheeks – and I explained to Frida that her mother's anger had made her awkward in taking care of her. Frida's screams abated as she listened and looked at me carefully. This is an example of the "chamber music of containment".

I label this aspect of containment its *maternal* component; to have an intuitive grasp of non-verbal communication such as voice inflections, temperature changes, facial furrows and tensions, etc. In the *paternal* component we supply words indicating what's on the baby's mind. This function relies on what French psychoanalysts refer to as the "law" or the symbolic order. The maternal aspect is rooted in the illusion that mother and child form a perfect union in which they understand each other without words. The paternal cuts through this illusion; every desire must be transposed into a wish, which must be expressed unequivocally. If the catchword of maternal component is empathy, that of the paternal is clarity. Therapy must rely on both these principles.

## 4 What does a baby understand? Eight-month-old Karen

In this chapter I take a mirror view of Chapters 1 and 2. Now I focus on what *the baby* might understand of our messages. I suggest that a baby grasps quite a lot of what we say and do not say, how we look or sound or smell, how we hold or not hold her, etc. Rather than understanding the *lexical* import of our communication, she is sensitive to its *emotional* undercurrents.

The baby is also an active interactor. Her challenge is to deal with those portions of the adult's messages that are unconscious or enigmatic (Laplanche, 1999a) – even to the adult. I will illustrate with eight-month-old Karen and her mother Miranda. Karen got the breast as soon as she whimpered because, as Miranda explained, she was "terribly sad". I, however, discovered other emotions; the two were angry with each other – though these emotions were unconscious to them. They were stuck in a cloudy mode of relating, which concealed their anger and disappointment. The vignettes indicate that Karen grasped the emotional import of some interventions I made. I will present a conceptual apparatus, which helps us understand the different levels of communication in psychoanalytic treatments.

In Chapters 1 and 2, I argued that truth is not a thing behind a curtain waiting to be "re-veiled". Chapter 4 approaches another epistemological mistake: since babies neither use nor understand words they are non-communicative. This mistake is grounded in an idea that words are the one and only way of communication. Unsurprisingly, our concepts of non-verbal communication are few and meagre. Furthermore, scientific discussions must use words to describe non-verbal communication. It seems as hopeless as to verbalize a sonata, a painting or a dance! The expertise of babies resides precisely in non-verbal communicative modes. Consequently, one doubts if letters or words can do justice to their inner life. Luckily, the discipline of semiotics or the science of signs offers concepts that help us up-grade the status of non-verbal communications. They explicate why sighs, smiles and groans are messages worthy of psychoanalytic interpretations.

## 5 A baby with a depressed mother: 16-month-old Beate

It is time to submit a lengthier clinical story. We will get to know 16-month-old Beate and her mother Nadya. She was a restless and anxious girl, grabbing for Mum's breast when something troubled her. They remained in joint treatment for eight months, and then Beate continued in child analysis. Treatment focused on her troubled relationship with her mother's breast, and on her fear of holes and of ghosts. Nadya's story about her postnatal depression enabled us to reconstruct Beate's earliest experiences. The present restlessness and phobias seemed linked with her earliest experiences of being with a sad mother who could not contain the girl's anxieties.

Peri- or post-natal depression is often depicted as something that strikes a woman out of the blue. I, however, have never met a depressed mother who did not tell me, when we probed deeper into her history, of emotional problems earlier in life such as depressions, burnout conditions, anxiety states, narcissistic personality traits, eating disorders, etc. This concurs with population studies indicating that previous depressions increase the risk of postpartum depression. For a summary, see Misri and Joe (2008). When they become mothers, they tackle the necessary psychological reorientation with defence patterns established long before maternity. A narcissistic woman finds it hard to love her child. A woman with a harsh superego feels guilty at the slightest sign of mishap in her child. An anxious woman will get up repeatedly at night to check if her baby is still breathing. Thus, the prefixes "peri-" or "post-" merely reflect that the depression is linked with the psychological readjustment around delivery. I see it as an expression of the new challenge to her identity as a sexual being, partner, caregiver and daughter, especially to her mother. Perinatal depression applies to women who have not managed to solve these challenges in ways that are satisfactory to themselves or their baby and partner. Some express their discontentment on a depression questionnaire. Others may score optimally but seem unaware of their suffering – or they feel ashamed and will "improve" their scores. Unless we interview them we will fail to understand if something is wrong and what that might be.

Chapter 5 looks at depression from the baby's point of view: how might Beate have experienced being with her depressed mother? I will argue that what affects a child is not the mother's depression per se; it is rather that her sadness, low self-esteem, guilt and self-preoccupation leave little room for her to contain the child's anxieties. This will have two effects. The baby is left alone with her confusion and anxieties, since there is no one "out there" to take care of the child's emotions. Second, she will experience the containing mother as absent-minded and self-centred, or as intrusive and insensitive. This will transform the container-mother into a frightening figure. Beate's case made me realize the importance of early treatment and what might happen to primal representations if they are not moderated in treatment. We will return to this question in Chapter 8 on primal repressions.

## 6 The infant "within" the adult: the case of Monica

I hope this book is relevant for therapists regardless of which age, gender or diagnostic category they are working with. This has to do with a vision of the mind that I call the "Babushka perspective". I refer to those wooden dolls with ever smaller copies tucked into each other, ending with a solid little figure in the centre. The metaphor is in line with Kleinian formulations of an internal world inhabited by internal objects (Hinshelwood, 1989). The innermost wooden doll corresponds to the infantile core of the mind – whether in an adult, a child or a baby.

Working with infants and parents has made me more familiar with these innermost "dolls" in adult analysands. They act like silent yet powerful forces concealed within diffuse symptoms, rigid character traits and pessimistic world views. Chapter 6 deals with a therapeutic stalemate. A young middle-aged woman, Monica, waged war in the beginning of every analytic session. She belittled me while describing herself as worthless. She claimed she could not talk to me but only sway her body while sighing, sweating and moaning on the couch. To me, she resembled an unhappy baby writhing and crying in front of a helpless mother – but when I suggested this to her she ridiculed me.

At that time, I was working with little Nic and his mother, introduced in Chapter 1. They enabled me to observe, directly as it were, the interaction between container and contained. Parent–infant practice brings us closer to understanding how these abstract descriptors materialize between mother and child. Nic and his mother made me see the parallels to my interaction with Monica. As long as she and I did not understand how we viewed the other person, we were caught in a deadlock. I considered my interventions well-founded and well-meaning, but Monica regarded them as the Truth imposed by some authority reluctant to admit his shortcomings. In Bion's terms, our relationship was far from commensal (1970, p. 95). Any intervention may be understood differentially at various communicative levels. The analyst can only hope to provide a reasonably accurate translation – from a more primitive to a more advanced level – of the wishes and fears imprisoned in the patient's "wooden doll".

## 7 The living fossil: Tristan's *Urvergessen*

Richard Wagner was a controversial figure, due to his notorious anti-Semitism and recklessness with benefactors and lovers. These character flaws went hand in hand with an astute capacity to portray his opera characters with great psychological depth and credibility. Many of them were struck by parental loss in infancy or childhood; Siegmund and Sieglinde, their son Siegfried and Parsifal. The most elaborated example of how an infantile trauma remains frozen in the individual to finally crush his life is the male hero in *Tristan und Isolde*.

Young Tristan is drawn towards destruction, dragging along Isolde and his foster-father King Marke. As he seeks to understand his infatuation with Isolde he realizes that all his life, he has been searching in vain for his parents. His father died before he was born and his mother during delivery. During his self-analysis Tristan coins a concept, *das Urvergessen* or primal oblivion. He refers to an enigmatic emotional state characterized by *Ahnungen* or intuitions. Tristan realizes he can never get hold of the memories of his parents. His infatuation with Isolde is a substitute for the lost mother. Needless to say, this project is doomed to fail because one object cannot be replaced by another without dire consequences. More importantly, Tristan overlooks a factor that I see as the prime reason for his disaster: a tremendous rage hidden behind his idealizations of Isolde and Marke. He has a vague *Ahnung* of it but cannot avoid acting it out through an aggressive suicide in front of the devastated Isolde.

This chapter is a preamble to the discussion of primal repression in Chapter 8. Tristan has inspired my thoughts on how the infant deals with traumatic events. My point is that they are registered but in such primitive forms of signification that the baby, and later the adult, can only have an *Ahnung*, an intuition or foreboding of them. Similarly to Monica in Chapter 6, Tristan is still affected by infantile trauma. In contrast to Monica, however, he does not receive any help in filling in these intuitions with more advanced signs, namely, the analyst's words of containment and reconstruction.

## 8 Classical concepts revisited I: primal repression

I sometimes hear from nurses or parents, "The mother will grow out of her baby worries". As I see it, however, we have good reasons not to postpone a therapeutic consultation in these situations. First, unnecessary suffering should be avoided. Second, as I argued in Chapter 2, the young baby's primal representations are still flexible and amenable to therapeutic interventions. Chapter 8 compares two cases. Tom started treatment with his mother Nina when he was eight months old. In contrast, Beate and her mother Nadya from Chapter 5 had been in dire straits for almost one and a half years.

Freud (1915b) used the concept *primal repression* to account for what may happen to our most remote childhood memories, the ones we did not register at the time and cannot recall later in life. Yet, he said they play an important role in forming our character. Not being able to recall something that you never registered – and is still central to your well-being – sounds illogical indeed! Unsurprisingly, primal repression has become a disreputable concept and I wish to re-formulate it into a clinically useful concept. In my reading, it covers emotional experiences that the baby once signified in stunted and undeveloped forms, and which thereupon were left behind during his semiotic development. I thus believe that those experiences, which later will develop into primal repressions, were once registered on the spot – though being only dimly accessible to the baby. This is precisely why these *Ahnungen* might influence the child, like "the deep waters beneath the earth … which never saw daylight but which, nevertheless, reflect a dull shimmer of whose origin we know nothing" as the French writer Albert Camus (1994, p. 300) expressed it.

Eight-month-old Tom wavered between clinging to his mother Nina and trying to separate and find a space of his own beyond Mum's body. Analysis inspired them to cut some sticky strings that had been tying them together. Tom's primal representations were still flexible enough to evolve when I interpreted his ambivalence between longing for and fear of separating from mother. In contrast, Beate was 16 months when starting analysis. We achieved substantial results during treatment, but part of her restless character remained untouched. I attributed this to the fact that primal representations had begun to succumb to primal repression during her first year, when she and her mother did not receive psychotherapeutic help. I speculate that if therapy had been instituted earlier, we might have had a better chance of reaching these early representations and thus enabling the girl to dissolve them.

## 9 Classical concepts revisited II: infantile sexuality

This book's main theoretical question is if parent–infant therapy may be integrated with classical Freudian theory. Today, infant clinicians rely mainly on attachment theory – whereas psychoanalysts rarely apply classical theory to babies in therapy. This is paradoxical since, as I claimed in Chapter 1, Freudian theory is based on inferences about the infant mind. For example, the concept of infantile sexuality is hardly ever used by infant clinicians, whereas analysts apply it to patients of any age group – except infants! I, however, will argue that it is vital for understanding emotional disturbances in babies.

I was brought to the topic from several sources. Once, little Frida (Chapter 3) suddenly smiled at me amidst her screams. Spontaneously I exclaimed, "One is totally charmed". In retrospect I realized that "charmed", with its sexual connotation, reflected my own repressed infantile sexuality, which emerged in the therapeutic encounter. The second source was mother–infant treatments in which I followed the mother in a lengthy therapy after the child had finished his participation. These treatments exposed the links between adult and infantile sexuality. Third, video-recordings of deliveries (Widström, Ransjö-Arvidsson & Christensson, 2007) made by the Division of Reproductive Health at the Karolinska Institutet in Stockholm illustrate the first moments of sensuous or, as I will argue, sexual contact between mother and baby. I have integrated these impressions with Jean Laplanche's (1989, 2002) psychoanalytic speculations on how a mother's messages contain wavelengths that are unconscious to herself and her child.

When the mother is not too uncomfortable with her unconscious urges, the enigmatic messages will nourish the baby's appreciation of his body and joie de vivre, that is, of *his* infantile sexuality. However, when the mother is depressed the situation is different. The natural gushes of touch and laughter, giggles and endeared looks are replaced by a frowning face, an irritable tone of voice or a brusque or passive way of holding the baby. Unacknowledged ambivalence may thus thwart the development of infantile sexual contact between mother and child. This is one good reason not to postpone a psychotherapeutic consultation once a mother seeks help.

## 10 Classical concepts revisited III: transference

Anyone familiar with psychotherapy knows that the patient may perceive the therapist in ways that are emotionally coloured. They often seem child-like, exaggerated and irrational, because the patient transfers onto the therapist emotions that stem from earlier epochs in his life. In this chapter I ask if the term for this phenomenon, *transference*, might be applied to babies in therapy. I will argue that a distressed baby might sometimes evince transference towards the analyst – provided he uses a direct baby address. Only such techniques entitle him to conclude that the baby is, for example, avoiding him because he represents a feared internal object. This was the case with 18-month-old Jennifer and seven-month-old David. They evinced what I name a *direct* transference. Prior to therapy their emotions were disguised beneath various distressing symptoms. In therapy, my attention caused their un-integrated emotions to be connected with me. In the child's mind the formula is: 'This guy puts me in contact with – or is the carrier of – feelings that I fear. If I shun him, I won't be afraid anymore.'

In contrast, *indirect* transference springs from the parent's unacknowledged transference to the therapist. A child intuits that his parent fears the therapist and then becomes fearful of him. The formula is: 'Dad becomes different with this unknown guy. I don't recognize Dad. This guy must be dangerous and I fear him.' The case of nine-month-old Vance in therapy with his father Henry will illustrate this. The boy's fear of me was initially due to the father's unconscious fear of me. The boy's fear was thus indirect. However, clinical reality is always complicated. When Henry's fear was analyzed, Vance's fear continued but now the mechanism was different. The emotional effects of an earlier separation from his mother had not been acknowledged by the parents. These primally repressed experiences now emerged and I came to represent this trauma. At this stage, the boy's fear was uninfluenced by the father's more relaxed state, and he was now in a direct negative transference.

I do *not* argue that every emotional reaction in a baby towards an adult represents a transference. I thus differentiate *transferences* from *transference-like phenomena*. The former are the ones related above. We can only infer them in the psychoanalytic situation, since this is the only place where our investigatory instrument is fully valid. In contrast, transference-like phenomena may occur at a visit to the nurse or to the neighbour. Similarly, when Andy's mother claimed he was angry with her she was describing – rightly or wrongly – a transference-like phenomenon.

## 11 Mother–infant psychoanalytic treatment: does it work?

Psychoanalytic practitioners and researchers doing systematic outcome studies have not always been on speaking terms with each other. Psychoanalysts often claim that the process is too intricate and its outcomes are too complex for any systematic evaluation to be possible or desirable. Researchers claim that analysts ought to subject their treatments to evaluations like any other practitioners. Analysts then claim that quantitative assessments merely skim the surface of the vast and intricate results of psychoanalysis. Researchers retort that they are, nevertheless, the best bet if we want to objectively compare different methods. Analysts reply that objectivity, either in the therapeutic process or in the evaluation of it, is an illusion.

Having worked many years as a psychoanalyst, I shared many objections to quantitative systematic evaluations. However, I began to change my mind. One reason was the increasing demand for proof from those who did not know about analysis from any personal experience. I thought their claim for evaluation "from outside" was justified. Second, proponents of other therapy modes based their claims on systematic evaluations. This increased my appetite for scientific comparisons of different methods. Third, clinical experience had taught me that no method suits everybody. Was it possible to investigate the results of psychoanalysis and find out for which people this method – or another one – would be the best one? To me this was the really important issue, rather than approaching the blunt question: "Which therapy is the best?"

I embarked on an RCT or a randomized controlled trial that compared MIP with the usual way of helping distressed mothers and babies in Sweden; the Child Health Centre care. Chapter 11 summarizes the study in an accessible and comprehensible way. It also gives some clinical pictures of the mothers and babies in the RCT. I want specifically to thank Rolf Sandell and Andrzej Werbart for valuable points of view on this chapter.

At this point, the book reaches its end and I hope to have reached my two major aims: to open a window into the internal worlds of babies and parents, and to inspire therapists to enter this clinical field. Several chapters build on published papers. I have taken care to integrate them into the general framework of the book. Chapters 1 and 2 were written specifically for this book while Chapter 3 builds partly on another article (Salomonsson, 2011). Chapter 4 revolves around a paper whose long title begins with Billie Holiday's words: "Talk to me baby, tell me what's the matter now" (Salomonsson, 2007b). Chapter 5 issues from a paper on an infant's experience of postnatal depression (Salomonsson, 2013a). Monica's case in Chapter 6 was presented in two earlier papers (Salomonsson,

2007a, 2009). Chapter 7 on Tristan and Chapter 8 on primal repression were written for this book, whereas Chapter 9 on infantile sexuality and Chapter 10 on transference have appeared as separate papers (Salomonsson, 2012, 2013b). Chapter 11 builds on the RCT reports (Salomonsson & Sandell, 2011a, 2011b, 2012; Salomonsson & Sleed, 2010).

## Acknowledgements

I want to thank all the parents who inspired my work with them and their babies and who allowed me to publish de-identified clinical material. Among my colleagues, I want first of all to honour the late Johan Norman, whose imaginative and courageous work awoke my dormant interest in the inner lives of babies. Other important sources of inspiration throughout the years were my co-authors Michelle Sleed and Rolf Sandell. Rolf, who taught me so much on statistics and psychotherapy research methodology, was also one of my supervisors for my dissertation project. The other two were Professors Per-Anders Rydelius and Andrzej Werbart. Professor Peter Fonagy at the Anna Freud Centre (AFC) in London offered much valuable help with the RCT papers. I thank them warmly as well as many other researcher and clinician colleagues: Christine Anzieu-Premmereur and Talia Hatzor at the Parent–Infant Program, the Columbia University Center for Psychoanalytic Training and Research in New York, Tessa Baradon and Angela Joyce and the PIP team and Mary Target at the AFC in London, Bernard Golse, James Grotstein, Alexandra Harrison, Miri Keren, Kai von Klitzing, Françoise Moggio and her team at Centre Alfred Binet in Paris, Eva Nissen and Monica Hedenbro at the Division of Reproductive Health at the Karolinska Institutet and, finally, René Roussillon and Edward Tronick. Writing a book takes its amount of concentration. My deep thanks go to my wife, colleague and research partner, Majlis Winberg Salomonsson, for putting up with my sometime absent-mindedness.

The RCT was made possible through generous grants from the Ahrén, Axson Johnson, Engkvist, Groschinsky, Golden Wedding Memorial of Oscar II and Queen Sophia, Jerring, Kempe-Carlgren, Mayflower Charity and Wennborg foundations and the IPA Research Advisory Board. The current follow-up project is supported by grants from the Children's Welfare Foundation and Signe and Ane Gyllenberg's foundations. The Wennborg foundation also provided a grant that enabled me to finalize this book. I thank them all deeply.

Finally I would like to thank John Wiley for their permission to reproduce the following articles in this publication:

Salomonsson, B. (2007a). Semiotic transformations in psychoanalysis with infants and adults. *International Journal of Psychoanalysis, 88*(5), 1201–1221. Copyright © 2007 John Wiley and Sons.
Salomonsson, B. (2007b). "Talk to me baby, tell me what's the matter now". Semiotic and developmental perspectives on communication in psychoanalytic

infant treatment. *International Journal of Psychoanalysis, 88*(1), 127–146. Copyright © 2007 John Wiley and Sons.

Salomonsson, B. (2011). The music of containment. Addressing the participants in mother–infant psychoanalytic treatment. *Infant Mental Health Journal, 32*(6), 599–612. Copyright © 2011 Michigan Association for Infant Mental Health.

Salomonsson, B. (2012). Has infantile sexuality anything to do with infants? *International Journal of Psychoanalysis, 93*(3), 631–647. Copyright © 2012 John Wiley and Sons.

Salomonsson, B. (2013b). Transferences in parent–infant psychoanalytic treatments. *Acc. for publication in International Journal of Psychoanalysis.* Copyright © 2012 John Wiley and Sons.

Salomonsson, B. and Sandell, R. (2011a). A randomized controlled trial of mother–infant psychoanalytic treatment. 1. Outcomes on self-report questionnaires and external ratings. *Infant Mental Health Journal, 32*(2), 207–231. Copyright © 2011 Michigan Association for Infant Mental Health.

Salomonsson, B. and Sandell, R. (2011b). A randomized controlled trial of mother–infant psychoanalytic treatment. 2. Predictive and moderating influences of quantitative treatment and patient factors. *Infant Mental Health Journal, 32*(3), 377–404. Copyright © 2011 Michigan Association for Infant Mental Health.

# Chapter 1

# What goes on in a baby's mind?

## One-month-old Nic

Sweet babe, in thy face
Soft desires I can trace,
Secret joys and secret smiles,
Little pretty infant wiles.

. . . . .

From thy cheek and from thy eye,
O'er the youthful harvest nigh,
Infant wiles and infant smiles
Heaven and Earth of piece beguiles.

From the poem "A cradle song"
(Blake, 1994, p. 107. Originally published after 1789)

What are babies thinking of? Or, if we restrict the verb "think" to more advanced beings than babies, let us reformulate our question: what goes on in their minds? To parents these questions seem redundant. They claim their babies display humour, joy, anger and other emotions – without clarifying on what grounds they base their opinions. Unhesitatingly they describe their children as wanting, disliking, loving and having other intentions – though they have never received any verbal confirmations from the young. The British poet William Blake also thought babies harboured desires, from "secret joys" to "infant wiles", which formed part of their enigmatic, distressing and endearing character.

What goes on in the baby's mind? In contrast to parents, therapists working with them and their infants must grapple with this crucial and complex question. Certainly, if we claim that our therapies work because *the parent* is affected by our interventions, the question is superfluous. According to this claim, she will be affected by our interventions and change her behaviour with her baby, who then functions better. However, today many clinicians (Baradon *et al.*, 2005; Dolto, 1985; Lebovici & Stoléru, 2003; Norman, 2001; Salomonsson, 2007b; Thomson-Salo, 2007; Watillon, 1993) believe that babies are not only affected via interventions to the parent. They also feel that they may be reached *directly* in a "dialogue" with the analyst. These observations force us to re-approach our initial question. Let us do this by first recalling the everyday example from the introduction: one-month-old Andrew and his mother in the kitchen. When Andy started crying his mother picked him up and then breastfed and comforted him. Nonetheless, Andy did not calm down but continued crying and glaring at Mum. She responded by saying, "Now, now Andy, aren't you angry at your silly Mum who didn't pick you up at once!?"

Why didn't Andy calm down immediately? Why did his mother speak of him being angry and her being silly? Concerning the first question, we might apply a biological perspective and claim that he simply failed to re-establish a physiological steady-state. This argument would apply to a newborn; he is "anterior to the organization of fantasies that bring meaningful structures" (Van Buren, 1993, p. 574). To be true, various research experiments have shown that infants only a few hours old can discriminate their mother's sensuous characteristics from those of other women (Beebe & Lachmann, 2002; Meltzoff & Moore, 1994; Reddy, 2008). We also know that they can imitate an adult's tongue protrusion and mouth opening (Meltzoff & Moore, 1997; Nagy & Molnar, 2004). On the other hand, such capacities do not imply that they are *fantasizing* about the parent. For the time being, we only feel certain that a newborn's crying represents biological regulatory processes. Whether it also reflects experiences that we might label "emotional" remains unverifiable.

Andy, however, has already reached one month of age. A subjective world seems to be dawning in him. His mother thinks his crying involves a primitive mind with direction and intentionality; he *wants* to cry *to* her because he is driven by something that's on his mind. How should we label this "something"? Psychoanalytic theory suggests our mind works with *psychic representations*. This term covers what we assume goes on in the individual's mind; that which he is about to *sich vorstellen*. The German reflexive verb means to put something "before oneself"; a splitting of the mind where one part is observing the other. When I think of "coffee" I envisage a black and slightly bitter liquid that I like drinking in the morning. This is my representation of coffee.

The infant researcher Reddy (2008) questions the concept of psychic representation for describing what goes on "inside" a baby. Such a term would suggest that we can gain objective knowledge of a baby's mind, from a "third-person perspective" as she labels it. Instead, his emotional expressions carry "an *interactive* meaning" (p. 79). When an infant is imitating an adult's tongue protrusion, this does not result from any subjective representation such as 'I feel like smiling and protruding my tongue just like that guy in front of me'. Instead, he is involved in an interaction or a game: 'This guy and I are doing a funny smile-and-protrusion game together'. The game demonstrates his primary intersubjectivity (Trevarthen, 2001) rather than any representations *inside* his mind.

I agree that we often interact with babies and thus shape our imaginations about what might lie beneath their behaviour. This was the method Andy's mother used to arrive at her conclusions. I also agree that babies are skilled interactors who observe emotional signals from the people around. Still, I argue that we may consider his representations separately. We tend to also assume representations in babies whom we are *not* interacting with. If Andy's father is in the next room overhearing that the boy is crying and if the two do not interact, he might nevertheless assume that something goes on inside Andy. Second, representation is a theoretical construct that is "*inferred* from the observable workings of an individual's mind" (Skelton, 2006, italics added). Nobody has ever seen a representation. Nevertheless we assume that people have thoughts, whims, feelings and intuitions; phenomena we subsume under the term representation: a "more or less consistent reproduction within the mind of a perception of a meaningful thing or object" (Moore & Fine, 1990). In psychoanalytic theory, it generally refers to unconscious mental phenomena. According to the French psychoanalytic tradition, representations form the essence of our being. In the words of Lionel Bailly (2012), "we are what we think and how we feel" (p. 6) and this is all built on experiences inhabiting our minds in the form of signifiers. They are sliding in and out of consciousness and held together in "a system of theories".

Any psychoanalyst might agree up to this point but then object: "Agreed, without the concept of mental representations any psychological theory would crumble. But what makes you think *babies* have representations? And how do you know they are involved in little Andy's crying? In my daily practice, I work with representations that my patient and I verify or refute in the therapeutic process. For instance, a man might report that he dreamt of a baby who was crying inconsolably. Due to the clinical background, I might interpret it as reflecting his loneliness, his anger with me, etc. Issuing from this response, we would then carry the analysis further. But I have no right to say anything about a real baby's crying!"

The logic beneath our colleague's argument is respectable and challenges us to investigate the notion of infant representations. I will now demonstrate that Freudian theory has always taken for granted that infants form mental representations. Freud was not perturbed by the fact that such representations were unverifiable. He assumed they contained passions and ideas and were directed towards another human being. In the beginning he called this person "extraneous help" or "the experienced person". Later, he switched to talking about the mother and her breast as being the first objects of the baby's representations.

In contrast, infant researchers such as Daniel Stern are more restrictive when describing infant representations. I will delineate his position and compare them with mine as it has been formed over years of psychoanalytic work with babies and parents. This chapter concludes that we need a special concept for conceptualizing representations in infants. Without it, our understanding of the infant's psyche becomes reductionistic and focused merely on behavioural manifestations. Chapter 2 will elaborate on some ideas by two French psychoanalysts, Jean Laplanche (1989, 1999a) and Piera Aulagnier (2001). Laplanche focused on how the baby is affected by the mother's "enigmatic messages". Aulagnier suggested the term "primal process" for the baby's mental processes. Finally,

I will suggest the term *primal representation* to answer our initial question: what goes on in a baby's mind?

Our perspicacious colleague above argued against representations in babies. However, he overlooked that it is impossible to draw a sharp dividing line between pre-representational and representational life. He might retort that this line is drawn when the child learns to understand and speak language. However, a simple clinical example indicates that this position is untenable. Ten-month-old Pierre has insomnia. His mother tells me she feels a bit lost after the family moved to our town. He is sitting silently in her lap but suddenly he starts crying while staring at me. Mother tells me this happens with other people, too: "He seems afraid but I don't know why." I might dismiss this as an unverifiable comment. I could state that I know nothing of what goes on in his mind or if he wants to communicate something. This view would concur with a strictly behaviouristic perspective but would contradict everyday intuition *and* basic assumptions in psychoanalytic theory. The scarce references to Freudian theory among present-day infant clinicians might intimate that classical psychoanalysis has been uninterested in infant psychology. We will now consult Freud's texts to investigate if this is correct.

## Freud on infant representations

When we read Freud's grand effort at integrating psychology and neuro-physiology into a psychoanalytic metapsychology, *Project for a Scientific Psychology* (1895/1950), the abstruse language may conceal its focus on the infant's psychological life. Freud describes the experience of satisfaction, which obviously is a psychological event, in neuro-physiological terms; as a neuronal discharge. But he adds that it cannot come about unless there is an "alteration in the external world (supply of nourishment, proximity of the sexual object)" (p. 318). This takes place via "extraneous help" by "an experienced person" who is drawn to the child's state "by discharge along the path of internal change" (idem). Put in everyday language, Freud explains that the baby keeps crying until the mother listens to him and comforts him. Another example of his struggle to describe psychological events in neuro-physiological terms is his suggestion that there occurs a cathexis of "neurones which correspond to the perception of an object" (idem). Today, we rarely say that the mother-object is cathected but that she has become a containing object (Bion, 1962a) or an attachment figure (Bowlby, 1969) – whichever terminology we prefer.

Though Freud does not yet speak of infant representations, such a notion is easy to discern already in *the Project*. For example, he suggests that when a baby communicates longing and distress to "the helpful person" (p. 318), s/he will perceive this object as hostile. Freud depicts a screaming and distressed baby with negative representations of the object. One gets the impression of Freud being a Kleinian before Klein! In *The Interpretation of Dreams* (1900), he focuses on another entity corresponding to the term representation: the wish. When a need arises in a baby, a psychological impulse will "re-cathect the mnemic image of the perception and re-evoke the perception itself, that is to say, re-establish the situation of the original satisfaction. An impulse of this kind is what we call a *wish*" (pp. 565–566, italics added). Evidently, to re-cathect a memory of a satisfying event implies to re-evoke an affectively charged *representation*.

Freud's infant focus is also evident in his works on hysterical symptoms, which he regards as a "re-activation of an infantile impression" (1909, p. 230). He depicts psychoanalytic therapy as a method by which the therapist provides "translations from an alien method of expression into the one which is familiar to us" (Freud, 1913, p. 175). He thus offered the patient interpretations that addressed what the hysterical symptoms might mean. Did he also think representations were involved in the symptoms? We have already hinted at a positive answer but will have to postpone a definitive conclusion.

In some works, Freud wavers between describing infants in biological and psychological terms. In a passage on infantile sexuality (1905b), it remains unclear if representations are involved when a "baby [is] sinking back satiated from the breast and falling asleep with flushed cheeks and a blissful smile" (p. 182). Another passage is clearer: anxiety in infants originally expresses "that they are feeling the loss of the person they love. It is for this reason that they are frightened of every stranger" (p. 224). Evidently, a baby who loves and fears people must have formed representations of them. Yet, in this passage Freud only speaks of infants old enough to distinguish parents from strangers. Therefore, we must return to his writings on "infants in arms" (Freud, 1925–26, p. 138). Their anxieties are conditioned by separation from the mother. They need not be explained on psychological lines but "can be accounted for simply enough biologically" (idem). Here, Freud denies representations in the newborn. But he is inconsistent; he labels such anxiety an "automatic phenomenon", a "rescuing signal", as well as a "product of the infant's *mental* helplessness" (p. 138, italics added). Obviously, he assumes that mental processes, that is, representations, exist in the very young baby. In other words, the term *hilflosigkeit* or help- lessness refers both to the baby's biological and psychological condition. Repeated moments countering this helpless state, those moments when the baby experienced satisfaction, have created the maternal object. "This object, whenever the infant feels a need, receives an intense cathexis which might be described as a 'longing' one" (p. 170). To conclude, the term "longing cathexis" implies that the baby has formed a representation of mother.

In *The Unconscious*, Freud (1915c) continues struggling with the *Vorstellung* concept as he seeks to understand the difference between conscious and uncon- scious experiences. He states that an instinct can only be represented by an idea (*Vorstellung*). Then he amends and suggests that it may attach *either* to an idea or appear as an "affective state" (177). Here Freud differs, more clearly than ever, between two *Vorstellungen*: thing- and word-presentations. Every representation originates as an unconscious thing-presentation. Later, a word- presentation is added and now it may become conscious or, alternatively, remain under repression. Tentatively, we might conclude that if unconscious thing-presentations are "the first and true object-cathexes" (p. 201), they would be the only ones existent in the infant mind. However, this conclusion creates problems. As Maze and Henry (1996) have remarked, a baby has many conscious representations that are not yet attached to words; their mother's voice, a dog's barking, the scent of milk or Pierre's anxious image of me. Such representations thus fall outside of Freud's bipartite division.

Freud was perhaps unaware of this inconsistency, but he realized another complication: the differentiation between thing- and word-presentations is far from clear-cut. Word-presentations also contain sense-perceptions, as when a baby is listening to the "sound-image" (1915c, p. 210) of the spoken word. Every word has a "thing-like" quality to it. If the dividing line between pre-representational and representational life is indistinct and does not coincide with the child's acquisition of language, Freud helps us in understanding why; a word is assembled from "auditory, visual and kinaesthetic elements" (idem). It is a complex representation whose meanings also reside in how it sounds, "looks" and feels. Our Andy is susceptible to these elements. When mother says, "Now, now, are you angry at your silly Mum" it might carry many meanings to him: 'Nice sound, good smile, she looks at me, nice breath', or with whatever words we must content ourselves to describing his representations.

To sum up, according to Freud's most prominent view, the infant forms representations. They are laden with affects and connected with experiences of internal, bodily events and/or with an external object. Melanie Klein has often been accused of – or commended for – being the first analyst to depict the infant's representations. Our survey indicates that this is historically incorrect. Freud's notion of infant representations was not a trivial whim or an abstruse speculation but a theoretical cornerstone. Many of his concepts were built on observations and assumptions about infants; the dream psychology (1900), the formation of the unconscious (1915c), the pleasure principle (1920), primal repression and repression proper (1915b), the primary and secondary processes (1911) and sexuality (1905b). We should also recall that, as Freud saw it, the psychological impact of infancy continues throughout life; our adult character is "based on the memory-traces of our impressions . . . The impressions which have had the greatest effect on us – those of our earliest youth – are precisely the ones which scarcely ever become conscious" (1900, p. 539). In other words, there is an infant within every one of us.

## Infant research versus psychoanalytic experience

Psychoanalytic theory thus holds that representations exist in infants. This challenges us with a new task, namely, to account for their content. Is Pierre really afraid when he is staring at me? If so, how does he envisage the doctor in front of him who gives him some friendly smiles interspersed with a brief comment or two? Similarly, what goes on in Andy's mind when he is picked up by Mum but keeps sulking and glaring at her? Is he overwhelmed by "bad" representations or is he simply in a bad mood that has nothing to do with any internal image of Mum? Is he about to catch a cold, which makes him irritable and surly? The latter suggestion is banal but evades our main task: whatever the reasons behind Andy's crying, we should try to describe what is going on inside his mind.

Let us begin by asking Andy's mother. She might suggest, "Andy was angry because I didn't pick him up quickly enough. Now he notices that I am comforting him, but he's still cross with me". In more abstract terms, she assumes that there is a divide between his "subjective psychic reality" (Stern, 1988, p. 506) (reflected by his persistent crying) and his "interpersonal reality" (the fact that he got the breast). Perhaps Andy also has a problem *inside* his subjective reality; he cannot handle two opposing ideas simultaneously ('Mum is nice' and 'Mum is silly').

Before we investigate these early mental phenomena further, we will recapitulate Fonagy's (1996) caution; infant behavioural observations confirm that psychoanalytic speculations sometimes have presumed capacities in the baby that are "outside the developmental timetable" (p. 406). According to this critique, psychoanalysts are so to speak hyper-creative. They imagine mental processes that babies are simply incapable of. The relevance of infant observation and research to psychoanalysis has been debated by Daniel Stern, André Green and others (Sandler, Sandler & Davies, 2000). Stern claims that research on infants is essential to inform us on their behaviour *and* their internal world. In contrast, Green insists that only findings from the analytic setting may yield valid conclusions about the inner world, that is, the subjective and unconscious realm which is the focus of psychoanalytic investigation.

I will argue for a third hypothesis; dialogues with mother and baby in *psychoanalytic therapy* may yield a basis for our assumptions about infant representations. The method of investigation is similar to the one we use with older patients; we observe behaviour, listen to comments and use our counter-transference to understand the workings of the participants' minds. In contrast, the infant researcher does not enter in a dialogue with his young subject. Accordingly, his conclusions are based only on behavioural observations and dialogues with mother. This being said, I also suggest that infant research may complement findings gathered in the psychoanalytic setting; it helps us understand the timetable of therapeutic accessibility in infants, as I will discuss in Chapter 2. It may also inspire analytic understanding similarly to other influences; poetry, analytic literature, neuroscience, our life experiences, etc. For example, the Still-Face experiment (Tronick, Als, Adamson, Wise & Brazelton, 1978) demonstrates glaringly a baby's reactivity in front of a mother with a lifeless and unresponsive face. To the analyst, it may function as a metaphor of postnatal depression and its consequences. Thus used, it may deepen his understanding of an adult patient's infantile trauma. It may also alert him to the heavy impact of non-verbal communication in the session. Another example is infant observation used in analytic training. Many students have noticed "the intensity of the impact of the experience, its lasting effects, and its centrally formative contribution both to a psychodynamic understanding of intimate encounters with other minds and relationships, and to the influence of such encounters on their own self-understanding" (Waddell, 2006).

My hypothesis is thus that neither infant research alone – nor observations nor reconstructions in adult analysis alone – will render a full picture of infant mental phenomena. We must also take into account the baby in psychoanalytically oriented parent–infant treatments. This idea emerged from a clinical case representing a magnified version of Andy's case. When I met a two-week-old boy, Nic, and his mother (Salomonsson, 2007a), I learnt she had had a wound on one nipple. We started treatment according to the mother–infant psychoanalytic method suggested by Norman (2001, 2004). I noted that though the wound had healed, Nic continued fretting and jerking. Something else than his mother's pain reaction must now guide his aversive behaviour. As I observed two distinct emotional atmospheres at the breasts, one calm and one agitated, I assumed he harboured two contrasting representations connected with breastfeeding. Alternately, a present representation was overshadowed by a specific memory that acted as "a more potent guide for interpreting the currently encountered 'interpersonal reality'" (Stern, 1988, p. 511). The question was if his memories only concerned the bruised nipple or if he had also sensed his *mother's* contradictory attitudes to breastfeeding and motherhood. If so, this might have yielded clashing representations in him that he could not handle.

Therapeutic encounters with Nic and other babies have made me hypothesize that (1) in parent–baby-relationship disorders we need to consider the mental processes of parent *and* baby and (2) we need a psychological concept for what goes on in the baby's mind, however primitive such mental processes must be. Let us now approach these ideas through the lens of the case of Nic and his mother Theresa, or Tessie as she was called.

## Nic and his mother Tessie: a case of breastfeeding problems

I will first outline the technique I generally use in these cases; mother–infant psychoanalytic treatment (MIP; Norman, 2001; Salomonsson, 2007a and b, 2009, 2011). Please bear with me if the description appears brief; I will return to it across the book. In MIP, sessions take place with infant and mother present. The number and frequency of sessions are flexible, from a few weekly sessions to one year of four-times-weekly analytic work. The reason for this elasticity is that the suffering and pathology of mother and child, as well as the mother's motivation and possibilities for continuing therapy, may vary considerably. Whichever length and frequency we decide on, the setting allows us to maintain a psychoanalytic attitude. I focus on unconscious manifestations of mother and child and I regard transference and countertransference as the central arenas in which they emerge. The method emphasizes containment (Bion, 1962a) of the infant and assumes that a troubled baby will be prone to look for such containment when he experiences my attention. Consequently, I try to establish a relationship with the baby to become that container. I achieve this through receiving and processing within the countertransference the distress that the child evokes in me – and then communicating it back in a form the little one can assimilate.

Needless to say, the baby does not understand the lexical content of interpretations. The idea is rather to utilize his ability to process the emotional wavelengths of the words, or their auditory, visual and kinaesthetic elements as Freud called them. As he gets captured by them, this may liberate distressing affects beneath his functional symptoms. The mother is emotionally affected by this interchange and will understand better how her baby's affects and symptoms are linked. This, plus the analyst's containment of her distress, may vitalize maternal care and mother–infant attachment.

My contact with Tessie and two-week-old Nic was initiated by a Child Health Centre nurse. At our first consultation, Tessie told me that she "almost regretted" having become a mother. She was frightened by fantasies that Nic might be killed in an accident. Her irritation and frustration were mixed with warm and loving feelings. I noted that during breastfeeding, he was jerking and tossing his head as if shunning the nipple. Alternately, he sucked it in entirely rather than rhythmically working on it for nourishment.

Due to the mother's panic and the boy's distress I suggested to Tessie that we meet four times weekly. She willingly consented and treatment started promptly. We soon discovered Nic's differential breastfeeding pattern; he nursed smoothly at the left-hand breast but shunned or jerked at the other breast. Since her wound had healed completely the breastfeeding pattern must be founded in their earliest interactions, which had been marred by her bruised nipple. In addition, I soon learnt about her ambivalence towards motherhood and marriage. She was a devoted and loving mother but also jealous and angry at her son.

I also got the impression that Nic had internalized his mother's contrasting attitudes. I therefore turned my analytic instrument, not only to Tessie's "ghosts in the nursery" (Fraiberg, Adelson & Shapiro, 1975) or projections onto Nic (Cramer & Palacio Espasa, 1993), but also to the ghosts that *he* seemed to harbour. I addressed her ambivalence towards motherhood and her own mother, but I also formed a picture of Nic's internal world by sensing how his communications reso-nated (Norman, 1994; Salomonsson, 1998) with infantile parts of my personality. I thus utilized concordant (Racker, 1968) aspects of my countertransference to understand his predicament. Similar techniques have been suggested by several authors (Baradon *et al.*, 2005; Lebovici & Stoléru, 2003; Pozzi-Monzo & Tydeman, 2007; Thomson-Salo, 2007; Watillon, 1993). For example, Thomson-Salo (2007) argues that "relating to infants in their own right usually seems to bring about a change in their thinking, feelings and behaviour, and the parents as well" (p. 965). MIP technique insists more on developing a specific analytic relationship with the baby. In Chapter 10 we will discuss if this will make the baby develop a transference to the analyst. Whatever conclusion we will reach then, at this point we realize that one main idea with MIP is to facilitate for the baby to direct his un-modulated affects vis-à-vis the analyst.

## Nic: a vignette from the fourth session

Five days have passed since we last met. Mother enters with Nic, who is now three-and-a-half weeks old. She seems more relaxed than she was at the previous session.

| | |
|---|---|
| *Analyst to Nic:* | You're looking at me, Nic. You haven't done that before. |
| *Mother:* | No . . . |
| *A to N:* | I got a glance right into my eyes! |
| *M:* | Yes, Nic, what was that? Do you recognize Björn a bit? |
| *A to N:* | Maybe you recognize my voice. But in your world, it's a long time since we last met. |
| *M:* | Yes . . . |
| *A:* | Hundreds of minutes ago . . . You look tired, Nic . . . Your gaze is moving towards the ceiling. Maybe you're falling asleep. |
| *M:* | He fell asleep right after we left home . . . I've been thinking a lot this weekend of what we talked about last time we were here. It was heavy. Yesterday and today, things got better. One of the big changes since Nic's birth is that I feel so constrained, even when going to the loo! I can't stand it that I must be there ALL the time for him. I want to go to the loo when I need to! |
| | [At this point, Nic groans and wrings his body.] |
| *M to N:* | Yes . . . ? |
| *A to N:* | You're groaning and wringing your body. You look sore, maybe you feel constrained like Mum. |
| | [Mother tucks Nic to a more comfortable position in his sitter but he is not satisfied.] |
| *M:* | That doesn't look comfortable, Nic. |
| *A to N:* | There's something that you don't like about this. You're turning away your head now, away from Mum. |
| *M:* | Yes . . . |
| *A to N:* | You look at some other place, out there somewhere. |

## Nic's representations

I assumed that Nic's groaning, wringing and gaze aversion were connected with Mum's discontent. I thus guessed he harboured representations of a distressed interaction. I also thought that when he sucked calmly at her left-hand breast, his representations resonated with her positive maternal attitudes. In contrast, his right-hand jerks and grimaces were propelled by representations that paralleled her negativity towards motherhood. One example of her ambivalence occurred when Nic sucked his finger instead of the nipple. In a tone of concern, irony and vexation she exclaimed, "No dear, there's no grub in your finger!" In the countertransference I felt uncomfortable, concerned and confused, as her message seemed simultaneously helpful, helpless and rejecting.

Nic's continuous fretting, however, could not be explained solely by the mother's irony. I concluded this as I observed that he also grunted when she was relaxed and tender. Thus, memory traces of contrasting emotional experiences had begun to settle. I addressed them by telling him "You have many feelings, Nic. Hunger hurts inside you. You sense Mum's wonderful milk. You also recall when you didn't like her breast because she said 'Ouch' when it hurt her. Your feelings clash. You don't want the breast and throw your head back. Then you get hungry and want the breast anyway. And Mum gets stressed". This exemplifies how I contain a distressed baby. Another example is found in the earlier excerpt when I told Nic that he was wringing his body, looking sore and feeling constrained.

Bailly (2012) suggests every individual has a system of theories developed from lifelong experiences. Such experiences are traumatogenic when one cannot transcribe them into symbols. A terrifying event may result either in a "hole in the signifying chain" (p. 7) or in a lack of fit with the individual's system of theories. "Incompatible pieces of information" (idem) will then be present in the psyche at the same time. This was Nic's dilemma. The mother's comment, "There's no grub in the finger", provided incompatible information; a mix of one concrete fact (milk does not emerge from a finger), one facet of the mother's emotional attitude ("I love you and I want to help you suckle my nipple") and yet another facet ("You are so tiresome when you are grunting"). Nic could not build up a coherent system of theories out of such a mélange. My address, "All this makes your feelings clash", aimed at clarifying this "breakdown of the transcription process" (p. 7).

Expressed in another terminology, I contained the child by paying attention to the mother–infant interaction, reflecting on its possible meanings, and *naming* the anxieties reflected in it. My words to Nic aimed at conveying that there was somebody on the other side of the fence trying to understand the confusion in him and his mother. I take this to be responsible for Nic's progress; breastfeeding normalized completely after a few weeks and he ended his participation in therapy after two months. Tessie wanted to continue in individual therapy because, as she put it, "I don't feel that I'm a very good mother". It lasted three years and centred round her anorectic tendencies, marital dissatisfaction and masochistic fantasy world. An ambivalent relationship with her mother was also analyzed. Her therapy enabled me to follow Nic's development via her reports. I also met him again once or twice. He remained a happy and sociable chap, and Tessie sent a final positive letter when he was four years old. It thus took years of therapy to help her ambivalence towards motherhood and femininity but only a few weeks to help Nic dissolve his ambivalent representations of the breast.

## A critical comment

At this point a critical point presents itself effortlessly: "The analyst's interventions do not affect the baby. They work on the mother whose anxiety decreases. When she calms down, this makes Nic calm down as well." This argument and my response are depicted in Figure 1.1.

Our critical colleague's view is illustrated by the two dotted lines running from the therapist to the mother and thence to the baby. He holds that my words, "You have many feelings, Nic", actually touch the mother. They alter her emotional balance and she becomes able to comfort Nic. I share this view but I claim that it only provides half the explanation. The other half is that the baby is also affected directly by my interventions. This argument is depicted by the continuous line from the therapist to the baby. How is this possible? I realize the difficulty in giving a tenable answer – but this difficulty equally challenges our critical colleague. He might argue that the intervention helped mother change her tone of voice, her way of holding the child, her muscular tension, etc. While this sounds quite reasonable, it cannot explain the therapeutic mechanism completely since our colleague would be left with the challenge to explain how the baby was able to pick up mother's new way of comforting him.

Thus, whether our colleague claims that mother is affected by analytic interventions and the baby picks up on this secondarily – or I claim that he may *also* be affected primarily by my interventions – we face the same challenge; to explain how the baby is affected by human interaction. I see no fundamental difference between my telling Nic, "You have many feelings" and Tessie saying, "Now, now, Nic, what's the matter with you today". They are communications on the same level and they affect the boy. To be true, Nic was not affected by my interventions' lexical content but by other communicative levels such as

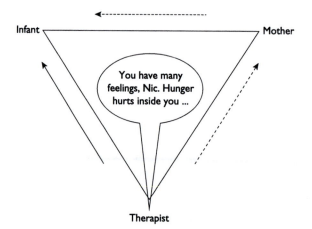

*Figure 1.1* A schematic view of the interaction between therapist, baby and mother.

my tone of voice, my facial expressions, my spontaneous hand gestures, etc. I suggest they conveyed representations that were less anxious and more contained. This made them differ from the ones he harboured – and/or which his mother communicated.

At this point, our colleague might be convinced that both of us grapple with the same question, of how the baby is affected by the mother's altered mental setup and/or the therapist's interventions. Yet, he might come up with another argument: "All right, we cannot settle by whom the baby is affected, but whatever the correct answer, it is only the baby's behaviour that is affected, not his internal world." To this I would object that if we want to understand our interventions' influence from a psychoanalytic vantage point, we must speculate on how they affect his *representations*. It is thus time to return to this concept.

## Representations in Stern's theories

I will approach infant representations from a theoretical perspective, beginning with one of the most cited researchers in the field: Daniel Stern. In *The Interpersonal World of the Infant* (1985), he speaks of the infant's earliest representations as "shapes, intensities, and temporal patterns", that is, "global qualities of experience" (p. 51). He depicts a baby with a "very active subjective life, filled with changing passions and confusions" (p. 44). She lives in "a state of undifferentiation" while struggling with "blurred social events that presumably are seen as unconnected and unintegrated" (idem). These experiences are accompanied by *vitality affects*. Indeed, subjectivity itself is constituted through them. Their "movement, dynamics, and temporal progression . . . imprint meaning onto the experience of a feeling, a succession of memories, or any mental process (Køppe, Harder & Væver, 2008, p. 169). Their meaning is *form*, for example, "surging, fading away, fleeting", etc. (Stern, 1985, p. 54). It is possible that they correspond to Freud's notion of "motor discharge", a phenomenon that is always included in an affective experience (1915c, p. 179). However, Freud imagined that some kind of thought was embedded in an affect. In contrast, vitality affects "do not reflect the categorical content of an experience" (Sandler *et al.*, 2000, p. 86).

As the child's self-development continues, she becomes able to average and represent pre-verbally important and recurring interactive events and experiences. She will create "Representations of Interactions that have been Generalized (RIGs)" (p. 97). In order to focus on how Stern's and my own views differ, I will leave the RIGs aside since they appear at a later age than that of Nic. Stern's "vitality affects" differ from the representations that I assumed were directing Nic's grunting and wringing. When I said, "There's something you don't like. You're turning your head away from Mum", I guessed his behaviour reflected some ideational content, albeit primitive. To bring out another divergence, Stern says a baby neither experiences the world primarily in terms of pleasure/unpleasure nor forms representations of a "good" and "bad" mother. To him, such notions reflect a tendency to "adultomorphizing" ideas about the infant's mind, that is, to impute processes in his mind that in fact stem from our adult fantasy world (Peterfreund, 1978). This critique is similar to that of Fonagy (1996) quoted earlier, that analysts tend to presume capacities that lie outside the baby's developmental timetable.

Though I respect the logic behind these objections, I have had many therapeutic experiences indicating that pleasure and unpleasure are essential categories in a baby's representations. Admittedly, I know as little as anyone else what the baby "really" thinks. I also agree that terms such as "the bad mother" or "bad self" are simplistic. Yet, they appeal to our intuition and prove productive to our therapeutic efforts. To approach this dilemma, we must wait until Chapter 2 with its section on semiotic theory. There I will discuss if we have any valid methods that might confirm – or disconfirm – such notions.

Stern returns to infant representations or "schemas-of-being-together" in *The Motherhood Constellation* (1995). They are constructed from interactive experiences, whereas "fantasies and imaginary elaborations" are added later (p. 81). Their affective dimension is described as "feeling shapes" or "protonarrative envelopes" rather than as having any content. Consequently, the infant has no wish-fulfilling fantasies and does not need to ward off unpleasant content "for defensive reasons" (1985, p. 11). In contrast, I argue that Nic's distress mirrors *representations with oppositional affective content*, which he must ward off. I thus hold that if vitality affects are not emotions, motivational states, pure perceptions and if they "do not belong to any particular content" (2010, p. 8), then this concept risks fixating "on the congruencies of pure form" (Køppe *et al.*, 2008, p. 175) and overlooking the affect's content and the human object that it may involve.

My critique of Stern's concepts of representations and vitality affects is however different from that of André Green (Sandler *et al.*, 2000, p. 86). To him, infant observations "cannot tell us anything about intrapsychic processes that truly characterize the subject's experience" (p. 60). Our survey of classical psychoanalytic theory proves the extent to which it is based on speculations emerging from Freud's – albeit unsystematic – observations of babies. My critique is rather directed towards Green *and* Stern for not making full use of experiences from parent–infant therapies. These settings evoke multiple data and make them interpretable. I do not claim that my interpretations are objective. Rather, they are based on my free-floating attention to the patients' communications and to my subjective reactions. Similarly to any other interpretation, they reflect my assumptions of what the baby and the mother are communicating about their internal worlds; in short, how I seek to understand what goes on in Nic's and Tessie's minds. I thus claim the right to assume an affective content beneath an infant's behaviour in therapy. Only the clinical course can validate or refute such assumptions. One could of course object that a baby cannot confirm an intervention; thus, my assumptions about the meaning concealed in a piece of behaviour must be uncertain. Yet, this also applies to adult work. A therapist who listens only to the literal content of a patient's words will go astray unless he also takes into account her ways of speaking, bodily position, demeanour, voice quality – and the parallel countertransference. This is another consequence of psychoanalysis being what Green (Sandler *et al.*, 2000, p. 86) called a "polysemic" (p. 71) enterprise.

Let us listen to another objection: "If psychoanalysis is a polysemic enterprise, then any sign could mean anything. A baby's cry might mean despair, hunger, happiness or nothing!" This is probably why Stern only allows us to attribute meaning to infant behaviour if the import is "apparent to anyone and [is] a normal part of common experience" (idem). This sounds fair enough, but how should we act in the therapeutic encounter? Andy's mother believed he was cross with her, Pierre's Mum thought he was afraid of something, and Tessie felt Nic was fussy. The therapist might of course refrain from interpreting these babies' behaviours because their meanings were not apparent or did not form a normal part of common experience. However, in doing this he would affront the mother's intuitions. He would also dispossess himself of the possibility of using his analytic instrument to understand the baby's internal world and how it has been shaped in interaction with the parents. As we will see in Chapter 4, little Karen is crying intensely and her mother suggests this is because the girl is sad. This sounds like common sense, but the analytic investigation will point in another direction; Karen is raging against her mother who is communicating in a muddled and feigned way.

To sum up so far, we have found that psychoanalytic theory assumes infants form representations but they have not been conceptualized consistently within that theory. Stern's vitality affect concept elaborates on their formal properties but little on their content. I have suggested, through the examples of Andy, Pierre and Nic, that a baby may be tormented by representations. On the other hand, Stern is right that our assumptions about what goes on in a baby's mind are uncertain. By now, we fear that we have reached a dead end; we can never prove any content of a baby's representations but cannot do without such a concept in parent–infant therapies. Evidently, these treatments pose philosophical questions on epistemology (how knowledge is gained) and semiotics (how the mind assembles knowledge by utilizing signs). We will approach these disciplines in Chapter 2. The purpose is to become better equipped to answer our main question: what goes on in a baby's mind?

# Primal representations

## Three-month-old Tina

In the first chapter, I argued against Stern's position (1985, 1995) that an infant's representations or vitality affects do not have any ideational content. I also argued against Green's stance (Sandler *et al.*, 2000) that only psychoanalysis with verbal patients entitles us to say anything about their internal world. I suggested that analyses with babies and mothers provide an additional investigatory instrument. It reveals that infants form representations that are tied to affects and to the human beings with whom they interact. I provided three examples. One was a commonplace example of Andy, a boy who did not stop crying when his mother picked him up and breast-fed him; the second was Pierre, who got scared of me during our first encounter and the third example was the clinical case of Nic. It might seem foolhardy to assume that a one-month-old boy throwing his head away from the nipple would be influenced by mental representations. Perhaps, a slightly older baby case may help making such assumptions more credible.

### Tina and her mother Nathalie

At the Child Health Centre where I work as a consultant I am asked to see Nathalie, a mother of three children. The reason for the referral is that her three-month-old daughter is screaming terribly. Furthermore, the mother cannot decide on the girl's name. Her tottering on this issue is tormenting her constantly. During our initial interviews, I learn about Nathalie's background. She speaks of her mother's self-preoccupation, her father's demanding character and her anorexia at the time of her parents' divorce when she was 17. After some interviews we start working twice weekly. I will provide material from two early sessions.

During the fifth session the girl is asleep in the baby carriage. Nathalie tells me about the christening last Saturday: "Finally, she got her name, Christina Jennifer Martine! My father told me his great grandmother was also called Christina. Martine comes from William's (her husband) family while Jennifer comes from myself. I wanted her to have a name containing the letters Na, to match my name Nathalie. I even fantasized she'd carry my name, but that would be weird! Christina is good. After all, it carries some of my own letters." I ask her what she wants me to call the girl and she responds with Tina, the name used at home. Tina is screaming less now compared with when therapy started. Mother regrets she is not as good at comforting her as William.

| | |
|---|---|
| *Mother:* | She gets her screaming attacks when we are about to take a walk. As soon as I put on her sweater it all starts. I don't understand why! |
| *Analyst:* | Could it have something to do with how *you're* feeling about going out? |
| *M:* | I don't think so. I don't feel anything special. Maybe I'm tense because she's tense. |
| *A:* | Some kind of vicious circle between you. And who knows where a circle starts? |
| *M:* | Yeah. Her screaming is terrible. At my son's nursery, they call her "the Fire Alert". |

The girl wakes up. Nathalie picks up Tina with a smile and puts her on her lap. Tina and I have eye contact for a minute. She is sleepy and smiles briefly. After two minutes she starts yelling. It is a terrible sound piercing my very marrow. I have a feeling of someone drilling my head and of my brain swishing about in my skull. Nathalie is tense.

| | |
|---|---|
| *A to Tina:* | You are screaming terribly and we don't know why. This must be very hard on you. How are things for Mum? |
| *M:* | I feel sorry for her. I don't understand why she's screaming. In these situations, only the breast will do. But I don't want to breastfeed her all the time, it can't be right! |
| *A:* | Tina, I also note that you don't look Mum in the eyes. You were looking at a painting on the wall but when your eyes returned to Mum you closed them. Well, that's not correct, sometimes you peer at Mum. I wonder why you don't look Mum straight into the eyes. |
| *M:* | Yeah, that's right. I wonder . . . |
| *A to the still screaming T:* | Tina, maybe you've got two Mums? One appears when you smile happily at Mum and look into her eyes. The other one you don't dare look at. You seem scared of her. |
| *M:* | When you mention two Mums I think of her names Christina and Tina. They're so different. Tina sounds nice and cosy while Christina is more . . . stern and old-fashioned. But it also contains "Stina", which I think has a gentle ring to it. I have made her confused by calling her Christina and Tina. I've been joking that she'll become schizophrenic one day. |

[The girl continues yelling. Mum can't take it any longer and offers Tina the breast. She takes it immediately. It is a calm and harmonious scene now and I add:]

| | |
|---|---|
| *A:* | Perhaps there is a third Mum? I got this idea now that you, Tina, are looking drowsy. |
| | Maybe "Drowsy-Mum" would be the third Mum. |
| *M:* | I think it is all my fault. After birth she always looked into my eyes when she was breastfeeding. But I was checking my cell-phone for text messages and emails while doing it! I feel guilty that I rejected her and that's why she doesn't look into my eyes! |

In the session the day afterwards, the girl is somewhat calmer and smiles at me. Then she resumes screaming, though without that piercing tone from yesterday. Mum and I begin using "Tina" and "Christina", not only to indicate the girl's name and nickname, but also to function as metaphors for parts of Nathalie's personality. "Christina" refers to her anorectic, well-controlled and elegant aspects, whereas "Tina" refers to a messy and spontaneous aspect. Nathalie finds it more difficult to retrieve the latter part within her. I also suggest to the *girl* that she starts screaming when she cannot find "Tina" in Mum's face. This seems to occur especially when Nathalie is blocking the "Tina-part" inside herself. She confirms that she feels her daughter's nickname is base and common, which makes her ashamed.

I formulate to Nathalie her dilemma of having a "Christina-armour" covering a "Tina-part" that cannot burst forth. As I use my two hands to personify the armour and the ensconced parts, I also make contact with the girl. Little Tina is looking attentively as I let my open left hand cover my clenched right-hand fist.

| | |
|---|---|
| *A to T while making the hand gesture:* | Mum has a little Tina inside and a big Christina outside of it, but sometimes her little Tina peeps through (I let one finger peep through the fingers of my closed hand). I wonder if you, Tina, notice this in Mum. You're following my fingers! Now you stretch out your hand as if wanting to shake my hand. Then you look away from Mum and that's very hard on her. It feels like a punishment to Mum. |

Some periods of screaming and calming down follow. The amplitude is slowly waning. I suggest to Mum we are working with two versions of "Tina" and "Christina"; one is 30 years and the other only three months old. Nathalie has one self-representation that is well-controlled and stern. Historically, it is linked to her anorexia and the parental demands during childhood. The other self-representation is more spontaneous and messy. I also use the two names to indicate how the baby experiences her mother; "Christina-Mum" is stern and rejecting, while "Tina-Mum" is warm and welcoming. I even conceive of a third representation in the girl; Drowsy-Mum. Tina starts screaming when she gets scared of Christina-Mum. Sometimes this happens because Mum is actually displaying some aversive attitudes vis-à-vis the girl. Sometimes, however, I cannot discern any such signals from the mother. It rather seems that the girl has a storage of all three types of representations, which – at least to some extent – live a life of their own.

Though it seems that Tina's representations are not always elicited by the mother's present behaviour, I attribute their genesis to Nathalie's corresponding self-representations. Already at the delivery ward Mum had problems in integrating her "elegant" and "base" images of herself with how she felt about her newborn. This was the point when she started brooding on the baby's names. My point, however, is that today we can no longer claim that the girl merely screams because of her mother's ambivalent ruminations. Now the *girl* has developed similar "infantile ghosts" or split representations of her mother. Not until we take them into account, and address her about them, will we be fully equipped to help the two. Only two sessions later, the girl's screaming had subsided considerably. In contrast Nathalie's anorectic anxieties, her ambivalence towards the girl and her perfectionist demands persisted and were dealt with in the ensuing therapy.

## Representations and semiotic theory

One often hears that in the psychoanalytic "talking cure", words are the prime conveyors of meaning. If therapy aims to "make conscious what is unconscious" (Freud, 1916–17, p. 435), and if words differentiate conscious from unconscious representations (Freud, 1915c), then verbal interchange is essential to bring treatment forward. This is why we encourage the patient to *tell us* whatever comes to his mind. Nonetheless, Freud knew that humans use other methods to convey meaning: "No mortal can keep a secret. If his lips are silent, he chatters with his finger-tips; betrayal oozes out of him at every pore" (Freud, 1905a, p. 77). He was referring to Dora's expressive playing with her little bag on the couch. Once again, we discover that psychoanalysis is a polysemic enterprise, as suggested in Chapter 1. Analytic interpretations also need to take into account *how* a patient conveys meanings; through her apparition and behaviour, and how her words sound and feel.

If we want to establish the meanings of a sigh, a smile, a cry or a wringing of the body, we need an epistemology that covers all forms of signs. To this end, C.S. Peirce's philosophy (Kloesel & Houser, 1992, 1998) is useful since it combines epistemology with semiotics, the science of signs. Peirce states that we can never secure any basic beliefs or genuine knowledge. All propositions are hypothetical and fallibilistic. Therefore, an interpretation can never tell the "Truth" but only reach a "highest-point" (Apel, 1995, p. IV). We do not reach certainty "by comparing *beliefs* with how things *are* . . . [but] by showing that these beliefs are required if our total body of beliefs is to be fully consistent and coherent" (Cooper, 1999, p. 8).

To get a coherent understanding of human communication, we enter an infinite circuit of induction, abduction and deduction. To exemplify, let us recall Andy in Chapter 1. His mother's inductive idea was: "Andy's crying. Babies who cry are hungry. So, he's hungry." She nursed him and he fell asleep. Her deduction ran:

"Aha, he was crying and I nursed him. He drank eagerly and calmed down. What'd I say, he was hungry!" She might be correct – but such deductions are also expressed by many mothers with breastfeeding problems. They interpret every cry as a sign of hunger and offer the breast to the child. We might therefore doubt her deduction and suggest: "Andy was crying, then breast-fed and now he is calm. Did he calm down because you provided milk, offered affection, helped release intestinal pressure, or . . . ?" Every such abduction yields new inductions ("Crying babies are either hungry or want contact") or deductions ("Next time he cried, I just stroked his hand without breastfeeding him. He calmed down. It seems that a cry indicates hunger or a longing for contact").

These terms build a conceptual platform for understanding what babies and mothers convey in their interaction. One way of defining a dyad's health is the flexibility with which its members move about in inferential circuits. A relaxed mother knows that the meaning of her baby's cry may vary. The relation between the sign (the cry) and what it means (hunger, longing for contact, tummy-ache, etc.) is *momentary* (Guiraud, 1975, p. 40). When she is confronted with such an object-sign relation she creates an interpretant, in this case her thought when she hears him crying. An interpretant may be "emotional" (Kloesel & Houser, 1998, p. 409) and focus on her feelings ("I get tense when he's crying"). It may be "energetic" and evoke an urge to do something ("I must breastfeed him"), or it may be "logical" and evoke a thought about what is going on ("Crying babies are either hungry or lonesome"). Each interpretant will become a new object to her mind ("Is he really crying like he generally does when he is hungry? No, today there's another ring to it"). This is how humans think, whether we are in psychoanalysis or in the kitchen with a baby; in an endless triangle of objects, signs and interpretants.

So much for the mother's imaginations about her baby. A more difficult question is if we may also speak of representations in babies. In the first paper, I began to answer it in the affirmative. I started with Andy and proceeded via Pierre to Nic's case. I argued that parent–infant-therapy is an instrument for interpreting representations, including those of the baby. I will now suggest that we may grasp some content of a baby's representations if we apply a *qualified adultomorphizing*. To follow my argument we must first recall two of Peirce's sign concepts, the icon and the index, which interest us particularly in connection with babies. When his mother approached Andy, he perhaps experienced her as an *icon* of distress: 'Mum's ugly face/harsh voice/unpleasant vibrations'. Icons "convey ideas of the things they represent simply by imitating them" (Kloesel & Houser, 1992, 1998). Andy maybe also experienced her as an *index*. If so, he would compare her appearance with other situations and take it to signify: 'Mum WANTS something from me that I don't want to do/have/be. GO AWAY, silly Mum'. An index conveys energy and "forces the mind to attend to that object" (p. 14). In therapy with Tina I got the impression that she experienced her mother as an incomprehensible icon, a mix of 'Tina-comfort' and 'Christina-rejection'. Mum's aspects, interpreted as indices, perhaps alternated between 'Tina-Mum wants you' and 'Christina-Mum admonishes you and shuts you off'.

What connects certain icons and indices to certain emotional meanings? The connections cannot be arbitrary. For example, a crying baby could hardly be interpreted as conveying happiness and joy. At this point, the concept of *analogic representations* becomes helpful. Rosolato (1985) exemplifies with the human gesture, which he describes as a dynamic bodily mirror of our emotions. Analogic representations copy the body's movements that accompany our emotions. Importantly, however, they are not mere blueprints of emotions and – in contrast to digital representations – they cannot be defined unequivocally. Rather, they function as parts in an "open system" (Corradi Fiumara, 1995, p. 64) in which all parts relate to each other. To exemplify; interpreted as a digital sign, a red street light always tells us to stop the car. In contrast, when we interpret a smile as an analogic sign it might convey many meanings; welcoming, derision, menace, meanness, desire, etc. Our interpretation depends on the network of signs in which we perceive the smile. To complicate matters further, any sign may be interpreted either in the analogic or the digital mode. The rush-hour driver who mutters "Damned red light" is reacting to the sign in the analogic mode – while hopefully stopping his car, obeying the digital signification.

Corradi Fiumara suggests analogic representations are our preferred tools for unconscious communication and that they utilize the body to convey affects and thoughts. Readers familiar with Susanne Langer (1942) recognize the similarity with her term presentational symbolism, "which is non-discursive and untranslatable, does not allow of definitions within its own system, and cannot directly convey generalities" (p. 97).

Now that we have sorted out analogic representations from the digital, we face another question: *how* do they convey meaning? We can summon an argument by looking at the host of linguistic metaphors that reflect such representations. They are common and easily comprehended by anyone. Let me exemplify: if I use the phrase "he banged his fist on the table", it is evident that I am speaking of an angry person. The metaphor copies the bodily movements of a decisive and angry person. If I say "I feel warmly for her" we understand which emotion my metaphor refers to, because it connects physical warmth with comfort and proximity with our loved ones. Such metaphors exemplify Lakoff's and Johnson's idea (1999) that the mind is inherently embodied. Many abstract concepts, too, are essentially metaphorical and based on sensuous language. We conceive of an important event as "big" or of a distressing situation as a "burden".

Such metaphors are built up in the following way, according to Lakoff and Johnson. First, the individual forms a "subjective judgment" (1999, Table 4.1, p. 50). When we "feel warmly for someone" our judgment centres round affection to which an experience from the temperature domain has been added. Once, the feeling and the sensorimotor domain were experienced as "conflated" (p. 49); a primordial stage when a baby experienced that to *have* an affect and to "*be* it" in his body was the same. Not until the two domains become differentiated will it be possible to transform primary experiences into metaphors or analogic representations. The child proceeds from having felt concretely warm when held affectionately by his parent to forming a general notion un-connected to temperature. As a teenager he will state: "I feel warmly for my friends and for human rights issues."

Infant research demonstrates that already the newborn possesses some assets that are needed to take part in analogic communication. His ability to imitate an adult's tongue protrusion and mouth opening (Kugiumutzakis, Kokkinaki, Makrodimitraki & Vitalaki, 2005; Reddy, 2008) indicates "intermodal perception" (Bahrick & Hollich, 2008) or "active intermodal mapping" (Meltzoff & Moore, 1977); he can observe an adult's grimaces and link them to his own muscular movements. As for affects, he seems to learn about them gradually by watching the parent's "marked" or exaggerated versions of the emotions they think he is harbouring (Fonagy, Gergely, Jurist & Target, 2002). This happens in daily life, as when Andy's mother picks him up with a special facial expression and vocal melody: "Are you *angry* at your silly Mum who didn't pick you up at *once!*?"

Still, the question remains: how do we adults intuit the representations beneath the baby's screams, smiles, sighs and body movements? The answer must be: through *our own* analogic representations. Mother understands that Andy's cry implies distress because she herself cries when distressed. She realizes that his smile after breastfeeding implies satisfaction because she, too, smiles when she is satisfied. I therefore suggest we understand babies via a *qualified adultomorphizing*, namely, by reclining on *analogic representations linked to our own bodily experiences*. Once, when they were created in our infancy they copied our affects' gestures and contents. Today, in front of the baby, we recognize the similarity between his behaviour and our representations.

In cases of baby worries, such qualified adultomorphizing has been compromised by parental projections onto the child. Nathalie cannot understand her daughter's screaming, because it is evoked by – and is a response to – her own "Christina part". Similarly, Nathalie's contempt of a spontaneous "Tina-part" within herself makes her repress it and thus it becomes unavailable to her daughter. Nathalie has an internal "Christina–Tina" conflict that extends to the girl. This results in confusion in the baby: 'Who am I, Christina-like or Tina-like?' Each name also represents an internal opposition; obsessive/well-structured and cute/base. We might express it: 'If I am Christina, am I proper or stiff? If I am Tina, am I cute or base?'

Needless to say, my suggestion that we recline on our analogic representations when trying to grasp the meaning of a baby's cry carries the risk of "hypersemiosis"; we might attribute too much meaning, or even an erroneous meaning, to a baby's behaviour. Indeed, as Tronick (2005) expresses it, meaning-making in any dyad is often messy and full of misunderstandings. To meet this problem in our therapies, we use inferential circuits. We observe the baby's behaviour and assume that he wants to communicate something – and that this is guided by representations of the parent or the analyst. Then we formulate an intervention, as when I addressed Nic about his clashing feelings. The response will determine the veracity of my guess and how to proceed with the inferential circuit.

Using inferential circuits to promote understanding has been central to psychoanalytic work ever since it was invented. To be true, Freud also used criteria of truthfulness "from science and from an idea of history deriving from science" (Kermode, 1985, p. 4). But many passages indicate that he also relied on a semiotic method of truth validation. One example is when he labels psychoanalysis a *Deutungskunst* (Freud, 1923, p. 238). *Deuten* is akin to when an augur or prophet interprets natural signs as harbingers of upcoming disaster. A semiotic perspective is also evident when he defines the drive as "the psychical *representative* of the stimuli originating from within the organism and reaching the mind" (1915a, p. 122, italics added). Similarly, he speaks of memories as being "registered in various *species of signs*" (Bonaparte, Freud & Kris, 1954, p. 173). Finally, his treatise on the Unconscious (1915c), as referred to in Chapter 1, terminates with defining the Conscious and Unconscious in semiotic terms; in terms of word- and thing-presentations.

During the last decades, semiotic theory has influenced many analysts working with adults (Chinen, 1987; Martindale, 1975; Gammelgaard, 1998; Goetzmann & Schwegler, 2004; Grotstein, 1980, 1997; Muller & Brent, 2000; Muller, 1996; Olds, 2000; da Rocha Barros & da Rocha Barros, 2011; Van Buren, 1993). For example, Grotstein (1980) sees the drive as a "messenger of information" (p. 495) that breeds signifiers for need or danger. He also regards affects as signifiers; they indicate how we feel about such internal information. Many French analysts unite Freudian drive theory with semiotic theory and apply such models to mother–baby interactions. They speak of the baby's cry as "a sign speaking to the mother" (Lebovici & Stoléru, 2003, p. 254). They emphasize the object's symbolizing function and the devastating effects when it falters (Roussillon, 2011). To specifically describe *infant* representations, other French authors have suggested terms such as "demarcating signifier" (Rosolato, 1978, 1985), "formal signifier" (Anzieu, 1990) and two others that we will investigate now; the enigmatic signifier (Laplanche, 1999b) and the pictogram (Aulagnier, 2001).

## Laplanche's "enigmatic message"

Is it possible to integrate classical drive theory with modern knowledge of mother–infant interactions provided by experimental researchers and psychotherapists? Jean Laplanche would have answered in the affirmative. His metapsychology incorporates "concretely the origins of human being; that is, the infant" (1989, p. 89). He refers to *real* babies, not to psychoanalytic reconstructions or infant-like parts of the adult personality. He retains one foot on classical psychoanalytic ground and places the other in mother–infant research and attachment theory – while being adamant that the latter does not expound on the unconscious mind (2002).

Let us first note that Laplanche defines the drive in semiotic terms; it is "the impact on the individual and on the ego . . . by the repressed thing-presentations" (1999a, p. 129). The mind is thus under direct pressure by representations, and only indirectly by whatever biological processes that might parallel them. Driven by a biological need, the baby sucks the breast. Propelled by a drive representation, he may simultaneously enjoy sucking it. The "object of function" (milk) then becomes displaced to the sexual or "phantasmatic breast" (Stein, 1998, p. 597). One of Laplanche's key points is that the baby's representations of this exciting breast emanate mainly from *the parent*. In this way, the Frenchman integrates drive theory with observations of mother–baby interactions. The drive arises in the baby because he mis-translates his parents' messages. The central term is *the enigmatic message*, which is "underlined, delimited, offered up, implanted . . . by the adult world" (Laplanche, 1999b, p. 64) – but whose full import the baby cannot yet grasp.

An everyday example: nine-month-old Rufus is being weaned. His mother wants to buy a new bra and the family visits a department store. In the dressing-room, she is trying on a beautiful bra while her husband is waiting outside with Rufus. She asks her husband to come and have a look. He looks through the curtain and says it looks lovely on her. But – Rufus also catches sight of it and starts crying. We might guess that he is tormented by a representation such as, 'This breast is closing down for me. It's hard. When I see her breast unexpectedly, I get enraged for not getting access to it'. We know there are undercurrents, which Rufus can only grasp dimly. 'Why does Mum show her breasts to Dad? They are *my* property! What's Dad got to do with them? Does he also get milk from them? Or is something else going on between them?' Rufus's mother longs to reclaim her breasts and the couple longs to bring them back into their erotic relationship. Of all this Rufus only senses a smile, a scent or a special tone in Mum's question: "Honey, what do you think of this bra? Isn't it nice?"

How are such enigmatic messages integrated? Laplanche suggests a two-step process. First, they are enclosed (*enclavés*; Laplanche, 2007, p. 205) in the baby's psychic apparatus; thus, he can neither process nor understand them. In a second step they reappear like a foreign body, which he must integrate or master. Only messages having passed this second step can be repressed. Figure 2.1 is a modified version from Laplanche (2007, p. 206). I have added the box referring to mother to emphasize that her messages have roots in her Unconscious; they are "compromised" (p. 100) by it. Tessie's comment to Nic, "There's no grub in your finger", was such a message; it was compromised by her unconscious rage and jealousy. Perhaps Rufus's mother, when calling her husband to the dressing-room, also harboured an unconscious intention of showing her son that their relationship was about to change.

When the mother's messages reach the infant's mind, this results in an initial splitting, as indicated by the horizontal line A in Figure 2.1. Messages remaining in the baby's "enclosed UCs" are subjected to primal repression. As yet, there is no line (B) dividing the pre- and un-conscious systems. Only when B is erected will dynamic repression become possible. Now representations surge towards consciousness and provoke repression, as indicated by the three dotted lines.

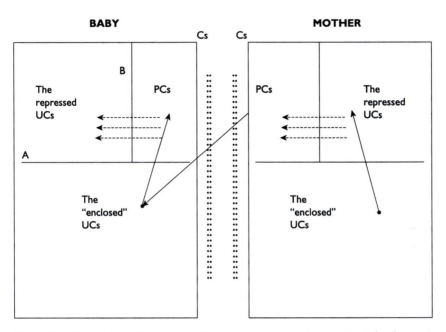

*Figure 2.1* The origin of the enigmatic message and its fate in the infant's mind. Modified from Laplanche (2007, p. 206).

The figure portrays a baby who is excited, confused, enraged and enamoured – and a mother who feels similarly though in line with her adult sexuality.

Laplanche's concepts unite drive theory and interactive concepts. There are, however, two problems. The term "enigmatic message" indicates that the mother's communication is bewildering to the infant, but it does not say what kind of representations it engenders in *him*. The enclosed message entails another problem; a message without meaning may be merely inscribed, but how could we say anything about meaningless phenomena? Similarly to Laplanche, Bailly (2012) differs between signifier and "raw experience". I claim that if raw experiences exist, they fall outside of any psychoanalytic discussion. Our investigatory instrument only allows us to comment on phenomena that carry meaning. As analysts we can comment on representations but not on pure perceptions. It is another matter that representations may be signified on different *semiotic levels*. This is precisely what makes the adult's enigmatic messages problematic to the baby. He experiences a tension between the different significatory levels of mother's communication. Rufus probably experienced this while peeping into the dressing-room; his mother's calling for her husband and the undercurrents of their intimate secrets.

In Rufus's case, there was a minute or two of crying and consolation. Then he was OK again. In clinical cases, the semiotic mix may create problems that neither mother nor baby can solve. On a word-symbolic level Nic's mother's comment, "There's no grub in your finger", aimed at comforting and guiding him in breastfeeding. On other semiotic levels her tone, phrasing, body movements and facial expressions contained other messages: "Stop bothering me . . . I wish I hadn't become a mother . . . I want the best for you . . . I'm so annoyed with this situation." These significations clashed and so did Nic's insufferable representations: 'I feel bad, I want it otherwise . . . Mum loves me, no, yes, no.' Possibly, his jerks reflected his effort at literally shaking them off himself. Little Tina was charged with a similar riddle; to integrate her mother's wish to be spontaneous and generous with her – and to reject and control her.

## Primal process and primal representations

I will now invoke Piera Aulagnier's (2001) concepts of the primal process and the pictogram. My hope is to solve the problem embedded in Laplanche's idea of the merely inscribed message and also to better conceptualize infant representations. To Aulagnier, the psyche's primary task is to create mental representations. They originate as the psyche of infant and mother meet. Similarly to Laplanche, she recognizes the inevitable "clash between what the infant perceives and [the] environmental stimulation" (p. xix), but she does not believe the adult's messages are simply inscribed in the infant psyche. Instead, she invokes *le processus originaire*, "the primal process", which produces these earliest representations in response to the baby's contact with mother.

To follow Aulagnier's argument, let us first briefly return to Freud. In *The Interpretation of Dreams* (1900), he suggested that the baby's original mode of reducing distress is to hallucinate that his wish is fulfilled. When this method fails he starts crying. He is then fed and his need is stilled. This is the beginning of wish formation. Aulagnier follows Freud but to her, the baby does more than just trying to "re-establish the situation of the original satisfaction" as Freud suggested (pp. 565–566). He also actively processes information that emanates "from a space [the mother] that is heterogenous to [the baby's psychical apparatus]" (Aulagnier, 2001, p. 17). He must metabolize it into a material that is homogenous with the structure of *his* psyche. This metabolization or transformation is the aim of the primal process.

The primal process works by creating *pictograms*. If Andy is breastfed and feels comforted, the "pictogram of conjunction" perhaps runs something like, 'Good Breast deleting Bad Mouth'. It is dual, since it consists of an erogenous zone with a complementary objectal part; mouth + breast. Nevertheless the baby represents it as singular and created by himself. In addition, it is connected with an affect. In the reverse "pictogram of rejection", 'Mouth–Breast' implies unpleasure. Pictograms are thus also dual in that they unite the represented object with the emotion linked to it, for example, 'Go away, Bad Breast and Bad Experience'.

Aulagnier, like Laplanche, emphasizes the role of the mother's unconscious representations in relation to the child. In her words, the mother sees her baby as a "shadow" of her projections. A child such as Nic faces the challenge of creating a pictogram out of Tessie's comment, whose word-symbolic content conveys a fact (a finger does not contain milk) while other significatory levels emanate from her projections ("Nic, you're exploiting me"). Perhaps his pictogram might be written, 'Come needed Good Breast–Mouth, go away Bad Breast–Mouth, I created both, I am bad, I suffer'. Similarly, for little Tina's muddled infant representations one might imagine pictograms such as, 'Come cosy Tina, go away stern Christina, you look alike, go away simple Tina, come proper Christina, I don't know who's who and what's what in either of you'. I suggest these representations, which were neither separated nor made conscious, were essential roots to the girl's screaming.

Nic's and Tina's cases demonstrate that a baby's discombobulated pictograms correspond to the mother's unconscious ambivalence towards her child. As therapy proceeds, we may talk with the mother about her mixed feelings. With the baby, we face further problems. Obviously, we know little of what he understands. We will soon return to this issue. The second problem is that he often seems to feel that *he* is bad. If he believes he created the pictogram he will conclude that its badness emanates from himself: 'I created both, I am bad, I suffer.' Symptoms such as whining, jerking, screaming and grunting may express a conviction that 'Breast-Me is bad and I must get rid of it'. My interventions to Nic addressed this: "You're grumbling and wringing your body. You look sore, maybe like Mum's feeling constrained." I conveyed that he was *not* bad and that his feelings and behaviour were interesting and needed to be talked about.

We are now ready to suggest a term that answers the question from Chapter 1: what goes on in a baby's mind? I have argued why we must assume that babies produce and work with mental representations. The problem has been to find the most suitable term for them. Sandler and Rosenblatt (1962) distinguish between "image" and "representation". The former is a rudimentary mental construct that is "indistinguishable from experiences of need satisfaction". In contrast, a representation has "a more or less enduring existence" and is "constructed out of a multitude of impressions" (p. 133). The authors restrict "image" to the newborn's biologically driven behaviour, whereas "representation" refers to a more advanced mental organization than in young infants such as Nic and Tina. I therefore suggest a term that falls developmentally between image and representation; *primal representation*.

Similarly to representation in the traditional sense, the function of a primal representation is "to perceive sensations arising from various sources, to organize, and structure them in a meaningful way" (p. 131) and to transform "raw sensory data into meaningful percepts" (p. 132). Still, there are huge differences between representations in the traditional sense and primal representations. The formal aspects of the latter are well covered by Stern's vitality affect concept but their affective dimension goes beyond "feeling shapes" or "protonarrative envelopes" (Stern, 1995). Primal representations have an affective content; they are *about* something or someone. Tina starts screaming in Mum's lap because she is afraid of, or frustrated by, various aspects of the maternal object. Nic's grunting at the breast reflects his confused representations of a mother who says friendly words in a harsh tone. Our main challenge with describing these representations is that our language is utterly insufficient. We need to imagine speech bubbles with interjections in a cartoon, chaotic shrieks in atonal music or the blurred dots of an abstract painting. Such imagery, however, only reflects the formal aspect of primal representations. To describe their affective content we must still rely on words. That is why I address both Tina and her mother with words such as, "You seem angry" or "This is hard on you".

## Primal representations, language development and therapeutic accessibility

I will end this chapter by using the concept of primal representations to explicate a phenomenon noted by many parent–infant clinicians: young infants in therapy seem particularly flexible in relieving themselves of distress. As their first birthday approaches, symptoms and character traits become more recalcitrant. The reason might be that negative parental influence has lasted longer and the mother's primary occupation (Winnicott, 1956) – her ability to "feel herself into her infant's place" (p. 303) – has begun to dwindle. Norman (2001) suggested another explanation; that the young infant's "unique flexibility in changing representations of itself and others" (p. 83) results from his undeveloped capacity to symbolize. The question emerges: what characterizes such undeveloped symbolization?

In my thinking, during the first year primal representations will be overlaid by more and more elaborate representations. Thus, words become linked ever more closely to iconic and indexical representations. This development has two sides to it. When a healthy baby such as Andy has passed his first birthday, he will calm down more quickly by saying 'Silly Mum', forgiving her, and becoming happy again. In contrast, distressed babies such as Nic and Tina may settle in their pathology and become more recalcitrant towards therapeutic efforts. One might object that this does not reflect any "psychopathology of a psychodynamic nature" (Stern, 1985, p. 202) in the baby. Accordingly, we should not address him with any intent of analyzing his inner world. I, however, think it is essential to also understand the baby's personal inner world. Of course, my position raises the question of how much language a baby understands. I will therefore approach experimental studies on infant language perception. The aim is to understand how the infant's developing linguistic capacities help to solder together primal representations and word representations and, in addition, how this will affect his therapeutic accessibility.

Infant researchers have investigated how language faculties develop during the first year. I will integrate their findings with a semiotic perspective. The newborn's experiential world consists of hazy images, buzzing sounds and poignant smells, all of which are probably connected with affective states. In semiotic terms, they belong to what Peirce calls Firstness. In this category there is "no comparison, no relation, no recognized multiplicity . . . no change, . . . no reflexion, nothing but a simple positive character" (Kloesel & Houser, 1998, p. 150). Phenomena are experienced in their "direct positive presentness" (idem). No sign has any specific meaning; all is marked by *semiotic fluidity*, which makes the category so hard to envisage. It is probably similar to Bailly's (2012) "raw experience" (p. 10). To quote Peirce: "Assert [Firstness] and it has already lost its characteristic innocence" (Kloesel & Houser, 1992, p. 248). Secondness, in contrast, is related to another experience; one stands against another. When Mum says hello to the baby, Secondness experiencing implies taking her words as a prompt or a reaction. It also marks a difference; Mum was gone, now she's here. Green (2004) describes it as a "brutal reaction to a force originating from the outside" (p. 112). Secondness is a prerequisite for the baby's development of linguistic capacities in the sense of differentiating the sounds, later also the meanings, of different words.

Infant research studies have clarified that the newborn experiences speech as a *special* kind of sound. He can discern phonetic contrasts in various languages (Kuhl, 2004) and classify them according to global rhythmic properties (Nazzi, Bertoncini & Mehler, 1998). He also seems to prefer the prosody of his native language (Mehler *et al.*, 1988) and his mother's voice (DeCasper & Fifer, 1980). Two months later he prefers real speech to similar but artificially produced sounds (Vouloumanos & Werker, 2004).

Yet, a young baby understands no verbal import. Instead he engages in face-to-face interactions with turns, smiles, vocalizations, arm movements and complex emotions (Trevarthen, 2001). Words are merely a comforter, an intimidation or a captivating sound, all depending on the emotional quality of these interactions (Markova & Legerstee, 2006). In semiotic terms, iconic and indexical signs have not yet been welded to their corresponding word-symbols. Vivona (2012), however, takes one step further and denies that a non-verbal period exists during development. She cites studies (Gervain, Macagno, Cogoi, Peña & Mehler, 2008) showing that already the newborn is more sensitive to perceptual patterns typical of infant-directed speech, such as *mama* and *dada*. Even babies as young as two months show a brain lateralization similar to that of adults when they listen to speech (Gervain & Mehler, 2010). Young infants also grasp that words, in contrast to general sounds, can be used for categorizing objects (Ferry, Hespos & Waxman, 2010). Vivona cites these studies while yet emphasizing that they do not say anything about the infant's word *comprehension*.

Vivona thinks we have underestimated infants' linguistic understanding. We have relied too much on observations that they derive meaning from "the music of parents' speech" and "the prosody or emotional tone" (p. 249). She argues that sensorimotor and linguistic representations are "inexorably linked" (p. 254). Thus, spoken language may carry with it reminiscences of dim bodily memories. This tallies with Freud's suggestion that a word is an ensemble of auditory, visual and kinaesthetic elements (1915c). Vivona concludes that the young infant is *preverbal* and *verbal* but not *non-verbal*. He has "begun to amass a vocabulary of acoustic word forms, to associate meaning to [them], to apply [them] reliably in novel contexts . . . and to understand speaking as a communicative act" (p. 256). Thus, there may be no self-experience that lies beyond the reach of language.

Some of Vivona's observations link well with my primal representation concept. I guess, for example, that Tina has different kinaesthetic and affective representations when her mother treats her as "Tina" or "Christina". Vivona's point that linguistic understanding develops earlier than hitherto assumed is also worth emphasizing. Nonetheless, I distinguish between periods during the child's first year. Many studies quoted by Vivona refer to children beyond six months of age. At this age an important change occurs. Babies who could earlier discriminate between consonants that are meaningful in *any* language will gradually lose this ability (Krentz & Corina, 2008; Werker & Tees, 2002). At ten months, they "prefer" their native language. Six-month-olds prefer American Sign Language to pantomime, since they discern that only the former has linguistic properties. Some months later, they prefer pantomime instead and regard sign language as foreign (Krentz & Corina, 2008). Their waxing estrangement vis-à-vis non-native language shows that semiotic fluidity is diminishing during the second half of the first year, and that the meanings of word-symbols are beginning to stick to their corresponding objects. If we point at a quadruped and say "dog" or "*chien*" to a five-month-old his reactions are similar, but saying "*chien*" to a ten-month-old American will evoke protests.

Vivona's clinical conclusions concern adult patients, which to me is an unnecessary restriction. Litowitz (2012), in a response to Vivona, suggests that babies learn to understand speech during daily activities with adults. The adult does not so much teach language; rather, "speech and other sign systems (such as gestures, body movements, facial expressions, songs) are simply part of these activities" (p. 269). I will issue from two suggestions by Litowitz to explain how I would apply Vivona's findings to baby patients: (1) the analyst uses language to reach "a shared understanding" (p. 272) with his patient and (2) "the child is extracting meaningful patterns from its environment visually and behaviourally" (idem) and from vocal sounds. I conclude that there also exists some "shared understanding" between analyst and baby. It does *not* consist in lexical comprehension. Rather, she notices the analyst's attention, empathy and intuition in trying to grasp what her communications might mean.

When I address one-month-old Nic, I know that in his primal representations the links between word-symbols, icons and indices remain fluid. Yet, his linguistic "appetite" makes him listen to language addressed and he will regard it as a special mode of communication. Its meaning is incomprehensible in the lexical, but not in its affective, sense. My words have a special impact, paradoxically, *because* they are incomprehensible to Nic but demonstrate my intention of comprehending his plight (T. Baradon, personal communication, 2012). They draw his attention to my words' affective message, including the calm reassurance that painful emotions may be talked about. This only becomes credible if I am sincere in my communication. Thus, I do not speak "bla-bla" to a baby. On a word-symbolic level, Nic would not differentiate "bla-bla" from "All this makes your feelings clash". But on an affective level the difference would be tangible and decisive for therapeutic outcome.

We thus end up with facing a paradox; a child seems easier to help when he does *not* understand our interventions' lexical content. I have sought to explain this by the semiotic fluidity during the first months of life; icons and indices remain un-attached to word-symbols. The main question in the first two chapters was: what goes on in a baby's mind? My answer is: primal representations. Sometimes they overwhelm the baby but may yield to external beneficial influence. This may occur when a moment of consolation or a feed of milk will finally turn a baby's emotional turmoil into quiescence – as with Andy. In clinical babies such as Nic and Tina, excruciating and contradictory primal representations govern their interactions and behaviour. The concept of primal representations helps us place the baby on a more equal footing qua patient in parent–infant therapy. He is still unequal in matters of biological development, psychological maturation and linguistic capacities. But he is equal in the sense that he forms representations, for which I have proposed the term "primal representations".

# Chapter 3

# Containment

## Maternal music and paternal words with three-month-old Frida

The vignettes with Nic and Tina in chapters 1 and 2 demonstrated how and why I address the baby as well as the parent. I emphasized that I do not believe a distressed baby literally understands verbal content. To provide an epistemological basis for this technique and to explain how communications flow back and forth in these treatments, I introduced a semiotic apparatus. One clinical example was when I told Tina, "You are screaming terribly and we don't know why. This must be very hard on you". I argued that she would grasp that I really wanted to understand what was going on in her, something she could only express by screaming. I also suggested that a baby might process the emotional wavelengths of the words. How does such processing come about, and how do these wavelengths appear in clinical reality? Obviously, a baby does not reach insight through reflecting on our interpretations. Some other working mechanism must explain the improvements that we register in these therapies.

Let us begin by taking a cursory overview of the development in psychoanalytic technique and theory over the second half of the last century. One notices a shift, which was actually inaugurated already by earlier authors (Ferenczi, 1931, 1933; Balint, 1949, 1952); I refer to an increasing emphasis on the analyst–analysand relationship. Nowadays, analysts study more keenly its impact on the therapeutic process, and we also think therapeutic improvement comes about, at least partly, by way of the relationship itself. Different analytic traditions phrase this emphasis on the patient–therapist relationship in various terms, such as the "intersubjective" trend (Beebe *et al.*, 2005; Levenson, 1983, 2005) and the object-relational in Winnicott's and the post-Kleinians' sense (Joseph, 1985; Rosenfeld, 1987; Steiner, 1993).

When Bion introduced the term *containment* he considered it to be the essence of analytic work. Though he based his ideas on work with psychotic adults, he anchored the model in what he imagined was going on between a mother and her distressed infant. Melanie Klein had focused on the workings of the baby's inner life but she had not elaborated on how they affected the mother and her response to the child's projected distress. Bion expanded Klein's model and focused also on the interaction between *two* inner lives; that of the baby and his mother. The term containment referred to what happens within the mother as she receives, processes and returns to the baby the anxieties, or "the contained", which he has projected onto her.

Norman (2001, 2004) brought Bion's containment concept into the parent–infant therapy room to describe what went on between him and the baby. Like many other therapists, he regarded the baby as an intersubjective being who relates actively to his primary objects from life's first moments. But he took one step further; he claimed that a distressed baby would look for containment from *him*, provided she was exposed to his intensive attention. Consequently, he tried to establish a relationship with her to become that container. His idea was that up till now, the baby had been suffering from affects that she could not integrate with more mature parts of her budding personality. Instead, they emerged as various symptoms that distressed both the baby and the parent.

Norman's argument raises a question: what do we actually do when we *contain* a baby? I will approach the question via a case, which will re-appear in the chapter on infant sexuality. It is taken from a video-recorded therapy session with 23-year-old Kate and her three-month-old daughter Frida. Between the vignettes, I will submit some theoretical remarks on containment, especially on its two aspects; the "maternal music" and the "paternal words".

## Frida: Vignette 1 – A crying girl

Kate, the mother, tells me Frida has been fussing all morning. She is sitting with Frida in her lap though holding her at some distance. Frida cries incessantly and wrings her body in distress. I move my chair closer to Kate's while trying to catch little Frida's eye.

| | |
|---|---|
| *Analyst to Frida:* | Oh my, something terrible is running around inside you! |
| | [Frida goes on crying against in the lap of her mother, who is rocking her briskly with visible anxiety. Mum tries to look Frida in her eyes, but she just goes on crying. I try to get eye contact with the girl, saying:] |
| *A to F:* | This is really hard on you. |
| | [Frida looks up the ceiling, then outside the window. She makes some quick blinking movements, as if closing her eyes.] |
| *A to F:* | Hello little friend, you're looking outside, at those trees outside. |
| | [I look outside, too, while Mum throws a quick and helpless glance at me. I look at Frida, while continuing talking to her. She goes on crying while Mum tries in vain to comfort her.] |
| *A to F and mother:* | Everything went wrong this morning! Mum got angry with me yesterday, and then you Frida got angry with her because she wasn't with you . . . How could you forgive her? This is really troublesome. Sheer hell! |
| | [Mum gets a bit more pensive and calm while Frida is still crying.] |

| | |
|---|---|
| *A:* | How does all this feel inside you, Kate? |
| *Mother:* | Terrible! |
| *A:* | You feel powerless. |
| *M:* | Yes! |

## Clinical background

My contact with Kate had begun eight months earlier, when she asked me for help with the aftermath of a rough and protracted adolescence. She was five-months pregnant by a young man she did not get along with. We started a twice-weekly psychotherapy dealing with problems with affect regulation; she could suddenly feel ashamed and gawky, unable to verbalize her internal situation or influence external events. These difficulties applied to any strong feelings such as anger, sadness, happiness and pride. Four months into therapy Frida was born. Delivery went well and though there was discord with Frida's father, her own family supported her firmly. Breastfeeding started smoothly and we soon resumed therapy.

Our point of departure was not a mother seeking help with her baby, but a pregnant woman with personal problems that she feared she would transmit to her future child. Until the session presented above, I had rarely addressed Frida. Most often, she rested peacefully on her mother's lap. But when Frida was two months old Kate started mentioning her fussiness. I assumed this was linked to Kate's difficulties with affect regulation. Kate often gushed with un-modulated emotions, as when she expressed her hopes for the future or her opinions about her family of origin. She would blush and her voice falter while tears were streaming down her cheeks. In such moments, she could not look Frida in her eyes and explain what was going on inside her – and it seemed that Frida was beginning to react negatively to this. I had begun pointing it out to Kate, but until now I had not observed any instant connections between her affective blushes and Frida's fussiness. Therefore, there had been little occasion for me to address the little one about how she reacted to her mother. To sum up, this was a therapy with a pregnant mother who then began to bring her newborn along.

During the session presented, however, I shifted to using an MIP approach with the two. Kate had worked up the courage to say I should have prepared her for the possibility of a phone call during yesterday's session. I had been expecting an important call and, for the first time in my professional life, I had left my cellphone switched on. In the midst of the session the phone rang. I apologized and left them for a few minutes. Upon my return, Kate vaguely conveyed that she had felt abandoned. It was easier for her to speak of sadness than of outright anger, a feeling I confirmed she had good reasons to harbour due to my breach of the therapeutic frame.

When Kate addressed this incident a day later, she was anxious and embarrassed and told me she almost wanted to run away. Then she reported that Frida had fussed all morning. While I received her critique respectfully and told her

I understood she was angry with me, I also reflected on Frida's morning trouble. I pondered if it resulted from her sense of abandonment by a mother who was preoccupied with anger at me. I thus guessed Kate's disappointment and anger had made her unable to contain her daughter adequately.

As Frida started crying, I decided to address her directly, to "retrieve those parts of the infant's inner world that have been excluded from containment" (Norman, 2001, p. 93). I did this by sharing with Frida her intense affective experiences this morning: "Your Mum got angry with me yesterday, and now you got angry with Mum because she couldn't be with you in the right way." I was addressing the unreliable containment both of them had been exposed to. I also formulated this as a problem with Frida's un-metabolized affects: "There is something running around inside you." Finally, I invoked her agency (Stern, 1985) in how she dealt with resentment and despair. I linked this with my empathy with her suffering: "How are you gonna forgive your Mum? Oh my, this was really troublesome."

What would Frida understand of these interventions? Did I not actually speak to her mother but via Frida, a question addressed in Figure 1.1 in Chapter 1? Or, if it really was Frida whom I was addressing, was she not rather affected by some-thing else than my verbal statements? If so, how could we conceptualize this "something else" and how it affected her? In the previous chapters, I answered these questions by using semiotic concepts. Here, I will address them by centring round the subject of containment. I will begin by formulating a question.

## Whom does the psychoanalyst contain?

I will compare two seemingly disparate situations: a trio of chamber music and a mother–infant therapy session. If two musicians are preoccupied with each other's phrases but inattentive to the third partner, it will result in vapid or shallow music. The forsaken musician might react with anger, despair or indifference. I use this scene to metaphorically portray a risk in mother–infant treatments; that we forsake the infant. When we ask a mother to tell us about her baby worries the little one might feel, 'Now, what about ME? I am also a member of this trio!'

Such abandonment of the baby occurs frequently. Over the years, I have witnessed scores of case presentations and video demonstrations at seminars and international congresses. Despite the therapist's intention to attend equally to mother and baby, in reality something else happens quite often: mother and therapist talk about the baby, whose activities go on relatively unnoticed until she starts crying or grimacing. Then the adults "wake up" and attend to her and even talk to her. A trio has emerged out of the duo – but often only for a while.

The therapist has many reasons to pass over the baby. He and the mother speak the same language and find it easier to understand each other compared with the grimaces, jerks and moans of a preverbal child. Second, a troubled baby's communications are anguishing to us adults. Her despair triggers not only the mother's infantile helplessness but also that of the analyst. This accounts for the powerful countertransferences in mother–infant treatments. The analyst reacts to being with a little person so incomprehensible and remote in development, yet so close to his own infantile self.

Though we wish to include the little one in a dialogue, we tend to forget. If we do it consistently, we will contain the mother while hoping that we simultaneously ameliorate the infant's suffering. This adult focus might be supported by the following argument: "Your trio metaphor may well illustrate the clinical interactions. Certainly, you should not neglect Frida and you should talk to her, too! But since she does not understand you, in reality it is her mother who is affected by your baby address." This objection was voiced already in Chapter 1. To substantiate my argument further, let me press the trio metaphor one more step. Who plays with whom in a trio? One musician's phrase may echo that of his fellow and yet foreshadow a phrase of another colleague. A trio where one part is merely accompanied by the two others makes boring music. So, whom does our musician actually address? Obviously both of his fellows, but his messages have different functions to each of them.

When I said, "Your Mum got angry with me, and now you got angry with Mum", this message had two recipients and several layers of meaning. Its verbal level suggested to Kate that her daughter reacted to changes within herself due to her anger with me. Of this level, Frida understood as little as a musically illiterate person would do in front of a musical score. This person, however, might "understand" music in the sense of enjoying, performing and being emotionally moved by it. Similarly, I believe Frida understood other levels of my address and that I would have curtailed my therapeutic arsenal if I refrained from this address.

The trio metaphor implies that our interventions will always affect both mother and infant. Technically, we have a choice of addressing either or both participants. There is an essential difference between looking Frida in her eyes saying, "This is hard on you" – or turning to mother explicating, "This is hard on her". Stern points out that as the number of participants increases, the therapy process becomes less linear and less predictable: "What happens is more spontaneously co-created, very sloppy, full of errors and repairs, and sudden direction changes" (Stern, 2008, p. 180). I think Stern would have agreed that this spontaneity and sloppiness is an essential ingredient of the "chamber music" of parent–infant therapy.

The analyst "musician" must listen to both of his fellow-players. If he focuses too much on the baby he may lose the mother's trust and the treatment altogether. If he focuses too much on the mother, the baby's anxieties will remain uncontained. In the end, this may also lead to a stalemate. Rather than prescribing when to address whom, I will outline the benefits and pitfalls of each alternative. Though this book brings out the infant address, I hasten to add that it will work only once the mother has understood our reasons for using it. If not, she may feel it is mumbo jumbo and get annoyed or offended. Kate and I had a lengthy therapeutic relationship and her working alliance had stood many tests of negative transference. But in newly started treatments, I try to gauge if the mother has grasped why I talk to her baby. If needed, I try to explain to her, though I do not overestimate the effects of pedagogy. Alternatively, I wait for a moment when the baby demonstrates that she is sensitive to the emotional communication. Then I indicate this to the mother. This way she witnesses first-hand that her baby is "a person", as one mother once expressed her surprised observation.

It is true that when we contain the baby, it may bring about "reparation of the mother–infant dyad" (Norman, 2001, p. 94). Sometimes, however, the mother's wish for being contained herself may disturb this reparation. If she feels left out by our infant focus, we should talk to her about it. The same is true if she is emotionally absent or overburdened by personal problems. Her claims of being listened to may arise from adult or more infantile parts of her personality. Whichever the case, her claims are justified. Sometimes, not much oversight is needed from the analyst for a snowball of negative maternal transference to start rolling, and then we are heading for an interrupted treatment. Mothers with baby worries are brittle. They often feel condemned that their love for the baby is not good enough. They are bewildered by forces they do not grasp. Their joy blends with guilt feelings and low self-esteem. Any intervention, whether directed to the baby or to her, may be read through the lens of "What does the therapist mean by talking that way? Is there something wrong with the way I treat my child?"

Our best lens for deciding on whom to focus is our countertransference. My oscillating focus on Frida and Kate was guided by spontaneous shifts in my identifications. Sometimes, I identified with Kate ("How does all this feel inside you, Mum?"). This occurred when I glimpsed her distress in front of the screaming Frida. Sometimes, I was more in tune with Frida ("Something terrible is running around inside you"). In those instances, I "was" the baby myself who was screaming helplessly because nobody understood me! The fact that we are thrown between primitive and more mature identifications is one reason for the often intense countertransference in parent–infant work (Golse, 2006).

## How does the psychoanalyst contain the infant?

I used the second person in "You got angry with Mum" because I wanted to personally reach Frida. One central aspect of containment is to convey to the infant one's full attention; not only by observing her but also by musing on and verbalizing what one guesses is going on inside her. To this end, the countertransference is of immense value when it resonates with the wave-lengths of the infant's anxieties. However, it is not a fool-proof source of information. It needs to be complemented by observing infant and mother after our intervention. We are back at Peirce's inferential circuit from Chapter 1. I guessed that Frida's anguish at home had to do with her mother's emotional unavailability due to her anger with me. However, until now my assumption remained unconfirmed. While containing Frida I got a new idea; her looking outside to the trees suggested that she, too, was making herself unavailable to mother's consolations.

Using the second person was not simply a matter of saying "you" to Frida – while I actually meant "she" talking to the mother about her baby. It implied that my entire communication spectre was bestowed on her; my vocalizations in a speech rhythm, the voice inflections with rises and falls and the sound quality of attention and empathy. I think that when we achieve *Einfühlung*, the "feeling-in" of empathy, our voice will be coloured by natural variations of piano and forte, crescendo and diminuendo, accelerando and ritardando, tenuto and sforzando – all those qualities that will transform the notes of a musical score into living music. The sum total of these qualities constitutes the emotional wavelengths of our communication with the baby – and it is these constituents that I believe the baby is able to process.

So far, I have addressed the auditory component of containment. It also comprises visual elements that capture the infant's attention; there was my look into Frida's eyes and my eyebrows being raised due to my specific attention to her. Video-recordings indicate that my facial expressions tend to inadvertently mirror those of the child. For example, I sometimes notice a sad look on my face when I am talking to a sad baby. Such expressions will only genuinely reflect one's countertransference, and will only be part of a well-functioning containment, if they are spontaneous and unfeigned. The same applies to the analyst's hand gestures and body movements. Many babies are captured by hand movements, probably because they reflect my emotional emphasis. When I told Frida, "This is really hard on you", I made an arm movement to emphasize my words. I noticed that she observed my arm closely.

If this "opera" (Golse, 2006) of sounds, gestures and mimics forms an important part of containment, how does it affect the infant? What makes her interested in doing "chamber music" with me and Mum? Why would she believe that I was addressing her suffering? To answer, I will invoke the "communicative musicality" (Trevarthen & Aitken, 2001) in the baby–mother interaction. The infant is "attracted to the emotional narratives carried in the human voice" and wants "to participate in a shared performance that respects a common pulse, phrasing, and expressive development" (p. 12). The analyst uses this aptitude to reach and interact with the baby. To depict the interplay of our containment and the infant's musicality is as hard as describing a musical experience in words. Throughout the book I have tried to bridge the chasm between the wordless and the verbal realms by way of concepts such as primal representations, analogic representations, presentational symbolism, icons and indices.

The concept of containment is also anchored in a semiotic vision of the mind. In brief, to contain is to transform signs. This becomes evident when we recall that the container metabolizes what Bion labelled β-elements, which, after all, are nothing but primitive signs. Containment results in a growth of the baby's α-function, as happened in my dialogue with Frida. Inspired by studies on parent–infant research and treatments, James Grotstein (2008) applies Bion's concepts to infants. He assumes she has a rudimentary (inherited) α-function with which she is "prepared to generate pre-lexical communications and to receive prosodic lexical communications from mother" (p. 45). I would only add: and the communications from the analyst. If I could formulate in infant language what was on Frida's mind as I was addressing her it might run, 'Me feel better', or to paraphrase the gospel tune, 'Nobody knows the trouble I'm in, nobody knows but that man'.

The idea of using musical metaphors to describe mother–infant interactions is not new. To Daniel Stern (1985), the newborn's emergent self is represented as "shapes, intensities and temporal patterns" (p. 51). He described vitality affects in musical terms and provided research evidence that infants can discern temporal patterns in their interactions with parents. Correspondingly, a mother intuitively makes the "temporal structure of their behaviour" (p. 84) obvious to the baby by singing and talking to her. Feldman (2007) also views time as a central aspect of emotions. Beebe *et al.* (2000) claim that timing and rhythm organize *all* communication and behaviour. There is the rhythm of the look, of the touch, of the breath and of the words.

However, let us not forget that I add one dimension – beyond the temporal structure – to the infant's affect. As I argued in Chapter 1, it also has some primitive content; it is *about* something pleasant or unpleasant. Frida's screaming expresses something that I label 'panic because Mum's here but she's not really with me'. Containment thus implies, not only to receive and hold the baby's anxieties, but also to try to understand what Frida is screaming about. Let us now follow if the session developed in a way that increased my understanding.

## Frida: Vignette 2 – "One is totally charmed!"

After Kate has expressed how she has felt powerless about Frida's crying, we speak about her sense of impotence with me and my cellphone and with men generally. Little Frida suddenly roars. This alerts me that I have left her out of focus. She is still sitting in her mother's lap with the possibility of facing me and Mum.

| | |
|---|---|
| *Analyst to Frida:* | Yes, we should also be talking about you, shouldn't we? |
| *Mother:* | Mmm . . . |
| *A to M and F:* | Things get screwed up for you both, well, if we are right about all this. Something else might explain what happened. Maybe a fart or poo-poo will come out of it! |

While saying this, I scratch my head somewhat nervously. The girl looks past me to her right-hand side, then again at my chest. I sense her vague efforts at contacting me.

| | |
|---|---|
| *A to F:* | Hello there, this was very troublesome to you! |
| | [The girl looks between her mother and me.] |
| *A to F:* | And all these things just kept running around inside you! |

| | |
|---|---|
| M *(looking at me confidently):* | You mean these things are linked: the physical and the psychic . . .? |
| *A to M:* | How does that idea sound to you? |
| *M:* | I think it is true. |
| *A to M:* | Mmm . . . Yesterday, you were angry with me. Perhaps you were also afraid of being angry. |
| | [The mother nods while rocking the girl, who is somewhat more at ease.] |
| *A to M:* | You were thinking, "How could I speak with Björn about it, and demand he had handled the cellphone in another way?" |
| *M:* | Yes! |
| | [The girl is calmer.] |
| *A to M:* | So you were gone from Frida (I point with my right hand between the two). |
| *M:* | Yesterday, yes. |
| *A to F:* | Mum was gone from you yesterday, Frida. |
| | [The girl closes her eyes a little and is more peaceful now.] |
| *A to F:* | Oh my, you are tired. But do you know something, little one: you are gone from Mum, too, because a while ago you didn't look into her eyes. It was as if you took revenge on Mum. I understand that. It's like when Mum didn't look into my eyes yesterday. I had to ask her, "Hello Kate, why don't you say anything, could we get into contact?" |
| | [The girl is calm now. Her gaze is clearer as she is silently looking out the window.] |
| *A to F:* | Mum just lifted you up, but I saw you looking away. And you, Mum, were sitting at home yesterday, looking away from Frida and thinking about you and me. Meanwhile you, Frida, were looking away from your Mum. Then you started crying and now you are so tired. |
| | [I nod my head slowly, spontaneously copying her fatigue. This captures the girl's attention. Mum smiles at her. The girl looks slightly away from me again.] |
| *A to F:* | Perhaps tomorrow morning you will have forgiven Mum. In a dream, maybe. After all, Mum is the best! |
| | [Mum looks lovingly at Frida who smiles faintly at her.] |
| *A to F:* | It seems you already started forgiving Mum. |
| | The girl gives me her first smile while looking into my eyes. |
| *A to F:* | Oh, what a smile, Frida. One is totally charmed! |
| | She goes on smiling for a little while and then resumes crying. |
| *A to F:* | Aha, the bad thing is coming back: 'Silly, silly, silly Mum! Next time, you gotta tell me when you are in a bad mood, so I will be prepared for it!' But you see Frida, Mum can't always tell you in advance, because she's only human. |

## Emotions and motions in the analytic discourse

In parent–infant work, we make use of the kinship between languages of music and of affects. They are connected via the *human body*. Coenesthetic (Spitz, 1965) and auditory perceptions rely on vibratory phenomena and therefore blend unnoticeably. We listen to music while sensing its vibrations and gestural affective motions. Music thus portrays affects by analogously imitating their bodily expressions (Salomonsson, 1989). In brief, we experience it as if music *sounds* similar to how emotions *feel* inside our bodies. The tonal waves of rise and fall, piano and forte, sharpness and mellowness, legato and staccato, correspond to similar affect waves in our psychosomatic beings. These thoughts echo Stern's (1985) description of vitality affects in "dynamic, kinetic terms, such as 'surging', 'fading away', 'fleeting', 'explosive', 'crescendo' . . . and so on" (p. 54). They also evoke Susanne Langer's (1942) idea that our inner life has formal properties "similar to those of music – patterns of motion and rest, of tension and release, of agreement and disagreement, preparation, fulfilment, excitation, sudden change, etc." (p. 228).

We may apply the links between music and affects to explicate how containment comes about in parent–infant work. The analyst discerns a happy from a distressed cry or the joie de vivre from the panic in a sudden jerk. He also differentiates a mother's panic, shame, hostility, love and guilt through her words, sighs, frowns and motions. He is thus "musical" in the sense that he understands emotions, that is, the motions of affects as they appear in the visual, auditory and proprioceptive modalities.

What then is Frida capable of? I think she captures the feelings parallel to my words. This comes about through the "timing . . . the scaffolding, the melody, on which verbal content is . . . superimposed" (Beebe *et al.*, 2000, p. 101). The music of containment thus holds Frida in a "sound bed". My intervention soothes her – but not because its words are to the point, since that would be impossible. It rather helps her when my expressions become increasingly coordinated as I work through my countertransference. The more I understand of Frida's predicament, the closer my speech and behaviour come together. I suggest she monitors this process in me, which gradually enables her to create primitive "acts of meaning" or "protolinguistic representations", as Bruner (1990) would call them.

At one point in vignette 2 I get scared that I have overlooked some gastrointestinal trouble – and I scratch my head. Consciously I want to address her experiences with Mum. Unconsciously, I get anxious that I am all at sea. This clash makes my words express one thing and my hands something else. My words mean, "This is not dangerous" while my gestures indicate, "Oh dear, what if I am missing out a medical calamity!" But, I resume courage and tell Frida "something that, at least for the moment, seems to be true" (Norman, 2001, p. 96). As Norman emphasizes – and my head-scratching also indicates – "this may sometimes be painful for the analyst to formulate" (idem). As I work through my anxiety the verbal, indexical and iconical levels of my intervention will come together into a containing Gestalt. In contrast, Kate's containing Gestalt had probably been inconsistent in the morning. Consciously, Kate wanted to soothe Frida. Unconsciously, she was dwelling on her anger with me. This made Mum's message "messy" (Tronick, 2005), which provoked anxiety and despair in Frida.

Another element may complicate containment; our messages to the child are inevitably "enigmatic and sexual" (Laplanche, 1997, p. 661), as we discussed in Chapter 2. They are imbued with connotations beyond ordinary linguistic usage and beyond our awareness. Our communications are thus "opaque to its recipient and its transmitter alike" (Laplanche, 1995, p. 665). This "fundamental anthropological situation" is caused by the asymmetry between adult and child sexuality (Laplanche, 2007, p. 99). When I tell smiling Frida, "One is totally charmed", I express my joy in our sudden warm contact. But the word "charmed" also addresses, though it was unconscious to me at the time, her budding sexuality. This undercurrent will never be brought to full awareness, neither in Frida nor me, and I do not think it marred my containment of her. We will return to Frida and infantile sexuality in Chapter 9.

One final comment on the auditory and visual elements of containment; the reason I have emphasized the musical aspect is that it is often neglected in psychoanalytic literature. Psychoanalysis began as a "talking cure" whose musical content has been treated somewhat half-heartedly. Conversely, visual impressions are downplayed in the analytic practice; the patient is placed on a couch and we have little eye contact. This has led to an emphasis on the word-symbolic aspects of signs in the session. I, however, believe our mind is born "rockin' in rhythm" to the mother's heart and bowels, her gait and speech and the ever-present humming from the blood vessels. Many infant therapists believe that auditory experiences form the primeval link between "the concrete state of somatic experience" and "the abstract mental activity linked to visual images" (Ciccone *et al.*, 2007, p. 17). After birth, these "sound objects" (Maiello, 1995) pave the way for the baby's interaction with the mother and will make rhythm the base of security. This becomes evident as we listen to a mother talking to her baby, talking in that soft yet rhythmic way, often in emphatic duplets: "There, there, what *are* we crying for, well, well, now, now." I think I did something similar when I told Frida, "Mum got angry with *me* yesterday and then *you* Frida got angry with *her*". This is the music that captures her attention and soothes her; this is what I call the maternal aspect of containment. Now, let us investigate it further and compare it with the paternal.

## Containment: maternal and paternal

Let us get back to vignette 2. At some instances I empathized with Frida's panic, as when I told her, "Mum was gone from you yesterday". At other instances, I addressed that she had played an active part with her mother. She had avoided

Mum's eyes and this was painful to Kate. These examples bring out the two different aspects of containment; the maternal and the paternal. In the maternal, we "hold" (Winnicott, 1965) the infant's anxiety. We are patient, empathic, imaginative and dreamy in order to approach her primal representations. This comes close to Bion's (1962a, 1970) model of containment, which is built on a mother's intercourse with her baby. In the paternal dimension (Quinodoz, 1992; Salomonsson, 1998) we represent the human order; there exist conventions and laws that regulate our interactions, and one must use words and unequivocal non-verbal signs to voice one's wishes.

When Bion (1962a) introduced the polarity container–contained he used a female sign (Venus) of the container and a masculine (Mars) of the contained. Thus, containment would be a feminine or maternal activity – while anxiety would be restricted to the masculine. A strange division! Only rarely did Bion bring in the paternal aspect of containment, as when he remarked that the containing mother needs to associate her reverie with love for the child *or its father* (Bion, 1962a, p. 36, italics added). He probably had in mind that the mother's vision of genital love and its delights counterbalances her fear that the child's nameless dread shall eat her up from inside. Her love of the child's father engenders erotic fantasies. Mars fills up the bosom of Venus and makes her happy, and Venus enfolds the member of Mars and makes him happy. If we transpose this imagery to the world of containment, we realize that it is a bisexual activity. The contained fills up the container in the form of anguished projective identifications. The container-mother is inspired by her reverie of the father to enfold the contained and make it contented. This helps the mother to not only calm the child but also to feel love for him/her in the midst of tears and screams.

If we look at containment from the outside, it seems to be an activity between mother and child. However, viewed from the inside, it is a triangular relationship; "the father is present in the reverie of the analyst-mother" (Quinodoz, 1992, p. 629). The analyst dreams along with the patient's fantasies without questioning them – but he also maintains the reality principle (Salomonsson, 1998). In maternal containment we build an illusory and idealized oneness with the patient. Here, words are used to uphold and confirm this state. In this mode, the analyst is "musical" in following the emotions of her affective language. He is in contact with his psychosomatic being when "dancing" with the baby. At times, he may feel that his intuitions are safely anchored. Other times, he feels at sea or panicky, as when I scratched my head with Frida.

In paternal containment, we negate the "maternal illusion" in favour of the reality principle. We acknowledge the borders between the parties and clarify that in order to cross them, one must use a common mode of communication; words that are clear and unequivocal. I prefer to describe this mode with Lacan's term *le Nom-du-Père* or the Name of the Father. To understand this term, let us start with his vision that mother and infant share an illusion of the "ideal primordial moment" (Lacan, 1998, p. 148). The baby demands that Mum should understand her secret desires – and Mum imposes on herself to understand them. Of course, this is impossible since "desire arrives signified otherwise than it was at the start . . . therefore, desire is always deceived" (p. 148). This is especially the case with a distressed baby such as Frida, who expresses her wishes in a confounded way. As Kate sighed, "I don't know what she wants. I try to comfort her but nothing helps".

The complaints of a frustrated mother should not, however, make us overlook the other side of the coin; the illusion that a mother satisfies every desire of her infant and the little one is her "phallus" making her a perfect human being (Porge, 2000, p. 135). The phallus refers to a mutually shared fantasy about completion and grandeur – regardless of the child's gender (Diatkine, 2007, p. 650). This is where the symbolical order and its representative, the Name of the Father, appear as a counterbalancing factor. It reminds mother and child that they are subject to the constraints of reality and to the law; neither of them is a bisexual and wondrous creature. The law prescribes that desire must be transformed into a wish, which can be granted or refuted by the Other. Frida must learn to express herself so that Mum understands her.

One might raise two objections against applying the Name of the Father to babies. We already dealt with the first one, that the baby does not understand words. It is easy to demonstrate that the Name of the Father is at work long before the child understands words literally. Nine-month-old Rufus, introduced in Chapter 2, wants to climb a little stool. He checks if his mother is watching him and when the coast is clear, he starts his climbing expedition. Though he does not understand the verbal import of her prohibition, he has grasped her commandment. Similarly, Frida reacts to my earnest address when I point through the window and convey that she is avoiding Mum's eyes. The second objection would be that Lacan did not include non-verbal expressive forms in *le symbolique*. As I mentioned in the previous chapter, post-Lacanian French authors have coined concepts for how the baby signifies his desire. I am referring to the "demarcating signifier" (Rosolato, 1978, 1985) and the "formal signifier" (Anzieu, 1990). They function as the baby's *porte-paroles* of *le symbolique*. When Rufus is sulking as mother discovers him on the stool, this is a signifier that he has grasped her message and that he feels ashamed and frustrated.

In many ways, the Nom-du-Père is bound to inflict psychic pain. One reason is that it reminds mother and baby that another object is involved in the mother's desire as well; the child's father. Her enigmatic messages intimate that, though she may call her baby the world's most beautiful person, there is someone else who comes closer to concretely fulfilling her desire. She is doing and feeling things with the child's father in private, which delimits him as being her sole lover. If she says "Baby, I love you" to the baby or his father, the words have very different meanings. When the parents look at, jest with or caress each other, they transmit wavelengths that the baby only vaguely understands. Sometimes, the baby intuits them and reacts with pain. We recall from Chapter 2 Rufus's outrage when Mum asked Dad to look at her new bra in the dressing-room. The Name of the Father causes pain in yet another way. It forces the baby to pay "the price of a loss" (Marks, Murphy & Glowinski, 2001, p. 194), a sort of customs duty for entering the world of symbols; he must express his desire in words. When he has accepted this, he has entered the cultural community. Dolto labels this relinquishment *symboligenic* castration (1982, p. 47). It helps the child become a member of the family and of the human community. Importantly, it must be instituted slowly and with the help of benevolent adults. Otherwise, "frustration will not be symboligenic, it will be traumatizing" (p. 61).

Expressed in these terms, the aim of paternal containment is to institute symboligenic castration. Accordingly it causes pain, as when I told Frida that she was avoiding Mum and taking revenge on her. My words described her intentions, her actions, and their consequences for her and her mother. I noticed that Frida got more relaxed and was looking out the window. She seemed interested in my comment despite its austere message, of which she perhaps captured an inflection of voice or a frown on my face. Her reaction might suggest that she was about to identify with me, the *porte-parole* of the Name of the Father.

## Frida: Vignette 3 – Oooh, oooh, oooh

This chapter began on a musical note and I will end it similarly, now that we have clarified the two constituents of containment. As the session reported above continued, Kate and I were talking. She felt more OK with the cellphone incident. However, it retained a place in her mind ready to be retrieved if she got disappointed with me again. I now turned to Frida.

| | |
|---|---|
| *Analyst:* | It's the same with you, Frida. You were quiet for a while but then something in your "soulbody" came up, running around inside you again. It all goes in loops (I make a circular hand movement). Mum was looking away, she was angry with me, she was busy with those things, and everything got stuck in your soulbody and you cried. |
| *Frida (looking at me):* | Oooh . . . Oooh . . . |
| *A:* | Yes . . . yes . . . |
| *F:* | Oooh . . . oooh . . . oooh . . . |
| *A:* | Yes, Frida . . . yes . . . |

The tempo of our rhythmical interchange was peacefully sinking from andante to adagio. While Kate relaxed and drew Frida closer to her, Frida and I were slowly rockin' in rhythm by the music of containment. She and I had become objects of musical interplay to each other. At that moment, our two voices in the chamber trio were doing some really interesting music while Kate's voice was pausing for a while. Some of the music consisted in our duet of "Yes . . . yes . . ." and "Oooh . . . oooh . . . oooh . . .". Other parts consisted in explanatory or paternal work, for example, when I said her "soulbody" was moving in circles.

To conclude; it is the combination of two elements – the rhythm of a maternal dialogue and the interpretative paternal words – that makes up helpful containment. To expand our musical metaphor; it is the combination of music and libretto that makes up an opera, whether on stage or in our consulting-room.

## Epilogue

Some weeks later, Frida had become a baby who expressed all sorts of emotions in a healthy and direct way. In attachment terms, an avoidant attachment to mother (Ainsworth, Blehar, Waters & Wall, 1978), in statu nascendi since her second month, was no longer to be seen. During the following eight months she was still present during mother's sessions. Then she started kindergarten and Kate continued with therapy on her own.

I end this chapter with a curious incident. When Frida was three years old, her mother once told me: "The other day Frida was fussy. I didn't understand why. She insisted, 'There is a bear outside the window'. I ignored it but she went on with it. At long last, I looked out and suddenly I realized the connection with you. Then I said 'Aha, now I see what you mean, yes, there is really a bear outside' – and she calmed down."

Needless to say, my name Björn means bear. Did Frida calm down because she knew that "Bear" was an important figure for her mother? Or did she have vague memories of her own, which were linked to having being contained by the "Bear"? Neither the mother nor I were certain, but evidently the girl did not relax until the mother acknowledged that there was a bear or a björn outside the window.

# Chapter 4

# What does a baby understand?
## Eight-month-old Karen

In this chapter we will explore more closely what a baby might understand of our interventions. I have chosen an older baby than the ones presented previously: eight-month-old Karen and her mother Miranda. She was able to respond to interventions in a more elaborated way than the babies presented so far. This will enable me to demonstrate more clearly my dialogue with her as well as to understand her role in these treatments.

## Karen and her mother Miranda: another case of breastfeeding problems

Talk to me baby, tell me what's the matter now.
Are you tryin' to quit me, baby, but you don't know how?
I've been your slave, ever since I've been your babe
But before I see you go, I see you in your grave.
I'm a good gal, but my love is all wrong.
I'm a real good gal, but my love is gone.

Billie Holiday's *Long Gone Blues* came to my mind as I was treating Karen and her mother Miranda. "Talk to me baby, tell me what's the matter now" depicted the mother's entreaties when she faced Karen's incessant crying and demand for the breast. Like the two lovers in the dirge they had become each other's slave, trying in vain to salvage their capsized relationship. During MIP treatment, I was able to discover the connections between Karen's disturbance and a derailed interaction with her mother. She communicated many unresolved intrapsychic and interpersonal conflicts with her mother. Truly she did not literally tell me, "what's the matter now". But her ability to express herself and to understand my communication was quite well developed.

In the previous chapters, I have emphasized that babies have an appetite for linguistic communication though they understand no verbal import. Instead, they engage in face-to-face chatting with dialogue-like characteristics such as turns, smiles, vocalizations and arm movements that express their emotions. Now I will examine further the infant–analyst communication by approaching the following questions. Colleagues often ask me:

- "You speak to the infant in interpretative work. How do you know the infant understands what you say to her?"
- "If she understands you, *what* does she understand?"
- "Given the infant understands some aspects of your communication, how do you know that you two understand the same aspects?"
- "Couldn't the infant's response simply be unspecific and un-interpretable reactions to your presence?"
- To sum up: "Does the infant really understand what you convey to her and do you understand what she conveys to you?"

To answer, we need first to continue building our theoretical framework for the communication in these analytic settings. One might claim this is irrelevant: "You simply rely on your countertransference to understand the baby's communication, so you need not delve into what a baby does or does not understand." Agreed, countertransference is vital for my understanding, but since the baby and I communicate in such different modes her cues are seldom easy to understand. Therefore, I need a more solid theoretical framework to understand the nature of our communications. In Chapter 2 I suggested we use a "qualified adultomorphic understanding" to guess what goes on in the baby's mind. I rely on my own infantile self and check to what extent its signals adhere to what I observe in the baby. Now, I will focus on *the baby's* understanding. I will apply developmental psychological research to account for how and when an infant develops her perceptual and cognitive communicative capacities.

In my exploration, I will use semiotic theory and developmental research as assistant disciplines. Compared with André Green's (Sandler *et al.*, 2000) position on infant observation and psychoanalysis, as referred to in Chapter 1, I am less of a "purist". I think we need other disciplines to understand the threesome communication in these therapies. Knowledge of experimental investigations of babies' communicative abilities will help us meet the criticism of "hypersemiosis" (Chapter 2); that we exaggerate what can be interpreted and what the baby understands of it. This position does not prevent me from regarding these therapies as truly psychoanalytic; they aim at understanding unconscious processes, use a strictly defined framework for investigation and view the analyst's subjectivity as an essential investigatory instrument. In this aspect, I am a purist.

## Mother–Infant Psychoanalytic work: some further comments

The MIP method (Norman, 2001, 2004) proceeds from four assumptions:

1   A relationship can be established between the infant and the analyst.

2    The infant has a primordial subjectivity and self as a base for intersubjectivity and the search for containment.
3    The infant has an unique flexibility in changing representations of itself and others that comes to an end as the ego develops.
4    The infant is able to process aspects of language (Norman, 2001, p. 83).

In Chapter 3 on Frida, I showed how I brought "the disturbance in the infant into the emotional exchange of the here-and-now of the session, making it available for containment in the infant–mother relationship" (Norman, 2001, p. 83). MIP draws from Winnicott, who used therapeutically the "fluidity of the infant's personality and the fact that feelings and unconscious processes are so close to the early stages of babyhood" (1941, p. 232). However, he stated it was essentially from the study of *adult* transference that we could "gain a clear view of what takes place in infancy itself" (1960, p. 595). Norman radicalized this position and talked to the *infant* about what he guessed was taking place in the infant himself.

The problem is that infants cannot speak and understand our words very dimly, if at all. In Chapter 2 we learnt about their "appetite" for language; yet, not until she is twelve months old will a baby understand some ten words, and she will begin producing her "first recognizable words between roughly twelve and twenty months" (Karmiloff & Karmiloff-Smith, 2001, p. 62). Balkányi (1964) used this developmental skew between language understanding and expression to explain why children faced with a trauma they cannot verbalize may run into emotional turmoil. To Norman, the infant's problem is not so much that she cannot verbalize the trauma but that it has not been contained. The mother might have said soothing words while simultaneously emitting unconscious messages with divergent meanings. This was illustrated by Frida (Chapter 3), who was left in a bewildering situation with her mother during that unfortunate morning. My interpretations aimed at containing this traumatic situation. The question is what an infant such as Frida might understand of them. I will soon return to this point.

Before I submit Karen's case, just a few words about the frequency of sessions. Norman emphasized the need of a high frequency, if possible four sessions a week. I have become less insistent in this aspect due to my experiences at the Child Health Centre. It may sometimes hurt or frighten mothers if I suggest high-frequency therapy. To paraphrase Holiday's blues, they turn to us and ask "Talk to me Doctor, tell me what's the matter with my baby". If we suggest a four-times weekly analysis she may take this to indicate, "I will tell you, Mum, what's the matter with *you*". To a mother who is already in a brittle narcissistic balance, due to her primary maternal preoccupation (Winnicott, 1956) and perhaps also depressive sentiments, this is of course frightening. Another argument for low-frequency treatment is that one may sometimes achieve substantial changes with brief once-weekly treatments. The urge in mother and infant to remedy the troublesome situation, the infant's flexible primal representations, the mother's "interior look" and "transparency" (Bydlowski, 2001) vis-à-vis her unconscious processes and her willingness to work hard in analysis; these factors contribute to sometimes making low-frequency treatments astonishingly instructive and efficient.

Having said this, high-frequency analyses are sometimes essential. A mother might be so terrified at her destructive impulses, like Tessie in Chapter 1, that only frequent sessions will provide adequate containment for her anxiety. The same goes for an infant who is depressed, sleepless or panicking at the breast – emotions that risk damaging the link to the analyst unless we meet frequently. High-frequency treatments also help us develop psychoanalytic knowledge of mother–infant pathology and communication. In Karen's case, I suggested a high frequency since both mother and baby seemed so distressed and helpless. Miranda had no clue as to "what's the matter now" with her baby and she had no adult she trusted in and whom she could talk to. Treatment lasted two months, with four sessions a week.

## Karen: Vignette 1 – A roaring girl

Karen is eight months old. She demands breastfeeding continuously and has severe sleeping problems. She cannot fall asleep without the breast. Any mishap makes Karen cry, and her mother is exhausted and helpless. Miranda tells me she has been worried about Karen's health. She knows that from a medical point of view it was not serious, yet she is distressed, which contrasts with her light tone of voice. Miranda does not let in my suggestion that the situation must be hard for her as well as Karen. I feel she blurs their identities, as when she is substituting "we" when speaking of either one of them. If I am right that Miranda fears her own affects about Karen's health, I feel she is not in a frame of mind in which she can contain Karen's affects. I ponder whether Karen's whining for the breast is related to mother's way of handling this complex situation.

While Miranda is speaking and I reflect on my feelings of our artificial contact, Karen whines and starts crawling. She tumbles on a little stool in my room and starts to cry.

| | |
|---|---|
| *Analyst:* | Now you fell down. |
| *Mother to Karen:* | Oh dear! You fell and hurt your head. |
| *A to K:* | Well, actually you look *angry* when you're looking at me. You might wonder what kind of man you have come to, with his silly chair . . . Yes? . . . But it wasn't that dangerous. |
| | [Karen calms down but whimpers still. Miranda describes how Karen wakes up at night and then only the breast will soothe her.] |
| *M continues, as if talking to K:* | When you wake up during the night, the only thing that helps is to get the breast at once. Otherwise you become *so sad*. |
| | [However, I get the impression Karen is annoyed.] |

*A to K:*               One might ask oneself: do you get sad because you don't get the breast? Or, do you get *angry*?!
                              [At this point, Karen roars.]
*A to K:*               Well, that does sound quite angry, I think!
                              [Karen stops crying.]

What entitles me to attribute such significance to Karen's communication? After all, she does not say she is angry with me. She roars. Which concept accounts most properly for such a communication? Traditionally, when psychoanalysts feel the patient conveys a meaning beyond the obvious, we say it appears in a symbolized form. Karen's roar would thus be a *symbol* of anger. I will now show that the vague definition of symbol in psychoanalytic theory gets us into trouble when we try to understand if and what infants are communicating.

## The concept of "symbol"

"Symbols can be conceived as being instruments of expressing our feelings to one another as well as being the instruments of meaning and understanding" (Silver, 1981, p. 271). Psychoanalytic theory has often assumed a constant relationship between "the symbol and what it symbolizes in the unconscious" (Laplanche & Pontalis, 1973, p. 442). As the jargon goes, a cigar always means a penis. Here, the symbol is formed on an analogy with the symbolized (Gibello, 1989, p. 37), it will revolve around bodily functions and existential issues and it will not evoke associations (Jones, 1916). This contrasts with Freud's original definition where *any* substitutive formation is symbolic; there is no condition of a constant connection conscious–unconscious but the symbol is simply regarded as a general conveyor of meaning. In this definition, "the deciphering of the unconscious is analogous to the one of a foreign language" (Anzieu, 1989, p. 10). An example is the elements of a dream that symbolize a defensive conflict (Laplanche & Pontalis, 1973, p. 443).

A third definition has slipped into clinical discussions nowadays. Some patients are said to have "difficulties in symbolizing"; they understand our interpretations concretely and their words are abstruse and convey affects vaguely. This definition comes close to Segal's "symbolic equation" (1957, 1991), in which part of the ego identifies with the object and is confused with it. This results in a crude and incomprehensible symbol.

A fourth definition was introduced by Lacan (1966). The modes of working of the unconscious are similar to a language. The problem is that his emphasis on words tends to overshadow other expressive modes that we humans use – and not only babies at that! This critique has been voiced as follows; the concept *le symbolique* tends to mute "expressions of affects, the investment of aesthetic objects, the representation and organization of images" (Arfouilloux, 2000, p. 25). This critique strikes especially hard concerning infants, since they express themselves without words. If the symbolic order is based only on a linguistic definition, we cannot apply it to an infant's communication such as crying and grimacing. Lacan later realized this shortcoming and introduced the concept of "la lalangue", infant babbling, (1975. p. 175), but he did not investigate it in infant practice or research.

None of these definitions of "symbol" will thus help us in explicating Karen's roar. It could hardly signify one unconscious content; a roar can signify many things and Karen seemed conscious of her emotion. It might symbolize her defensive conflict but her roar expressed her affect openly and it is unclear what would be defensive about it. Obviously, she had difficulties in symbolizing, but when is a roar complex enough to merit being called a symbol? As for Segal's symbolic equation, this term also seems inapplicable since Karen conveyed anything but a muddled border between us.

Finally, to state that the roar belongs to *le symbolique* in Lacan's sense would be incorrect, since a roar is not a linguistic expression. Yet, Karen's response to my intervention, "Well, that does sound angry", indicated that she had grasped some aspect of my paternal containment. Her roar was a rejoinder to my address that she was angry with Mum. If we could liberate *le symbolique* from its tie to linguistics, we might find a concept to designate Karen's roar. Guy Rosolato (1978, 1985), and also Eco (1968) and Corradi Fiumara (1995), divide communication into two dimensions: digital and analogical. Lacan had focused on digital language; speech consists of discrete units assembled in accordance with linguistic laws. Rosolato emphasized the analogical aspect of communication; tone, intensity and other nuances of the word stream. We recall from Chapter 2 how he described the human gesture as an analogic representation, a dynamic bodily mirror of emotions. When I hear Karen's whining and combine it with my impressions of mother's feigned communication, I guess she is angry underneath. As I tell her this, she roars. I take her roar to "copy" her anger, and I interpret this analogic representation because it corresponds to my own representations of anger. Actually, my "qualified adultomorphic understanding" is but a specialized version of a tool that every parent uses to understand the infant.

Thus, infants grasp aspects of statements such as "That does sound quite angry, Karen!" If only we could find one general term for how meaning is conveyed between humans, it would become easier to conceptualize how and what a baby is grasping in such an interchange. Such a term should be unburdened by dichotomies such as conscious/unconscious, verbal/non-verbal and separate/fused object. From this term, a terminology should branch off to cover significations on different levels of consciousness, complexity and object status. To this end, I suggest the term *sign*; Karen's roar is simply a sign of an affect – at whichever level it is signified. Defining that level comes at a second step. Throughout the book, I have used the term "sign" without really defining it. Now the time has come.

## "What is a sign?"

"This is a most necessary question, since all reasoning is an interpretation of signs of some kind" (Kloesel & Houser, 1998, p. 4). The philosopher C. S. Peirce set aside *the sign* as a general term for invoking meaning. Out of this term branches a multitude of sign types of which "symbol" is but one. His most concise definition of a sign runs: it is

> a thing, which serves to convey knowledge of some other thing, which it is said to stand for or represent. This thing is called the object of the sign; the idea in the mind that the sign excites, which is a mental sign of the same object, is called an interpretant of the sign.
>
> (p. 13)

The experiences involved when we perceive something as a sign are classified into three universal categories: Firstness, Secondness and Thirdness. Firstness was defined in Chapter 2 as an immediate experience unrelated to other experiences. Secondness was defined as being related to another experience; one experience stands against or is compared to another. Thirdness applies to perceptions of laws, conventions and regularities. These terms thus cover human experiencing in its entirety, from its crudest to its most elaborated forms.

Our experiences are essentially signified in three ways: as icons, indices and symbols. These terms were also introduced in Chapter 2. If my impression of Karen's anger was a Firstness experience of "Anger", I experienced her face as an icon or "image" (Kloesel & Houser, 1998, p. 273) of anger. If I compared Karen's mien with faces in other situations it would be an index of anger. I placed my experience in a context of dynamic interaction. An index "stands for its object by virtue of a real connection with it, or because it forces the mind to attend to that object" (p. 14). Finally, my words to Karen, "That does sound angry!" were word-symbols. They were "associated with their meanings by usage. Such are most words, and phrases" (Kloesel & Houser, 1998, p. 5). "A symbol is a sign which refers to the Object that it denotes by virtue of a law" (p. 292). This is the major sign type that Lacan includes in *le symbolique*.

Signs are building blocks for thinking; "we think only in signs" (Kloesel & Houser, 1998, p. 10). Peirce emphasized that signs refer to anything from a colour spot to a verbal statement. He also emphasized that they do not cover their referents in a fixed way. A roar is not always a sign of anger, and a cry is not an eternal sign of sadness. Further, as I suggested already in Chapter 2, one sign can be interpreted on all three levels: as icon, index and symbol. Interpreted as word-symbols, "That sounds angry'" described Karen's wrath. This did not preclude her from interpreting me on an icon level, perhaps as 'Friendly Man interested in my feelings'.

Semiosis, the attribution of meaning, is an endless process. My immediate interpretant, that is, thinking about what Karen's roar signified, was emotional. I felt she was angry with me because of the stool incident. Having realized this, I felt affected by her anger. Now, my interpretant was energetic. Finally, I could reflect on the word "angry" as a logical interpretant and ask if it aptly described her emotion. Let us say I suddenly suspected that I was exaggerating. This idea could function as an emotional interpretant in a new train of thoughts. The semiotic process can be described as an infinite series of triangles where one

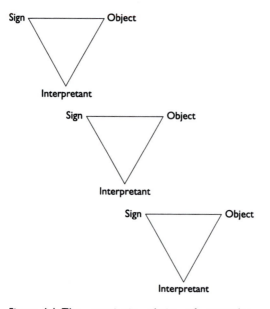

Figure 4.1 The semiotic chain of triangles.
Adapted from Sheriff (1994, p. 35).

corner hitches on a corner in the next triangle of interpretant, object and sign. Figure 4.1 is adapted from Sheriff (1994, p. 35).

The triangle places the sign in a meaning-chain with no fixed anchoring point. No sign is defined *per se* but only in relation to other signs. Even the interpretant of an icon is based on some kind of code (Eco, 1968, p. 208). After all, I used my personal code when I experienced Karen's angry face; she looked like other angry people I have met. This subjectivity emerges clearly when we recall that to her mother, in contrast, it was an icon of a sad baby. We realize that only the inferential circuits mentioned in Chapter 2 will establish which interpretation is – not "true" since a true interpretation is a myth –the most fruitful one.

## The semiotic process: mother and child, analyst and analysand

I began this chapter by letting my interlocutor ask: "Does the infant really understand what you convey to her and do you understand what she conveys to you?" If I need a code to interpret Karen, the answer seems negative. On the other hand, I have suggested that a "qualified adultomorphizing" may help us to interpret the infant. But an adult who is addressing an infant is not only interpreting *to* her. S/he is also engaging *with* her in an interaction to create meaning in a mutually evolving process. Several models of the intersubjective process of meaning-making exist (Beebe & Lachmann, 2002; Muller, 1996; Stern, 1985; Trevarthen & Aitken, 2001; Tronick, 2005). For example, Muller describes how infant and mother intuit each other's communication while developing their semiotic capacities. Through mutual mirroring with the mother, the baby builds up representations of icons and responds; Mum frowns – he frowns. Later, indexical signs come to the fore; Mum frowns – he understands that she feels something about him. He feels affected and responds. Finally, mother and child take part in a traffic of word-symbols; "It's time to go to bed" – "I don't wanna."

How do infants make meaning out of all the expressions they meet with? Bruner suggests that verbal communications become "acts of meaning" (Bruner, 1990) and that babies actively search for "certain classes of meaning to which human beings are innately tuned and for which they actively search" (p. 72). These "protolinguistic representations" (p. 72) are structured like narratives and function as early interpretants to the child. In other words, our dialogues in the session are little unfolding stories. "Once upon a time there was a little girl Karen. Then she stumbled on a stool. She got angry and roared."

Karen thus grasps some narrative-like quality of my interventions. But, had we not better reserve the term "narrative" for language? No, responds Langer (1942), who denies that humans only understand discursive or linguistic expressions. This erroneous idea, she says, is based on two misunderstandings: "1/ that language is the only means of articulating thought, and 2/ that everything which is not speakable thought is feeling" (p. 87). "There are things which do not fit the grammatical scheme of expression ... matters which require to be conceived through some symbolistic schema other than discursive language" (p. 88). I interpret Karen's communication like an image or a dance, or what Langer calls a presentational symbol. This "wordless symbolism, which is non-discursive and untranslatable, does not allow of definitions within its own system, and cannot directly convey generalities" (1942, p. 97). We recognize the similarity to Corradi Fiumara's and Rosolato's term analogic representation.

By now, we have several concepts explicating how babies and adults understand each other. However, they would be meaningless unless we included the interactive object. It is only by interacting that a baby climbs the semiotic ladder. Bion's account is pertinent: a baby listens to her mother, who has discerned a state of mind "before the infant can be conscious of it, as, for example, when the baby shows signs of needing food before it is properly aware of it" (1962a, p. 34). She responds, "What is the trouble my dear, are you hungry?" The baby calms down when he understands mother's icons and indices conveying her containment. This description goes for the analytic process as well. It is a continuous, sometimes successful and sometimes abortive, effort at meaning-making. Let me exemplify with a second vignette, in which I will indicate sign levels of our three-way communication.

## Karen: Vignette 2 – Why are you angry?

In the second session, Miranda criticizes Karen's father in a pleading way.

Karen whines, once cooing "Maeh-Maeh". [Unclear icon: Sad Face + indexical request: Treat Me Like A Poor Creature + possibly an effort at forming a word-symbol "Mama".]

| | |
|---|---|
| *Analyst:* | Yes . . .? [Symbol-question: What Do You Mean? + encouraging index: Go On, Express Yourself, Karen! + Icon: Attentive Face.] |
| | Karen roars. [Distinct index: I Am Angry With You! Feel It!] |
| *A:* | Yes . . . Now you sound furious, I think. [Symbol-interpretation: You Are Angry + index: Go On, I Am Interested And I Am Not Afraid Of Your Anger.] |
| | Karen whines again. [Resumes iconical and indexical signification to elicit analyst's response: Feel Sorry For Me! I Am Sad!] |
| *A:* | Maybe there are two darned people here! [Symbol-interpretation: You Two Are Angry + indexical communication: I Am Not Scared Of Your Anger.] |
| *Mother:* | Mmm. [Symbol comment: I Agree + indexical comment: I Am Thinking About What's Happening Here.] |
| *A:* | One mother mad with father . . . [Symbol-interpretation + Index: I Am Reflecting.] |
| | Karen frowns and roars distinctly. [Icon and index now match: Angry Face And Voice + I Want To Tell You Both I Am Angry.] |
| *A:* | . . . and one Karen mad with me and Mum because we talk so much. [*Etc.*] |
| | [Karen cries angrily.] |
| *A:* | Is it in a situation like this that Karen wants the breast? |
| *M:* | Yes, now it's time for the breast . . . |
| | [Karen cries again.] |
| *A to Karen:* | Karen, I think . . . I think you are angry. |
| | [Karen cries more angrily.] |
| *M:* | Yes, now she is not sad, now she is angry! |
| *A to K:* | Shall we try to find out; what are you angry with? |

Miranda now interprets the girl more succinctly and Karen creates more unequivocal signs of her emotions. Earlier, the signs were distorted since there was no contact between emotions and memories of when they arose. Instead, they were tied to craving the breast. One part of her psyche expressed symptoms and stormed with affects. Another part silenced her anger in favour of whining. After this cleavage, symptom and personality were fixated and a repression was about to be established, and, Miranda got stuck in stereotyped interpretations: "She's so sad".

We may now answer the questions in the beginning of this chapter: "How do you know the infant understands what you say to her?" She understands it in a developing semiotic interaction with me and mother. "What does she understand?" She understands my communication as icons and indices. Not until way beyond her first birthday will the words' lexical import start to become meaningful to her. "How do you know you two understand the same aspects of communication?" Through an inferential circuit of induction, deduction, and abduction. Observing my countertransference, as well as the communications of mother and child, help me in pursuing this circuit.

## The infant's understanding of emotions: findings from developmental research

It is sometimes claimed that the therapist should use the same kind of phrasing to the baby as does her mother; so-called *motherese*. This will help the infant "to identify linguistic units in continuous speech" (Fernald, 2004, p. 58). Furthermore, it seems to have a calming effect on the child. However, my reason for addressing Karen is not so much to calm her, but to contain her anxiety and to speak about its content. So why do I use words whose symbolical, digital or lexical meaning she cannot understand? My response is that she understands emotional communication. We will look at some findings from developmental psychological research that support such a supposition.

In the Still-Face experiment (Tronick *et al.*, 1978), the mother is playing with her child and then suddenly keeps her face still. The effect is dramatic. The infant stops smiling and looking at her mother and becomes distressed. The mutual exchange and creation of meaning is replaced by the infants' "self-organized regulatory behaviours to maintain their coherence and complexity" (Tronick, 2005, p. 303). Muir and co-workers (Muir, Lee, Hains & Hains, 2005) focused on the baby's emotional reactions in the Still-Face. They showed (D'Entremont, 1995) that three-month-old babies react to a change from happy to sad expressions in the adult. If such young infants can "read" and sort different facial emotional expressions, then eight-month-old Karen is already an expert reader of emotions. This explains her problems in understanding her mother's enigmatic messages, as when Miranda is angry but muddles this emotion with a cuddling and spurious pity. In such situations, Karen cannot fuse what Mum conveys consciously and unconsciously or, in another framework, what her diverging sign types mean.

The advantage of Karen's emotional "literacy" is that she reacts to a sincerely conveyed therapeutic intervention. This presupposes that my iconical and indexical expressions concord with my word-symbols. If not, her emotional understanding is hampered. Concordance comes about when "the analyst's tone of voice and her gestures and the lexical meaning of the words express the same meaning" (Norman, 2001, p. 96). When I speak with Karen the words' content concords with my emotional expressions. When I look like and sound like the words I am telling her, this indicates that I am sincere. This helps her to release herself from her mother's discordant communication. This is why I use plain and simple language, which I do not season with any childish intonation.

Many stumbling-blocks prevent the analyst from being sincere. If I fear that Karen or her mother cannot stand any mention of anger, I will probably show this iconically even if I am silent. If I speak to Miranda following her logical interpretant that Karen is sad, while ignoring my emotional or energetic interpretant that she is angry, I will be insincere as well. If I look encouraging but feel sad about their communication, I will repeat the happy-face-sad-voice-experiment of Muir and co-workers. To be sincere, one must continuously examine the countertransference.

## Communication and therapeutic action

The two summarizing questions were: "Does the infant really understand what you convey to her and do you understand what she conveys to you?" I hope to have clarified my reasons and provisos when I answer both questions in the affirmative. Karen understands my communication on the iconical and indexical levels that accompany my verbal interpretations. She is affected by my efforts to understand her and to express sincerely what I think goes on in her. I understand this on the basis of her and her mother's communications as well as my counter-transference. I have also accounted for infants' perceptual and cognitive tools for understanding linguistic and emotional communication.

Sometimes I am asked if this method works simply because the mother listens to my dialogue with her infant and identifies with me. This question touches on the discussion of Figure 1.1 in Chapter 1. Indeed, Miranda's pensive position and growing resistance to panic when Karen cries prove that she has identified with me. I think her identification wells forth from double sources. She is a first-hand witness of Karen's struggle with her affects during sessions, moreover I also interpret their interaction. Miranda will thus understand more of the girl's inner world and of her own contributions to their emotional climate. This will give her experiences an under-the-skin quality, which promotes her identification. Having stated this, I hope to have shown above that the method also works by affecting Karen directly.

To play the devil's advocate, what if Karen changed in a beneficial direction simply due to normal development? However, some arguments support that she needed interpretative work to catch up with development. When Miranda first brought her to our sessions, Karen seemed helpless and immature. It was as if her psyche tried to delay repressions from settling. Without therapy, what could have enabled development to resume its normal course? After all, Karen had been crying and craving almost all her life. This changed radically during treatment and I have described the therapeutic mechanisms that helped her get back on track of a normal development.

## Karen: Vignette 3 – Playing at the milk-bar

The final snapshot shows how the semiotic process between mother and child has developed. Karen arrives at the twelfth session newly awakened and a bit hungry.

She is a little cross but keeps herself together. She looks at me earnestly and I wait. Unexpectedly, she crawls to a cupboard and reaches for a door knob. She knocks at it and moves her hand to her mouth, as if drinking. She gives a laugh, which Miranda meets with: "You're having a drink at the milk-bar, aren't you!" Karen's play shows she has integrated my interpretations of her anger with Mum's breast and her fears about this feeling. Miranda's pun "milk-bar" shows that she is no longer ensnared by Karen's demands for the breast. It is also a sign of her identification with me, since I sometimes use such playful language.

This incident exemplifies the problems with the concept of *le symbolique*, as related in the chapter's beginning. Karen's play is mute, no words are uttered, and yet it is quite an expressive communication. She transposes the breastfeeding situation to one where the door knob signifies the nipple and the cupboard the milk reservoir or the breast. It is thus a communication within the analogic realm, a gesture or a presentational symbol – and it is strictly pre-verbal. Karen also conveys that she, at least during this game, has accepted the symbolic order. Importantly, she does *not* convey this in the sense of verbalizing a wish, because this is still beyond her capacities. However, her game indicates that she is about to accept that certain rules govern human interactions; mother is the proprietor of her breasts and Karen has to ask for them rather than insist on them. Unsurprisingly, during treatment Miranda decided to stop breastfeeding, a process that met with brief initial protests but then ran smoothly.

To quote from Billie Holiday's *Long Gone Blues*: "Talk to me baby, tell me what's the matter now." Or, to express it differently: "Signify to me baby, and I will translate your icons and indices into more comprehensible signs and convey them to you. Your protolinguistic representations of emotions will form a narrative, which we will explore together. Our dialogue becomes a dance, the presentational symbolism of which we will interpret." The latter formulation aptly describes communication in parent-infant psychoanalytic work. On the other hand, it would make a lousy blues title. But that's another story.

# Chapter 5

# An infant's experience of mother's depression

## Sixteen-month-old Beate

Can a father see his child / weep, nor be with sorrow filled?
Can a mother sit, and hear / an infant groan, an infant fear?
No, no, never can it be.
Never, never can it be.
From the poem "On another's sorrow"
(Blake, 1994, p. 62. Originally published in 1789)

Analogic representations, presentational symbolism, icons, indices, protolinguistic narratives; our list of complicated and perhaps abstruse concepts has become quite lengthy. The reader might exclaim: "OK, I believe babies understand some human communication. When I think of it, I always believed it! I didn't need philosophy to justify my telling a baby that she looks cute in her little cap! I was never interested in semiotic concepts but OK, the ones you have provided give us a theoretical backbone. Thank you, but I didn't need all these terms, neither for talking to babies nor to understand that they sometimes suffer and need help. I am still not convinced that your interventions affect the baby *directly*. Perhaps, you should provide a coherent description of a therapy. Do it and I might become more convinced!"

To meet this request, I will present a mother–toddler treatment, which ended in a classical child analysis. The aim is also to bring up some reflections on how an infant might experience her mother's depression. Beate was in treatment from 16 months to three-and-a-half years. At first, I worked with her and her mother ensemble, since they were living in "a certain unconscious oneness that is based on the unconscious of the mother and of the child being in so close relation to each other" (Klein, 1959, p. 248). I wanted to reach two minds that seemed to function with one singular muddled unconscious. My help consisted in helping them consolidate their respective personality. When this had been sufficiently achieved, we shifted from MIP treatment to child analysis, in which Beate and I worked alone.

Developmentally, Beate was in a stage of transition – from non-verbal and bodily to more verbal modes of expressing her unconscious fantasies. At first, she was anxiously craving for the breasts of her tired and resigned mother. Then she developed a fascination and a fear of holes at different places. Finally, she revealed her fears of nightly ghosts and monsters. The termination of the analysis was inaugurated when she began to link these ghastly creatures to concrete spots in my office. This enabled me to interpret her fears within the transference. We could now speak about them directly, and she was able to handle them with greater frankness, ego-strength and self-esteem.

## Beate: Vignette I – Grabbing the breast

A mother, Nadya, phones me about "some problems" with Beate, 16 months, an only child. At our consultation, I meet a shrill-voiced, spindly, alert, tense and officious girl who uses very few words. She behaves in a peculiar way; she picks a stool from the loo, returns to the consulting-room, runs to the waiting-room to get her ball, returns again, plays with Mum for half a minute and then pulls back into a corner. Her behaviour gives a jumbled and distressed impression. After a minute, she wants to leave again and I decide to address her.

| | |
|---|---|
| *Analyst to Beate:* | You want to leave. I wonder why . . . |
| | [Beate avoids me anxiously. She throws the ball to Mum but leaves Mum sitting with it in her lap. Mother looks embarrassed and strained. Suddenly, Beate approaches Mum and starts tearing at her blouse. She wants the breast, and she gets it.] |
| *Mother:* | (sighs) It's often like this . . . |
| *A:* | Is this why you came, to get help with this breast problem? |
| *M:* | Mmm . . . As soon as she got her own will, these problems started. |
| *A:* | You still nurse her. Is it full-time? |
| *M:* | Yes. If I were to decide, it would be morning and evening only. She doesn't really suck the breast, she's just got to have it. |
| | [At the next session two days later, Beate continues anxiously to enter and leave my room. She throws some toys to Mum but never engages in play. She shakes a doll as if it had a bell inside, grabs for some fruit in a bag and then for the breast.] |
| *Mother sighing to the Analyst:* | "She tends to tear things out." |
| *A to B:* | Something seems to ache inside you, Beate. I wonder what it could be. |
| | [Beate avoids me and continues leaving and entering the room. In the countertransference, I feel more and more powerless as Beate interrupts our dialogue. I discover that whatever therapeutic frame existed in the beginning of our contact, by now it is quite disrupted. I tell Nadya, to explain the change of frame I feel necessary:] |

A:                    The next time Beate wants to leave, I'll tell her to stay. Then
                      we'll gather things in the consulting-room, so we can talk
                      about them.
                      [As Beate wants to leave again after some minutes, I
                      address her calmly.]
A:                    I want you to stay in the room.
                      [Beate obeys but starts grabbing at Mum's breast and inside
                      Mum's mouth while giving me an eerie smile.]
A:                    I guess you think I was nasty when I told you to stay. I can
                      understand that. But this is the room where we work.
                      [The third session, two days later again, Beate hesitates to
                      enter. Firmly, Nadya carries her over the threshold. She is
                      stunned by Beate's reaction when I told her to stay in the
                      room: "It's a relief to see she can obey." Beate's play does not
                      start and she listlessly avoids me.]
A to B:               You don't want to look at me. Last time, I told you to stay
                      here. You didn't like that. You got angry with me, and now
                      you are afraid because of it.
                      [Beate's possessive focus on Mum continues. Sometimes, she
                      dares to look at me reproachfully, but only from mother's lap.]
A:                    I think you are angry with me, "Mr. No". You are looking at
                      me, but only when you're sitting in Mum's lap. You feel safer
                      there. To be angry and afraid, those things scare you. We
                      could talk about them so you won't have to be afraid of them.
                      [Beate wants the breast again, but this time Mum puts her
                      down. Beate starts crying and then she grabs Mum's cellphone.
                      Mum looks ashamed and distressed as she lets Beate play
                      with it. I describe to Nadya that it is confusing to Beate when
                      she has it halfway with the phone, Mum gets annoyed and
                      they end up quarrelling. Nadya sobs.]
A:                    You got sad?
M:                    Yes, I did.
A:                    Perhaps you felt I criticized you.
M:                    No, that's not it. It's more like ... it's so hard, this whole
                      thing.
A to Beate and
Nadya:                So there are two sad people in here: Beate and Mum.

## Comments on vignette I

When I said "there are two sad people here", I took into consideration Beate's
state of mind and her mother's self-esteem. A mother easily feels hurt, ashamed
and a failure when her suspicion is substantiated that the child's behaviour
expresses an underlying disharmony with her. Nadya wanted to make Beate's

childhood better than her own, but she was also brittle, phobic and depressed. Had I not acknowledged her strivings and spoken about her guilt and shame, I would soon have lost her and Beate. That is why I asked her if she felt criticized.

Now let us look at Beate and what she communicates. With the terminology from the previous chapters, she transmits iconical and indexical signs. There is much exhortation in her behaviour. She seems to convey, 'Look at me, do something, I am a naughty and strange girl, can you see beyond all this?' Her running in and out of my office is an icon of 'Distressed girl'. I also think it signifies an energetic wish to concretely get rid of her distress by running away from it – a project doomed to fail. I thus take her behaviour to be an index, which, as Peirce says, forces my mind "to attend to that object" (Kloesel & Houser, 1998, p. 14).

What about Beate's shaking the doll as if it had a bell inside, and her restless grabbing for the fruit and the breast? This scene plus her mother's comment that Beate tends to tear things out make me guess that the doll and the bag contain some concrete object that worries and occupies Beate. My intuition is anchored in the Kleinian and Bionian traditions, which makes me conceive of it as an icon of "Dangerous pieces of thoughts within a brittle container". This is why I tell her, "Something seems to ache inside you. I wonder what it could be".

I believe that if I speak sincerely with Beate, she will understand our emotional communication. When I say "I guess you think I was nasty", I act like any parent speaking in what I call "sincere pretence". Parents believe their babies understand *something* beyond the literal content. In addition, I address the baby's emotional intentionality. I am able to do this because my training has made me acquainted with my own unconscious – and it is not muddled with that of Beate. In contrast, Nadya wanted consciously to stop breastfeeding but could not say no to Beate's cravings. As it emerged later, she unconsciously felt weaning would harm the girl. Nadya identified Beate with the naughty and hopeless daughter she felt she had been in her parents' minds. She never wanted Beate to feel the same. The result was, unsurprisingly, that Beate became "quite hopeless", as Nadya put it. Thus, her messages were imbued with mixed and unconscious currents. My position outside this muddle enabled me to notice and address the emotional intentionality of both parties.

In Chapter 4 I argued against using "motherese" with the baby, because such communication may appear – and in fact also be – insincere to the child. Another counterargument is the necessity for the analyst to stand outside the muddle of the unconscious of mother and child. Motherese may be beneficial with children in other situations, but in therapeutic work I think it is inappropriate and counterproductive. Therefore, I speak simply and sincerely with Beate, as when I tell her to stay in the room. This is an instance of paternal containment; to uphold the therapeutic frame. It is also important to confirm her anger due to this intervention. Accordingly I tell her, and this time more in the maternal mode, "You got angry with me, and now you are afraid because of it". My words, with their ensuing non-verbal expressions, capture her attention. I believe she notices the difference from her mother's way of communicating and that this brings her relief.

Another way of describing their muddled unconscious is Seligman's observation (quoted in Silverman & Lieberman, 1999, p. 181) that projective identifications occur "as readily from the parent to the child as from the child to the parent". Therefore, I talked to Nadya about her anger with Beate, her projection of a bad girl-self onto the baby, her guilt and hopelessness – and to Beate about her rage with mother and her ensuing bad-girl self-image. When I told her to stay in the room, she experienced this as a threat and sought refuge at the breast. However, it did not comfort her. In a Kleinian interpretation, Beate feared she had assailed the breast through her repeated cravings. In response, it did not "want" to console her. She had not been nice to the breast and therefore it would revenge on her. This I addressed with interpretations such as "You got scared of Mum's breast after you grabbed it". We will now see how her breast problems were associated with a deficient containment due to the mother's postnatal depression.

## Beate: Vignette 2 – Falling through the "Escato"

At the end of the second week in analysis, and by now the three of us are working four times weekly, Beate places a stool in an armchair. She sits down on what now looks like a throne, though without any evident joy. With an anxious expression and an imperative look at me, she repeats "Dinnn . . . Dinnn". What does she mean? Her conflicts with her mother have probably prevented her from developing such capacities. What is the function of the sound "Dinnn"? I interpret it as an index of a manic defence, meaning something like 'Björn, I order you to feel that I am a happy girl!' I am guided to this interpretation by the mixture of her imperative grin and sad eyes.

She leaves the throne to investigate the armchair, an oblong cushion on a wooden frame. She pulls it away and now the chair looks like an H. She starts climbing through its lower opening below the crossbar. This reminds me of situations when she has been sitting in mother's lap for some seconds, only to impatiently sneak out of it. Neither Mum's lap nor the armchair provides containment; they cannot hold her distress and return it in a metabolized form. The armchair game could be interpreted as a non-specific way of getting rid of her distress, but her insistent playing makes me suspect that she wants to communicate something more specific. Figuratively speaking, her anxiety seems to seep through the hole of the chair instead of being held by a solid and reliable frame. We will now follow when we reconstructed how this failing container was linked to Nadya's depression.

I will leap six months into treatment. Twenty-two-month-old Beate is now better equipped to express herself in words. I regard this as a therapy effect. As she has calmed down and developed more trustful relationships, she has become able to absorb language and express herself verbally. One day, as is quite common, Beate is active initially. It is difficult to get in contact with her. She bangs a tiger doll on the play table. The game results in a little wound on her finger. Her mother puts a Band-Aid on it. Beate says, "Pat Mum", but Mum says, "You are hitting me", which matches my impression; she shows some signs of violence.

| | |
|---|---|
| *Mother:* | When we got home yesterday, Beate, you were happy and said you'd been talking to Björn. Now you don't want to talk to him. |
| *Beate:* | It's the wound. It's blood. |
| *Analyst:* | Mum told you something about me and you answered about the blood. |
| *B:* | Mum told. Mum told. |
| *A:* | Sometimes you want to bang the tiger doll, sometimes you want to talk. |
| *B:* | Old wound is there. |
| *A:* | What kind of wound is it . . . |
| *B:* | Old wound. |
| *A:* | Baby wound? |
| *B:* | Mum. |
| *A:* | Where is Mum? The wound is old. Where was Mum when you were little? |
| *B:* | Mum is crocodile. |
| *A:* | Was Mum like a crocodile? Were you afraid she wouldn't like you since you were biting and hitting her? (Turning to Nadya) It must have been hard for you having these angry feelings about Beate when she was hitting you. |
| *M:* | Difficult to say, it's so hazy when I think about these times. |
| *A to M:* | Like an old wound. |
| *Mum nods and* | |
| *Beate fills in:* | Old wound. |

Beate and I are now in good contact and the mother listens intently. She has started speaking about her depression. Up till now, she has been secretive and afraid that I would condemn her. I start receiving more material for reconstructing their early relationship. Beate's rephrasing her cut in the finger into "Old wound" inspires my interpretation that she is referring to their early or "old" contact. "Mum is crocodile" leads me to assume there is an oral aggressive element in their relationship. After a while, Beate says:

| | |
|---|---|
| *B:* | Girl in ambulance car. Doctor car. |
| *A:* | Earlier today, you did not want to talk to me. Now you do. I'm a doctor. |
| *B:* | A girl doll (she indicates that I put a Band-Aid on it, which I do). |
| *A:* | You banged the tiger today. You got a wound and Mum put a Band-Aid on it. Perhaps you want me to put Band-Aid on your old wounds. |
| | Beate looks confidently at me and smiles. The session ends on a calm note. |

The next day, Beate runs into my consulting-room calling out "Escato! Escato". Nadya explains that they had seen an underground escalator on repair. Beate stood rooted at the spot. Mother had to explain that "the hole" was there because some workers had taken away the escalator to fix it. Beate seems fearful and thrilled.

B:              Will it be good again, Björn? Escato not dangerous!
A:              You want me to say it's going to be OK. Yes, they will repair it.
                You are afraid of the escalator. I wonder why.

Beate and I talk about what scared her with the "Escato". Was it the workers in helmets? Beate shakes her head. Was it the noise? "No", says Beate, "It was the hole!" Meanwhile, she gets fascinated with a little hole in the upholstery of the H armchair and puts her finger through it.

The reasons that "old wound" and "Escato" are scary to Beate will appear as Nadya continues to speak about her postnatal depression. It is excruciating for her since, after all, she was responsible for a baby and now fears it has affected the girl.

Mother:         I felt worthless when Beate was born. There was a time when I felt
                the social services might as well come and take her away from me
                . . .

As I reflect on Nadya's account of her postnatal depression, Beate's "Old wound" and "Escato", and her preoccupation with the hollow armchair and its hole in the upholstery, I get a visual image of a baby in front of her mother who is physically present but emotionally unavailable – like a hole. The mother is depressed, but to the baby she might rather seem like a hole unable to provide containment. When the baby seeks comfort from this hole- or wound-mother, she is overcome with a fear of disappearing into her.

Shall I dare speak about this? Will Beate understand? Will Nadya feel offended and guilt-ridden? I feel we are at a decisive moment in treatment. If my image has any validity, it shows Beate's original traumatic situation. Though it is painful to convey my impressions and Nadya is weeping, I agree that "even the most horrible things that go on between mother and child lose some of their destructive force when formulated, sincerely, in words. Children are seldom surprised by the truth when they already have intuitively grasped what is going on" (Norman, 2001, p. 96). I begin with addressing the mother:

A to M:         Maybe your depression was like a black hole to you.
M nods and
B fills in:      Beate, Mum's girl, falling down.
A to B:          Yes . . .?
B:              Mum's girl go doctor.
M:              Come to think of it, lately Beate wants to sleep on top of me. She
                says she will crawl inside my tummy.

| | |
|---|---|
| *A to B:* | You want to crawl inside Mum's tummy. Once, you were there. |
| *B:* | Come out of Mum's tummy. Girl falling into hole. Blood come. |
| *A to B:* | Mum says that when you were a little girl, she was very sad. She couldn't help you as much as she wanted because she was so worried. Now, when she speaks about it, she is crying. (Beate listens attentively. She is serious and calm. I continue) I wonder how you felt then. I think of the escalator hole. You are so afraid of it and talking to me a lot about it. I wonder if Mum was like a hole when you were little, one that couldn't be fixed and that scared you. You had so many things inside you, so many feelings. But maybe Mum was like a sad hole who couldn't listen to you as well as she wished. |

[Mum cries softly in a mixture of relief, guilt, sorrow and hope for their future. A dialogue goes on between my words and Beate's earnest attention. Evidently, she cannot verbally confirm my reconstruction since the implicit memories of her earliest interactions with Mum remain repressed. Yet, I think it is vital to address them. It will be the first time that someone speaks to her about serious events without guilt, accusation, shame or prevarication.]

## Comments to vignette 2: reconstructing the original trauma

What justification did I have for reconstructing Beate's original trauma? Basically, I used three sources: Nadya's story, Beate's play and remarks and my visual image of a baby in front of an object experienced as a hole. Nadya's story was about pain, feelings of inadequacy and guilt. She suspected that Beate had been affected by her depression but did not know how. At this point, Beate's contribution was of substantial help. The H chair game and its link with the preceding Dinn game and the similarity with her restlessness in Mum's lap put me on the track. I began to conceive of the chair as a deficient container, though I kept this idea to myself. Meanwhile, new expressions such as "Old wound", "Mum is crocodile" and "Doctor car" added substance to my conception of how she might have experienced containment in her "old" days of infancy.

My visual image of the baby and the hole-mother finally appeared during the Escato incident. Its validity can always be questioned since it was produced in my, not Beate's, mind. However, if such an image arises in the context of careful analytic work and if we do not overtax its informative value, it may help us to understand unconscious processes. Anthi (1983) notes that the increasing emphasis on free associations in psychoanalytic technique has led to a shift in interest from visual to verbal material. However, to quote Freud (1923), we should neither "forget the importance of optical mnemic residues" nor deny that thought-processes may become conscious "through a reversion to visual residues" (p. 21). Similar ideas were also expressed regarding dream-formation (Freud, 1900).

Freud thus points to the close connection between verbal and visual thought processes. I regard visual images as an important facet of the "psychoanalytic instrument" (Balter, Lothane & Spencer, 1980). They condense "various elements in the patient's emotional experience" (p. 489). Provided the analyst uses fantasy in allowing them to be spontaneously created – and judgment in interpreting their meanings – they may inform on emotional processes that otherwise might have escaped his attention.

In other terms, the visual image of the baby and the hole-mother was a result of my analytic α-function. Ferro and Basile (2004, p. 677) describe a chain of events in the analyst's mind; from a visual image or ideogram, via α-function to dream work. S/he may take one step further and verbalize the image in an explicit intervention, as I finally did. Bion's words are pertinent; "interpretations are really 'imaginative conjectures' about the missing pages" (1987, p. 179). Nadya's depression and Beate's experience of it was in truth a missing page – mostly so to Beate but also to Nadya – and I tried to help them fill in some of its essential words.

I assume Beate's affects had begun to transform when she experienced that her mother's containment was deficient. At first they emerged as a general restlessness and anxiety and, later, as a fear of holes. Several analysts suggest that traumatization may lead to a lack of psychic representation; in Cohen's (1985) words, to "an absence of structure and representable experience in a region of the self" (p. 178). The patient cannot represent her wishes and thus cannot modify them by intra-psychic defences but only by "need-mediating objects" (p. 180). This description corresponds to the start of treatment when Beate could only cling to the breast. Evidently, she did not want milk but containment – which, however, she did not get. If such a situation persists, "no representations of need-satisfying interactions . . . provide the basis for symbolic interaction with the world and for goal-directed behaviour" (idem). This was illustrated by Beate's speechless and incomprehensible behaviour. Green (1998) formulates a view similar to Cohen; if the container cannot assimilate projective identifications the individual will suffer "a haemorrhage of the representation, a pain with no image of the wound but just a blank state . . . a hole" (p. 658).

In contrast to Cohen and Green, I emphasize that a hole is indeed a mental representation. We cannot articulate anything about a thing that lacks a representation, since "we think only in signs" (Kloesel & Houser, 1998, p. 10). The hole is a sign though it is primitive, iconic and scary. If not, it would be a "merely inscribed message", a Laplanchean concept challenged in Chapter 2. I emphasize this, not only because of my wish to be clear about semiotic matters; I am also driven by a technical consideration: the more Beate and I can invent elaborate signs of her present enactments and past assumed experiences, the more we will be able to talk about her "hole". The sign appears in treatment as play and words, which indicate the despair of a little girl in front of her depressed and unavailable mother.

During infancy, Beate seems to have suffered from the relative absence of an attentive and containing mother. The therapeutic action does not reside in these memories reaching consciousness – because that is not possible. Instead, therapy helps through containment that includes my reconstruction, in cooperation with Beate and her mother, of the original trauma. Beate creates new representations of it via the armchair play, the Escato fear and expressions such as "old wound" and "Mum crocodile". Analysis thus helps her to signify the trauma in a more elaborate way. This enables her to approach the containment "hole" in a roundabout way. The final vignette will illustrate that we reached this phase only after the ghosts had begun to haunt her in the transference relationship.

## Beate: Vignette 3 – Can a ghost see a crayon stroke?

When Beate turns two years of age, she and her mother have been in MIP treatment for eight months. Nadya's depression is gone and she easily accesses feelings of love, appreciation, interest and anger towards her daughter. Beate is vivid and can get angry when things do not go her way. She also feels immense warmth for her mother. Her breast-grabbing is gone and she has started kindergarten.

A new symptom appears. Beate wakes up in tears and runs to her parents' bedroom, "because of ghosts and monsters". When I ask her about it, she jumps into mother's lap and becomes quiet. She uses Nadya's presence to resist further probing. There is no longer any mother–child-interaction disturbance that seems meaningful to address. Beate has an internalized problem with the ghosts, and she fusses with Nadya to avoid uncovering them. I suggest we continue in child analysis and Nadya is relieved. At first, Beate is afraid of being alone with me. After a week she accepts, both because Nadya insists and because Beate trusts me. Beate and I will work together in child psychoanalysis for one and a half years. She begins hesitantly to speak of ghosts and monsters that haunt her at bedtime.

*Analyst:* I wonder about the ghosts and the monsters at home . . .
*Beate:* I can't tell you.
*A:* You don't know what they look like . . .
*B:* No. They don't show themselves!
*A:* Maybe you're afraid of them.
*B:* Yes, very much so . . . They come when I fall asleep . . . and . . . they're up there, too.
   [She points at a roof ventilator in my office.]

I link the nocturnal creatures to occasions when she and Mum have quarrelled during the day: "It seems these awful ghosts come into your room when Mum thinks you've been nasty and you're angry with Mum." These interpretations do not lead us far. Neither do we get any further when I link the ghosts at my ventilator to situations when she has been angry with me. One such instance was when I held back her efforts at running in and out of the consulting room. Clearly, this made her unruly and annoyed.

One session, however, Beate inadvertently makes a tiny red crayon stroke on my table. She becomes terrified and looks up at the ventilator.

*Analyst:*    You got scared?
*Beate:*    Yes!!
*A:*    Is it the ghosts?
*B:*    Yes. There are ghosts *and* monsters!
*A:*    You didn't want to paint my table. It just happened. Maybe the ghosts and monsters think you did it on purpose because you're angry with me. We know that you are, sometimes. Then, you think they will do something mean to you. It's not easy for you, this ghost thing.
*B:*    They have no mouths. They could eat me up.
*A:*    Because they think you are a bad girl.
*B:*    But I am not!
        [After some hesitation, Beate grabs the crayon anew and makes her first ghost drawing.]

I ask her to tell me more about it, but she is still too scared. After a while, she makes a second drawing:

*Analyst:*    The ghost has a very tiny mouth . . .
*Beate:*    Didn't you know that ghosts don't have mouths?!

*Figure 5.1* Beate's first drawing of a ghost.

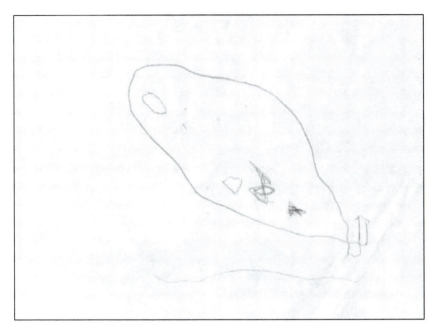

*Figure 5.2* Beate's second ghost drawing.

To emphasize her point, she makes a third drawing, in which she scribbles intensely across the ghost's mouth.

*Analyst:*  Aha, the ghosts have no mouths . . .
*Beate:*  Of course not. That's because they eat you!

The mouth-less devouring ghost is a bizarre object. By deleting the mouth, Beate has amplified its hideous and voracious qualities. In other words, the presence of the frightening mouth is emphasized by its mysterious absence. I take this to portray that Beate is struggling with what Bion (1965) describes as "the relationship of the no-thing and the thing". He speaks of the normal personality who is "capable of tolerating a no-thing [and who] can make use of the no-thing, and so is able to make use of what we can now call thoughts" (p. 106). In such a situation, a child can think about the absent breast and realize that it is out there somewhere and will return later. In contrast, a more disturbed patient, when hearing the analyst saying the word "point", will behave as if the point marks the place where the breast was. "This 'place' seems to be invested by the patient with characteristics that less disturbed people might attribute to an object they would call a ghost. The point (·) and the term 'point' are taken as sensible manifestations of the 'no-breast'" (p. 76).

*Figure 5.3* Beate's third ghost drawing.

Beate is similar to Bion's patient; not because she is psychotic but she is so little and has experienced a hole in containment. The mouth of the mouth-less ghost is a manifestation of the "no-breast". It represents her hunger for reciprocity and her rage against the container when she is not contained adequately. It also signifies the vengeance invoked on her because of her hunger and rage. Vengeance will come to her from a container transformed into a ghost. In the last analysis, this mute creature is also a painting of her mother's depression.

## The infant of a depressed mother: a psychoanalytic model

The poet William Blake asked, as quoted in the chapter's beginning: "Can a mother sit, and hear / an infant groan, an infant fear?" He answered, "No, no, never can it be". In the case of a depressed mother, we must unfortunately object. What torments the most is her difficulty to really feel the pain of her baby. This may have consequences for the child. In Beate's case, I have indicated how her symptoms – from her initial restlessness and breast-craving to her subsequent fears of holes and ghosts – were related to how she experienced containment coloured by her mother's postnatal depression. If we want to extend her case into a general model, the following must be emphasized:

- Postnatal depression does not *cause* certain infant behaviours or experiences. We may rather speak of a "circular causality". Maternal negative mood "compromises the child's functioning and makes the mood even more negative" (Tronick, 2007b, p. 377). Innate factors in the baby, such as temperament difficulties, may also contribute to the mother's sense of hopelessness.
- The infant is not disturbed by the mother's low-keyed affect per se but by the experience of a faltering maternal containment.
- Every infant who is seeking containment projects onto the mother his/her negative emotions. The problem for a depressed mother is that she finds it so hard to receive and process them. As a result the infant's emotions remain in an un-metabolized state. They frighten the baby who gets restless and fretful.
- The frightened baby seeks comfort again from the mother – and may now experience malfunctioning containment once more. Alternatively, s/he is reminded of earlier such situations. As a result, s/he avoids their mother or becomes pushy and fretful. Needless to say, this increases the mother's despair.

I assume these points apply generally to interactions between a depressed mother and her infant. The following two points were discovered in Nadya's and Beate's case.

- The baby may experience insufficient containment as a hole or a void. This may appear clinically as fears of being alone, breastfeeding difficulties, sleeping problems, etc.
- At a later stage, the child may seek to counter the void experience by creating phobic objects, which represent a defence formation. It is more bearable to be afraid of a phobic object than to be constantly restless or in emotional contact with the void experience.

To establish this model's generalizability, we need to investigate other cases. Norman (2001) describes analytic work with six-month-old Lisa and her mother, who was hospitalized for depression during Lisa's third and fourth month of life. Lisa avoids looking into her eyes. He interprets that she is avoiding a mother whom she feels has been ruined by depression. In parallel, mother's psychic pain is increased by Lisa's avoidance. She becomes reluctant to open up emotional links to her daughter. Like Beate and Nadya, this dyad was locked in mutual avoidance. Since Lisa was ten months younger than Beate she had neither had the time nor developed the mental capacities to develop phobias. She was in a primary relation to her mother and used a "pathological defense in infancy" (Fraiberg, 1982) of avoiding looking at the frightening object. The same conclusion could be drawn from Calvocoressi's (2010) case of a seven-month-old boy with his depressed mother. He looks at the ceiling and smiles to an unknown observer without any "expectation of a response from his mother" (p. 40). I did not notice such gaze avoidance in Beate, probably because she was old enough to physically withdraw from her mother. This masked her avoidance of a closer emotional contact with Nadya. Further, she was able to develop more elaborated defences such as the ghost phobia.

Emanuel (2006) reports that a baby may "unconsciously experience a depressed mother's inability to receive and contain its feelings as a lack of willingness to do so, or hostility towards it" (p. 252). She suggests that a baby may defensively "intensify its efforts to evacuate the persecutory sensations which threaten to overwhelm it, to attempt with greater force to gain entry to the mother's mind so that its communications can be received and understood" (idem). Emanuel's idea tallies with my hypothesis that Beate clung to her mother's breast to check if she had damaged it. Nevertheless, I do not emphasize the baby's experience of the mother's hostility as much as her insufficient containment.

To explore my model's relevance to other cases, we need to investigate lengthy high-frequency parent–infant treatments. Only such in-depth studies will allow us to investigate the infant's experiences and formulate psychoanalytic models of them. One might also probe the model on published case studies – provided one differentiates studies based on psychoanalytic techniques from those that rely on supportive interventions. The more the technique relies on the uncovering of unconscious material, the more it will enable a psychoanalytic investigation of how an infant might experience being with her depressed mother.

## Summary and follow-up

I end this chapter by pointing to the complex challenges with distressed dyads. Who is in the most dire straits, today and in some years' time? This thorny question has no simple answer. Our challenge is not to grasp either the child's communications or the parent's suffering. It is to do both! In principle, I regard the baby as the major patient, since she is at the mercy of the adult world's empathy and has few other spokesmen. When the child's distress has abated, the parent may sometimes continue treatment on his/her own, like Nic's mother Tessie did (Chapter 1). In other cases, I end simultaneously with mother and child after a few months.

With older children, symptoms are beginning to settle, as in Beate's case. If so, the child needs more attention of her own and we may embark on a child treatment. When I first met Beate she was craving for Mum's breast and behaving in a bizarre and anxious way. At 17 months, she played with an armchair. At 22 months old she revealed, by telling me of her panic at the Escato, how much she feared a gruesome and engulfing container. At two years and beyond, she feared it would return on her in the shape of nocturnal terrifying creatures. Mouth- and word-less, they attacked her for being a bad girl. I helped her in naming, and thus containing, her conflicts with the container. Then, she could open her mouth and tell the ghosts that she was not bad.

Three years after treatment, I received a mail from Nadya.

> Beate is six years old now and is well. She is active and has a lot of temperament. Sometimes, she is taxing when she wants it her way, but when our wishes clash we are able to solve it. She sleeps well and is not afraid anymore. The other day something remarkable happened at the breakfast table. Suddenly Beate said, "Mum, when I was little I was afraid of an escalator in the underground. Isn't that weird?!" She said nothing more. I understood what she was referring to, of course. I asked her to tell me more, but she just shook her head saying "How weird"! Then it was time to go to school. I thought about you and wanted you to know about the event.

Beate's insomnia, fearfulness and phobia are gone. In contrast, character traits that I have linked with her infancy experiences still remain, a topic we will discuss in Chapter 8 on primal repression. The mail also speaks of the fate of her memories. Unlike the memories from infancy, the Escato events stemmed from the verbal period. What remained to six-year-old Beate was no longer a fear of an escalator but only a memory and a feeling of "Isn't that weird?".

# Chapter 6

# The infant "within" the adult
## Interacting with Monica

So far, we have been dealing with babies and their parents. We will now leap to analytic work with adult patients, with the aim of bringing out the kinship between the two fields. This affinity is a consequence of the "Babushka perspective" mentioned in the introduction. Our earliest experiences seem to go on living within us and emerge especially in emotionally charged situations; when we are scared, in love, enraged, hungry, sleepless, lonely, jubilant, etc.

The analyst is a like Babushka doll, too. Hopefully, he has learnt to recognize and "taste" its layers and put words to them. However, when he assumes responsibility for a patient he may forget the complexity of his own Babushka. Just as we expect parents to be less childish and more conscious of their failings than their children, the analyst expects a similar maturity from himself. Sometimes, though, he is drawn into dire straits in clinical work. Such situations can make infantile layers meddle with his interactions with the patient. Treatment may then resemble a struggle between two baby Babushkas.

The doll metaphor may lure us into thinking that the patient has access to her earliest experiences in the form of explicit memories. This is incorrect. Rather, we may sometimes reconstruct that a present feeling is a *transformation* of a primeval experience. If so, what constitutes such a transformation? This question emerged as I was treating Monica, 35 years of age, in psychoanalysis. Some time into her treatment, I started analyzing Nic and his mother Tessie (Chapter 1). This experience helped me get out of a stalemate in Monica's analysis. The mother–infant work made me grasp more of the interaction between container and contained. When I transposed this insight to Monica's analysis, it took a more fruitful turn.

## Monica: Vignette 1 – Moaning on the couch

Monica bursts out on the couch, "I can't bear it! Now I'm here again, it's terrible. Oh, God! I would do anything to come to my session, but then I can't stand being here. Ahhh . . . we really have a problem". Her legs sway from side to side as she brushes her forehead and moans. It is hard to watch her panic and frustration. I interpret her resentment for my having abandoned her since our last session and her bewildered and bitter feelings when we meet again. She reacts with indifference. I get an internal image of a baby who is longing for mother and screaming and moving in panic; a magnified version of Andy in Chapter 1 who keeps crying after his reunion with mother. When I convey such imagery to Monica she replies, "Your baby thing doesn't tell me anything!" I feel helpless and annoyed, doomed to witness her jerks and sighs and yet declared unable to help her.

Monica sometimes speaks of her childhood. She recalls her mother's emotional unavailability and stern attitude as well as her own hatred towards her father. Her childhood was "wonderful until my father one day told me to help out at home. My world collapsed. At that time I was already ten years of age!" She triumphs, proving that my infant imagery is rubbish. Another negative reaction occurs when I speak of her separations reactions vis-à-vis me. I observe that she jerks and moans mainly in the beginning of sessions and especially after weekend breaks. I interpret that when she returns to me she is longing for closeness and consolation but cannot calm down. Monica feels such comments are meaningless at best, insulting at worst. She is not a baby, and she needs weekend breaks – from me!

Let us pause and reflect. When I perceive Monica's body movements, why do I think of an unhappy baby? Might I not as well have thought of a sexually excited and frustrated woman? After all, she often conveys her erotic desire and declares that I cherish similar feelings – though I do not dare acknowledge them, as she claims. I have, however, two reasons for voting on the baby impression; first is her way of speaking of sexual excitement or anguish. Her flat moaning voice, her swaying legs, her sweating forehead; no, this is not the body language of an excited woman. Second, I feel neither the pleasure or excitement nor the shame or timidity that would come to me in front of a desiring woman. I rather feel helpless and tormented, which I assume is a *concordant* identification (Racker, 1957) in the countertransference. In other words, my feeling resonate with those of Monica. Racker describes this phenomenon as an interchange of introjections and projections between analyst and patient. My task is to discern what in Monica actually belongs to me – "this part of you is I" – and what in me actually belongs to her – "this part of me is you" – (p. 311).

Early in the analysis, Monica brings three dream fragments. In the first, her friend Maria stands with her baby at a railway station. In the second, a man hugs her from behind, saying, "I know what she wants. She wants the breast". In the last dream, a man seduces her. She resists but he puts his penis into her mouth and urinates. Monica is upset; the revelation that she wants the breast is humiliating. She wants a man's body, not a woman's breasts! The thought of his urine in her mouth is just frightening. When I ask for associations to Maria, she is silent. She is brought up in the Catholic faith and I suggest the name might be associated to Virgin Mary and Jesus. Monica finds this far-fetched and shrugs her shoulders.

When I describe her baby helplessness, I can stand her deriding or intellectualizing response. What is harder to bear is my own helplessness. I get uneasy, forced to sit still despite my own jerking feelings. In Racker's (1957) terms, I switch to a *complementary* identification: "The patient treats the analyst as an internal (projected) object, and in consequence the analyst feels treated as such; that is, he identifies himself with this object" (p. 312). I identify with a harsh, dismissive object that derides her infantile wishes. This object seems connected with her mother. Recently, Monica had been telling her during a conversation that she felt sad. Her mother replied, "Pull yourself together. Just go on with what you are supposed to do". Monica felt hopeless. In my complementary identification, it is as if I am snapping at her; "Pull yourself together, Monica!"

She senses my irritation and is afraid that I am fed up with her. Indeed, sometimes I feel that way. She experiences me as a man seducing her while mocking her for wanting the breast. However, I do not realize that she views my interpretations as if I were forcing mocking jets of urine into her. Consequently, the meaning of the dream of the urinating man eludes me. In brief, I do not grasp our interaction in the psychoanalytic field (Baranger & Baranger, 2009; Civitarese, 2008; Ferro, 1999; Ferro & Basile, 2011).

## A change in technique

During the fifth semester, some events clarify how she experiences me when I interpret our drama of a helpless mother and an inconsolable baby. During summer, she had an ice cream with her parents. She panicked, rushed to the toilet and took a tranquilizer in secret. Some time later, she had an anxiety attack with her boyfriend. She told him about it, he embraced her and things felt better. I comment on the different feelings and outcomes in the two situations.

*Monica:* The relations with my parents and with my boyfriend, they're so different. What kind of relation should you and I have? One in which I . . . we . . . I . . . pester and nag? Or something new?

*Analyst:* You waver between "I . . . we . . . I nag". Maybe you are not sure if our relationship is *your* responsibility or *ours*. It makes a difference if you feel that I want to assist you and try to understand your panic – or that you must deal with it on your own.

*M:* "Understand?" What mockery! If you understood me, you wouldn't have taken this long summer break.

We speak from different vantage points. I empathize with a baby and her mother – but Monica feels I am criticizing her. In Racker's terms, I think of my countertransference in concordant terms while Monica views my interventions as directed by a complementary identification. She views me as a mother who, while pretending to care for her baby, calls the doctor: "Take care of this baby! I'm finished. I need some vacation!"

## Analysis of the patient: analysis of the interaction

Monica's expression "I . . . we . . . I" is a succinct description of the variations within psychoanalytic *field*. This term explicates that everything said and experienced in the analytic situation expresses the conscious and unconscious fantasies of both participants. We tend to think of an "I" and a "you" in the consulting-room, but in reality there is more of an intersubjective "we" than we dare admit. Some intersubjectivist psychoanalysts (Beebe & Lachmann, 2002; Lichtenberg, 1983; Stern, 2004) are also distinguished infant researchers. They claim that mother–infant interaction studies enhance our sensitivity to the mutuality in the therapeutic process. They describe the therapeutic process as a "moment of meeting" (Stern, 2004) rather than as a therapist treating a patient. In the words of Seligman and Harrison (2012), this perspective "emphasizes the process of mutual recognition, in which one person 'sees' another while feeling separate, even while the very act of seeing the other as separate affirms the connection in the relationship" (p. 340).

There has been a tendency among intersubjectivists not to focus on the *individual* unconscious. I object to this for two reasons. First, every therapist constantly shifts between focusing on the patient and on the interaction. At times, the patient is an *object* of our thinking. At other times, she is a *subject* with whom we "co-construct" (Beebe & Lachmann, 2002) meaning. This has nothing to do with which therapeutic philosophy we adhere to but with how our "negative capability" (Bion, 1970, p. 125) handles the uncertainties in analytic work. Second, this polarity is not a recent discovery. Perhaps Ferenczi (1931, 1933) was the first to fully comprehend that the psychoanalytic process is more intricate than a doctor's investigation of his patient's unconscious. To him, it was – and should be – an encounter in which both participants were struggling with unconscious urges during sessions. Balint (1949, p. 121) continued to investigate the analyst's contribution to the psychoanalytic situation. A later contributor, Betty Joseph, described the patient's attempts "to get the analyst to act in a manner appropriate to his unconscious projection" (Bott Spillius & Feldman, 1989, p. 48).

To give an instance of the sometimes false opposition between the inter- and the intra-subjective perspective, consider this fragment: After the "I . . . we . . . I" episode, I felt freer to reflect on the opposition between "my" baby theme and "her" erotic theme. Monica obviously felt freer, too. She revealed a fantasy that I, when seeing her swaying legs, masturbated behind the couch. If we look at this fantasy from an intersubjective perspective, it reflected her suspicion that I was masturbating while pretending sympathy – whereas she was pleading for help from an analyst who kept his sweets for himself. If we look at it from an intrasubjective perspective, we could say that her erotic desire was rooted in fantasies about a tantalizing nipple – later followed by a penis with similar qualities – that pretends to reach and calm her. Actually, these two interpretations are complementary rather than contradictory.

A theory that bypasses the dialectics between analyzing the patient (the "intra-perspective") and the relationship (the "inter-perspective") remains incomplete. To understand our involvement with the patient and the "confusion of tongues" (Ferenczi, 1933), we need inspiration from many sources: self-analysis, supervision, studies, literature, opera, etc. Parent–infant work adds observable examples of a derailed interaction. During Monica's treatment, I started psychoanalysis with two-week-old Nic and his mother Tessie, introduced in Chapter 1. We shall now follow how this case helped me and Monica in our intersubjective stalemate.

## Little Nic as my supervisor

As we recall, in my first meeting with Tessie she reveals her maternal ambivalence while Nic jerks and tosses his head as if shunning the nipple. They are already on the brink of a "malady of interaction" (Golse, 2006, p. 187). She thinks Nic dislikes her and he cannot handle such projections other than by shunning her. Tessie bursts out, "When he doesn't clutch the nipple or bites it without sucking, I panic. Where's the design for all this? Why can't he stop crying and start sucking!" Her rage *and* commitment is evident and already in the third session I suggest, "When you fear Nic will be injured in an accident, I guess you also fear the thought that you want to get rid of him. 'Adult Tessie' and 'Baby Tessie' want different things." Tessie cries in confirmation, but we do not get trapped in a sadomasochistic relationship like I do with Monica. Nic contributes to the malady of interaction by becoming afraid and withdrawing during breastfeeding. This adds up to his resentment against mother. Their intersubjective problem can be summarized; Nic, with his contradictory intentions, is seeking a mother who is assailed by *her* contradictions.

The sessions with Nic and Tessie take place at a time when I am working with Monica. Witnessing the dyad heightens my attention to the twosome in my work with her. Nic and Tessie function as an internal model of the dyad of "baby–Monica" and "mother–me" with our mutual ambivalence. When Monica feels I am like a fed-up mother, our relation resembles that of Tessie and Nic. To paraphrase Tessie, it is as if I were thinking, "Why can't Monica stop moaning and start sucking my interventions!" Accordingly, she thinks the interventions are actually my method of projecting distress into her. As she puts it, "We really have a problem".

I now begin to think Monica and I suffer together but, nonetheless, we try to remedy the situation. I might feel fed up sometimes – yet maintain interest in our interaction. She suffers – but may also reflect on her accusations. She muses, "Why do I deny you a summer vacation? Can people care for each other and yet part from each other now and then? It feels as if I am running to you *and* away from you. I guess that's why I am lying here kicking about". She is running towards an idealized analyst full of bounties and away from a fed-up and mocking one, all at the same time.

## Transformations

What does it mean when I suggest that Monica is jerking like an unhappy baby? Do her jerks continue directly as a symptom from infancy? Is their link with infancy a mere subjective construction without any general explanatory value? Or, do they represent a transformation? Monica has brought no history of jerks earlier in life, so the first possibility is not substantiated. The second clashes with my countertransference impressions. Not only do I feel that her behaviour on the couch resembles that of a distressed baby; she has also told of her torment in front of crying infants in cafés and other places. She also harbours fantasies of a blissful merger with me; such impressions make it impossible to reject my associations to a baby. The third alternative remains; her jerks represent a transformation. What does that term imply?

Bion (1965) devoted an entire book to his transformation concept. He exemplifies with a portrait of a landscape. The reason we understand its meaning is that during the transformation from landscape to painting, "*something* has remained unaltered and on this *something* recognition depends" (p. 1). This Bion calls the "invariant". Similarly, he says, the analyst interprets the patient's symptoms and dreams as transformations of invariants. Transformations "are not a matter of the analyst's mere individual opinion" (Sandler, 2005, p. 765). In fact, they conserve "seminal features of the material or immaterial fact, object or person observed" (p. 767).

What is the seminal feature or invariant essence that is embedded in Monica's jerks? Let us first approach the question in a general sense. To Bion, a transformation arises out of an invariant of $O$. The problem, as I see it, is that he grounds $O$ in Kant's concept "thing-in-itself". If so, what is a symptom or a painting a transformation *of*? To Kant, objects are not accessible to us in themselves but only through their appearances. No matter how deeply we explore an object, "we deal with nothing whatever but appearances" (Kant, 1996, pp. A45, B63). "It would be easier to run away from one's shadow than to reach [the thing-in-itself]. Every effort to reconstruct it has already gone astray" (Ahlberg, 1967, p. 475).

On this point, Bion is inconsistent. A clinical event may be "as a thing-in-itself and unknowable" (1965, p. 12). Here, he agrees with Kant; we cannot know the thing-in-itself. Other times he dissolves the border between an experience and the thing-in-itself: "The experience (thing-in-itself) I denote by sign $O$" (p. 13). At another instance, he hopes "to discover from the invariants in this material what $O$ is" (p. 15). However, he also says that $O$ cannot be discovered; "it can be known about, its presence can be recognized and felt, but it cannot be known" (Bion, 1970, p. 30). This contrasts with his formulation about an analytic session, in which "a week-end break, $O$, exists" (p. 17). The term "week-end" reveals the analyst's idea that his schedule influences the patient emotionally. $O$ is already endowed with a meaning.

Bion's alternate ascribing transcendental and experiential qualities to $O$ creates problems; how should we name Monica's jerks? If we subscribe to the transcendental view, her jerks are the invariant "Baby-*O*", a thing-in-itself. Unknowable infantile invariants would thus hide within her jerks. If the invariant were an infantile experience we would have to wait for Monica's memories to confirm the roots of her symptoms. It is more practicable to suggest that her movements *appear* like baby jerks and that I interpret them to *signify* some infant psychic reality, because I once jerked myself or because I have seen many babies jerking. This I will experience as if – although I have no rational grounds for believing that – an invariant baby experience has been transformed. I may *feel* that her infant self is preserved like "the pearl in an oyster" (Mark, 2001, p. 351) but, logically, it is an impossibility.

Thus, Monica's jerks are transformations of a *present* emotional state. They are signs that I perceive and interpret. This argument is in line with Kant. He would protest if we claimed there is an invariant flower in a painting that makes us conclude what it depicts. "The order and regularity in the appearances that we call 'nature' are brought into them by ourselves . . . without understanding there would not be any nature at all" (Kant, 1996, pp. A125–126). We perceive the world and invent concepts such as "flowers" or "baby-like jerks". This process of combining perceptions via concepts into thoughts is possible because our fellowmen provided signs from birth onwards. They once taught us, "This is a flower" or "This jerking baby is unhappy".

We now realize why the Babushka imagery must remain a metaphor, *une façon de parler*. It helps us understand the infantile-*like* qualities in Monica, me and other human beings. There is no baby inside any of us; it just appears that way. To be true, there might be links between implicit or primally repressed memories from infancy and our adult internal world. Importantly, however, we can only assume such links via reconstructions, "through inferences derived from implicit (unconscious) semantic and procedural evidence" (Solms & Turnbull, 2001, p. 169). In the next chapter, we will follow Tristan's lonely struggle with this problem.

## Signifiers of infantile experience

As I described in Chapter 2, a sign could be a word, a smile, an admonition, a frown, a squeak – anything that incites thinking. Peirce's tripartite semiotic apparatus [three signs, three interpretants, three experiential categories – for summaries, see Muller & Brent (2000), Olds (2000), Salomonsson (2006), Sheriff (1994)] – is well suited for covering both conscious and unconscious representations (Winberg Salomonsson, personal communication, 2006). For example, when I tell Monica, "As I see you jerking, I am reminded of an unhappy baby", my word-symbols signify her misery. However, *her* interpretant indicates that she views my comment as an index: "Lie still for Heaven's sake. You're not a baby anymore!" Or, it issues from my voice as an icon of "Annoyed Man". Meltzer reminds us that the analyst's behaviour, "verbal and otherwise", may have "the impact of actions rather than communications" (Meltzer, 1992, p. 42). This division between action and communication dissolves once we realize they both have semiotic properties – both are signs. As Olds puts it, "every-thing a therapist does has semiotic implications at one level or another" (2000, p. 524).

Many psychoanalysts have invented concepts for how a baby signifies his perceptions. Freud spoke of "*Wz*" or "*Wahrnehmungszeichen*" (1892–99; 1950, p. 234) – "signs of perception". He had in mind primal, unconscious and loosely arranged registrations. As Balestriere (2003) sums up, "This primary material is conceived as non-repressable, foreclosed, non-fantasizable. Nevertheless, it acts upon everyone's psychic and/or somatic life" (p. 63). In Peirce's terminology, *Wz* corresponds with icon and index. Compared with Laplanche's concepts brought out in Chapter 2, it corresponds to the "enclosed message" (2007, p. 208). In Rosolato's (1985) terms, it is a forerunner to a "demarcating signifier". This concept covers corporal expressions, affect and drives, as well as perceptions and sensations that make up "the peculiar quality of a lived experience" (p. 14). It also covers the "gestures, the mimic and the prosody which complete the functions of the word" (idem). Demarcating signifiers emerge before the child acquires language. Their meaning derives from pairs of opposite emotions – good/bad, pleasure/unpleasure. Out of such dual experiences, a network of signs and meanings branches out, which it is our analytic task to investigate.

When I included Monica's view that I was attacking her with interpretations I moved from using a demarcating signifier to a "formal signifier" (Anzieu, 1990). I was no longer only addressing her psychic pain but also that she thought the container/form was untrustworthy; me, the annoyed analyst. As I also learned with Nic, an interpretation needs to focus on the patient's troubled feelings at the breast – or on the couch – as well as his/her notion of the incomprehensible containing object; a sad mother pulling her breast back – or an annoyed analyst snapping at his "impossible" patient.

Bion's concept, "β-element", also signifies infantile experiences. It covers "phenomena that may not reasonably be regarded as thoughts at all" (1997, p.11). I suggest it expresses the individual's emotion *and* its level of signification. It is a sign, though the patient *feels* it to be a thing-in-itself (Bion, 1963, p. 39). It is an icon or index "waiting" to become signified at a higher level so that the individual can reflect on it through word-symbolism. Being a primitive mental sign, the β-element is a thought, however catastrophic, fragmented and thing-*like* it may appear to the subject. Thus, Monica's jerks represent β-elements. If we assumed that her mind has not signified them at all, we could say nothing about them. Psychoanalysts investigate mental phenomena that are unknown – not unknowa-ble or un-signified. When we claim that a patient evacuates β-elements, it is a metaphor. She *thinks* she evacuates them because she has signified them as a thing that must be evacuated. Freud noticed "how much more concretely children treat words than grown-up people do" (1909, p. 59). Monica treats my interpretations like a child. She feels they clog her only trusted safety valve; the jerks through which she is evacuating what she experiences as unwanted "things" inside her. This is another reason why she detests my interventions.

## Containment and translation

If we view transformation as a semiotic concept it will be easier to understand what we are doing when we contain the patient. As Stern has remarked, containment does not come about via some medium "through which the fantasies of mother and infant could communicate and affect one another" (Stern, 1995, p. 42). We have to de-mystify the containment process; it is something we *do* with the patient and within ourselves. In Chapter 3, I focused on its "maternal music" and "paternal words". Here, I emphasize its similarities to the work of translation. The container, whether a parent or an analyst, suggests names or signs with the intention of ameliorating the panic and making it thinkable. By my words, intonations, looks and silences, I invent new signs of Monica's anguish. In Nic's case, I translate the possible meanings of the icons and indices that he and his mother are transmitting. This activity includes how I look and sound; the sum total constitutes my translation of the present emotions – from one significatory level into another.

Must I then always express myself unequivocally, free from projective identifications, and with all affects fully conscious? No! All semiotic interchange develops by way of messiness (Tronick, 2005), imperfect contingencies (Fonagy *et al.*, 2002) and misunderstandings. We can only hope that our interpretations provide a reasonably accurate translation – from a more primitive to a more advanced level – of the baby's wishes and fears. This translation is of vital importance to the baby. In Bion's model, she gets frightened when she projects terrible feelings but mother rejects them. The baby will then reintroject, "not a fear of dying made tolerable, but a nameless dread" (1962b, p. 309). What is intolerable about this dread is not only its affective strength but also that a baby has such undeveloped signs to think about it. Containment provides her with new ways of thinking, as when I say, "Nic, I think you are so scared of all this". The new meaning is not the words in themselves – because they are meaningless to him. It is rather my calm mode of speaking and earnest attention to the boy's torment.

We should, finally, remind ourselves that we are not translators sitting in a box talking through a mike to a receiver. Containment is a bi-directional process. Nowhere does this become clearer than in mother–infant work. In such therapies we have, as it were, the container and the contained in front of our eyes. Such experiences may help us become more sensitive to analyst–patient interactions and more conversant in addressing them. As the final vignette will show, this can sometimes move the analysis in a positive direction.

## Monica: Vignette 2 – The hen or the chicken?

One session towards the end of the seventh semester, Monica gets jerky and anxious on the couch.

*Monica:*   It's impossible to be at ease with you! *It doesn't work!* It feels like you're putting demands on me. Already after one minute! It reminds me of a party the other night. We were playing charades with songs. It felt like a demand, too. I couldn't think of one single tune to impersonate!

[We talk about this experience. Then she comes to think of a lecture. She was responsible for the microphone, but something went wrong and there was a noise in the loudspeaker. A lady rebuffed her.]

M:    There was something wrong with the set-up! I thought, "What am I doing here? I don't feel welcome anywhere. I long for my home country . . . " But that's an illusion. When I was young, somebody asked where I came from and I replied, "I come from the world!" I was talking like a teenager . . . but it was important to answer that way.

Analyst:  You wanted to tell them you don't feel welcome anywhere; not at the party, at my office, in any country. This feeling is there all the time inside you.

M:    And then everything gets complicated, since I behave in a way that makes people annoyed. I don't know which comes first, the hen or the chicken.

A:    The hen or the chicken?

M:    Well, the hen and the egg . . .

      [In the countertransference, I get a shivering feeling as I think about a cold and white eggshell.]

A:    Am I the hen who doesn't want you and cannot stand you, chicken? Is that why you feel unwelcome and hardly can stay with me? In your family, you were the youngest of many siblings. I wonder if you had a feeling of being the unwelcome chicken of your hen mother.

M:    . . . Sometimes I think about death; not suicide, but dying to get free. Maybe to be reborn, leave the bad things behind me, start anew . . . But I can't start my life anew!

A:    OK. But we're talking about bad feelings. At home, perhaps the feeling was, "Now Monica's fretting again! Why did we conceive her?" Here, "Why did I receive her in analysis?" Can you express this awesome fear openly instead of having it running around in your body and creating so much distress?

M:    . . . Mum once bought us chickens. The wings were made of figs and the beak was an almond. Oh, how I wanted to save them instead of eating them! On that occasion, Mum was friendly and really wanted to brighten up our day.

The next session, Monica imagines that I have taken away a little picture hanging over the couch. Recently, she has begun playing with it in her thoughts, imagining it depicts a game of peek-a-boo. Today, she experiences that I took it away because I was annoyed with her playing around with it. She takes up courage:

Monica:  It feels as if I've been in a prison for a long time. The prisoners were grey and gloomy. Now some light is seeping in. I feel I am sharing something with you. This homeless feeling, I have no words for it. I'd like to be silent . . .

*Analyst:*  . . . instead of talking it away. I guess you often talk to make me appreciate you, but then you fear I'll like you even less. Then you babble more and we end up in this terrible circle. The reverse, I guess, would be a hen that lets its chicken babble, pick up a worm or two, or be silent.

*M:*  You know, I like that hen and chicken image!
[She turns silent for several minutes. This has never happened before.]

*M:*  I almost feel guilty, lying here and enjoying myself. I feel like I got a piece of candy from you. Yes, like that chicken of figs and almonds!

When I assume her mother has harboured rejecting feelings I base it not only on Monica's information but, more importantly, on complementary identifications in the countertransference. To the extent that the mother harboured feelings similar to my vexation with Monica, it is the *covering up* of these feelings that was harmful rather than their existence per se. Any mother can harbour terrible thoughts about her baby. Still, she can have loving feelings, too. What harmed Monica was probably that the mother did not acknowledge any negative feelings, and that Monica prohibited herself from acknowledging her intuitions about the family atmosphere.

*Monica:*  Things feel different now. I wonder what happened . . . I have always felt I am intruding in your office. I don't have any place!

*Analyst:*  You have come here, squirmed on the couch, and feared that I am annoyed. Yes, sometimes I have been annoyed with you. But is that dangerous to you? Isn't it rather that if you don't pronounce your intuition, or if I don't dare to realize what I feel, a terrible feeling will remain inside you?

*M:*  You scare me! I'm still afraid to talk about it. It's important to talk about it with respect, like when you speak to a baby.

*A:*  When Mum sneered, "Pull yourself together, go on with what you should do", or when you sensed I was annoyed, you felt treated disrespectfully. You feared our feelings but what you really should fear is our insincerity – and that you don't acknowledge that you notice it.

*M:*  I tried to re-make my parents. I can't teach them to respect that baby. I must teach myself!

A little later, she reveals a memory. One day little Monica was fussy and Mum yelled, "Get away, you monster!" She has been concealing this memory, fearing that once she told me she would break down or I would sympathize with her mother.

*Analyst:*  It has been especially hard on you, since you felt I thought of you as a monster, too.

*Monica:*   That monster thing is much larger than me!

*A:*   Only if you don't dare naming your suspicion, "Björn thinks I am a monster!"

The next session she relates a lengthy dream. I will just relate a detail. During an art seminar she is supposed to tell the group what she thinks of a painting. A resigned woman whispers, "We're all *livegna* (serfs)". Monica retorts, "No, we are all libido"! Her friends chuckle at her pun. She shows a new ability to speak up about libidinal feelings without fearing that she evokes the "Get away you monster"-feeling in me. She continues associating to the dream. The painting reminds her of Michelangelo's *Creation* in La Capella Sistina. She has always been moved by God's finger touching that of Adam: "This is Genesis, isn't it?" This comment ends the last session before Christmas. It indicates the upcoming separation between the "fingers" of analyst and analysand. Compared with her earlier rage towards my summer vacation, this separation is not only saddening to her. It is also necessary for something new to be born; a child ready to go out in the world to find a libidinal object.

## Affective disclosure

As seen in this vignette, I disclosed to Monica an aspect of my countertransference; I had been irritated with her jerking and moaning. Certainly, "self-disclosure can be just as presumptuous and intrusive as interpretations or silence" (Maroda, 2000, p. 247). On the other hand *affective* disclosure can be vital, because "for the analyst to attempt to stifle her naturally occurring emotional responses is to deprive the patient of exactly what he is desperately seeking" (Maroda, 2002, p. 107). Mother–infant work lays bare the sometime disastrous effects of concealed ambivalence and of feigned devotion. As described in Chapter 1, Tessie's ironic comments and peevish voice with Nic evoked strong countertransference; not because she was ambivalent but that she was insincere about it. The same could be said of Miranda's spurious comments about Karen in Chapter 4. The fact that these mothers did not disclose their affects in a genuine way did not prevent me from sympathizing with their plight. If we denied that such an atmosphere negatively influenced their babies we would blame it all on the young; on the other hand, to deny that the babies were also active participants in these spurious interchanges, though they were just as unconscious about it as their mothers, would imply blaming it all on the mothers.

The point with the final vignette is thus not to blame Monica, her mother or me. As for her parents, I knew about them only via Monica's story. In contrast, I knew quite a lot about my unacknowledged negative feelings against her. When we became able to talk about them, she evoked the fingers of creation and separation. In Michelangelo's painting they belong to God and Adam. In the last session before separating from me, in order to return home to celebrate the birth of an infant Jesus, it related to mother and her, as well as to me and her.

# Chapter 7

# The living fossil

## Tristan's *Urvergessen*

In the previous chapter, we followed how Monica and I struggled with finding a better way of working together. She reminded me of a distressed baby – but she thought such interpretations were insulting. One of the topics in that chapter was; what justifies our assumption that a patient's worldview or symptoms resemble that of an infant? We will now turn to a literary figure, the male hero in Richard Wagner's opera *Tristan und Isolde* (1865). Like Monica, he struggles to understand the connections between his present torment and his infancy. In contrast to her, however, he has no one to help him in his fatal pilgrimage towards his interior. This is one reason that he succumbs in the end.

Let us start with the plot. Tristan, a young likeable man meets Isolde, a fair woman whose betrothed he has just killed. When their eyes meet they fall in love. Yet, they never touch each other or speak about their feelings. Instead, Tristan leaves her and returns home. He persuades his foster father, King Marke, to marry her and offers to bring the future bride home. Upon returning, they accidentally drink a potion that rekindles their love. Nevertheless, she marries Marke. One night Tristan and Isolde secretly decide to make their love materialize by reuniting in death. Marke and his royal escort discover them. In the ensuing battle, the young man gets wounded by intentionally avoiding defending himself. On his sickbed, he yearns for Isolde to die with her. When they reunite, he instantly dies and then she as well. Marke is devastated and declares he would gladly have renounced the woman to his beloved foster son.

This is the drama of *Tristan und Isolde* in its essence. Though it centres around two lovers, I will concentrate on Tristan; his history is more clearly portrayed than Isolde's – and he is reckoning with a question that interests us particularly: infantile trauma and its sequelae in adulthood. His father died before birth and his mother immediately afterwards. He has known about this catastrophe all his life. Only now, during his struggle with his "*Urvergessen*" or primal oblivion, does he realize its consequences. I will argue that his self-analysis is courageous but incomplete. The libretto speaks movingly of Tristan's lifelong depression, gentle disposition and courage. We will unravel more adverse traits such as self-centeredness, disloyalty, inconstancy and a complex of unconscious rage and guilt towards Isolde and Marke. Tristan manages to link the infantile trauma to his depression and yearning, but its connections with his self-centred, enraged and guilt-ridden propensities remain unconscious.

Tristan blames the misery of his life on the parental losses in infancy. I will emphasize how these losses were inadequately handled, especially through his uncle's way of containing little Tristan. This has led him to suffer from what I suggest are the effects of *primal repressions*. This concept has fallen into disrepute, due to Freud's incomplete definition (Freud, 1915b, 1915c) and its seemingly logical inconsistency. I will argue that Tristan may help us understand it from a new vertex. In Chapter 8, I will focus further on the concept and argue that it is essential in clinical work with infants and adults.

## The enigmas of Tristan

Like his other works, Wagner conceived both the music and words of this opera. In fact, music often appeared prior to the words (Zuckerman, 1964, p. 8). Though the second act contains a lengthy dialogue between the lovers, Wagner said that "almost nothing but music is happening" (Lindner, 1912, p. 325). The opera's *Leitmotifs* refer mainly to emotional states. This is in line with its psychological focus:

> I plunged into the depths of the innermost processes of the soul. Then I created, unhesitatingly, out of this innermost centre of the world, its external form . . . Life and death, the entire meaning and existence of the external world, depends here only on the internal mental processes.
>
> (Lindner, 1912, p. 19)

When I now proceed to analyzing only the libretto, I am aware that this will give an incomplete idea of the personae. However, a thorough musical analysis would be a project exceeding the scope of this book.

The opera is set in some unspecified medieval time. Tristan is a young man of noble birth and a nephew to the old King Marke of Cornwall. The childless king took the orphaned boy under his wing at birth. Tristan was recently sent to war against the successor to the Irish throne, Morold. Tristan slew him but was wounded in the battle. By chance, he came under the care of Isolde, Morold's betrothed. When she recognized her fiancé's assassin, she wanted to kill him; but when their eyes met she released him. This presents us with the first enigma of the story: Tristan and Isolde instantly fell in love. Why did they not consummate their love?

Some time later, and this is where the opera actually starts, Tristan has been sent by King Marke to Ireland for a second mission; to ask Isolde to become his queen. Marke is unaware of their earlier encounter. Actually, he has been persuaded by Tristan to woo the princess. In the first act, Tristan is bringing her home. She is furious with his reserved manners and silence about their earlier encounter. She seeks revenge and requests a deadly potion for Tristan and herself. To save their lives, her servant Brangäne substitutes the deadly poison with a love potion. Immediately after having sipped it, they realize their love. Meanwhile, they land in Cornwall and Isolde becomes queen. We encounter the second enigma: the bond between uncle and nephew is warm and trustful. King Marke is old and wishes Tristan would find a woman and succeed him on the throne. Why does Tristan persuade Marke to marry Isolde instead of confiding in his foster-father and tell him that he loves her?

In the second act, Tristan and Isolde arrange a nocturnal meeting. It evolves into an ecstatic encounter – whether it is consummated or not has been eagerly debated. They decide to die together, but they are disclosed. The broken-hearted king tries to understand Tristan's betrayal. The third enigma emerges: Marke asks Tristan in earnest for an explanation. Why is his response so veiled that Marke cannot understand it? Why does Tristan then prepare a near-suicide by becoming an easy victim of the sword of Melot, the vassal who betrayed him?

In the third act, Tristan is lying wounded in his ancestral castle in Bretagne. Impatiently, he is waiting for Isolde to die with her. Through an exasperated and courageous self-analysis, he discovers that his yearning for Isolde is an after-effect of the parental deaths. The losses have made him depressed and constantly yearning for salvation. Tristan concludes such salvation is possible only by dying with Isolde, which also implies to reunite with his dead mother. This was already hinted at in the second act when he asked Isolde to follow him to "the dark land of Night, out of which my mother sent me". When Isolde appears towards the end of the opera, she is ready to use her medical skills on Tristan. However, he dies in a seeming suicide. She sings her "Liebestod" hymn and expires. A fourth enigma emerges: when Isolde returns to cure Tristan's wounds in order to die with him, why does he tear off his bandages, bleeding to death in front of her and thus abandoning her?

The enigmas can be summarized: Tristan is heading towards self-destruction, a state he idealizes as a union in death with Isolde, while dismissing the fact that he killed her fiancé and mortified his uncle. He connects the enigmas with the parental losses, while I focus on how they were contained during infancy. My analysis includes not only his present depression but also his self-centredness, ruthlessness, fury and guilt towards his loved ones. In this emotional maelstrom he is bound to succumb while drawing his loved ones along. We will follow this process and start with the lovers' ecstatic dialogue in the second act. Their clandestine meeting results in a decision to die together. I will use a translation from the internet (Wagner, 1865), which I have corrected when it missed some detail of the German original.

## Day and Night: transformations of metaphors

In the second act's love scene, two metaphors are born and eagerly discussed: Day and Night. As their meanings evolve, the lovers will arrive at their resolve to die together. At first, daylight is a concrete obstacle to their union. At long last nightfall arrives, ushered in by Isolde's quenching the torch. This is the secret signal for Tristan to rush into her arms. He moans of the Day that has prevented their embrace, but he also sees it as an impersonated agent: *Der Tag*, the Day, is opposed to their union; enviously and mercilessly it exposes the pangs of their suffering.

In a second transformation, the Day symbolizes worldly achievements and the hunt for glory. Tristan curses "Day's bright orb of worldly honour, shining upon me with the brightest radiant glow". Such strivings have prevented him from realizing his true feelings for Isolde. The Day is now only an internal force, which the two lovers discover that they have harboured and cherished – until the potion revealed their true feelings. Tristan realizes that the Day has awakened his envy and zeal, which has threatened his happiness and resulted in "the despondence which began to make honour and fame a burden to me". When he was wooing Isolde on the king's account, these forces guided him. In short, the Day signifies emotional truth *concealed* and has thus caused Tristan's depression. The Night comes to signify emotional truth *revealed*. Tristan exalts "*das Wunderreich der Nacht*", the wonderful realm of night: "In darkness my eyes might serve to see [the Day's deceiving beams] clearly."

Now, Night also begins to imply the night of death, "where, all-eternal (*ur-ewig*), true alone, love's bliss smiles on him". Here, the prefix *ur-* enters for the first time. It means primal or original and will reoccur during the opera, finally in Tristan's *Urvergessen, ur*-oblivion, of his infantile trauma. When Night has come to signify *ur-ewig*, it picks up yet another meaning: the maternal bosom or womb. By being taken up in it, Tristan hopes to be released from the world. He asks Isolde to follow him into "the dark land of Night out of which my mother sent me". After the connection Night-bosom has been established, Night's connotation with *Liebestod* ("love-death") is emphasized. The lovers now sing of "sweet death, yearned for, longed for *Liebestod*". There, they will enjoy the *urheilig, ur*-holy, warmth of the Night where there is "no evasion, no parting, just we alone, ever home, in unmeasured realms of ecstatic dreams".

When Tristan asks Isolde to follow him to the bosom of his dying mother to reunite with her, I interpret this to be an idealized version of an infantile disaster. His depression expresses a wish to reunite with a sanctified maternal object, which simultaneously brings the child to life and entices him to return to death. Isolde functions as a representative of the maternal object that shall accompany him, as he imagines, to the womb. He plays out his infantile trauma in reverse; he brings Isolde back to where his mother gave him life only to abandon him forever. The consequent rage, which ever since Freud's *Mourning and Melancholia* (1917) we regard as a basic contributor to depression, is concealed behind the eulogy of dying with Isolde. As for the paternal object, it remains mysteriously mute, but we can trace its shadow in the way Tristan kills Isolde's betrothed and betrays his uncle.

Other interpretations of the opera are possible. Roger Scruton (2004) regards the lovers as performing a sacrifice with religious dimensions. He depicts Tristan as "the orphan and outsider who has wandered the world in search of a love that only Isolde could provide, loving him, as she does, with the total and predestined commitment that a mother too must feel" (p. 63). I, however, find the maternal object to be coloured by his idealization and rampageous hatred. To Scruton, their sacrificial death is the consummation of their love. In my reading, they mistakenly believe that their love is exalted and that only death can liberate and unite them. As Scruton correctly reminds us, they are prisoners in a social and political cobweb, but they are also imprisoned in a cobweb of personal unconscious impulses. We witness the tragedy of two youngsters who cannot stop the avalanche of their unconscious urges. This is set in motion by Tristan's character, which we will now look at more closely.

## Tristan's character

The libretto portrays Tristan as a sad, courageous and loveable young man. Other passages point to his lack of consistency and fidelity. In the closing seconds of the second act, he suddenly rages against Melot, who denounced him. If his consistent intention were to exalt love by dying with Isolde, why does he behave like any lover caught in the midst of adultery? I take this question to be valid even though Tristan later lets his sword fall to become wounded by Melot.

If this example indicates more of a rash and youthful temperament, others point to more consistently narcissistic traits. I refer to Tristan's self-centred and exacting attitude when addressing Isolde and his friend Kurwenal. In the second act's love scene, Isolde emerges as a passionate woman – but he responds by complaining against the Day with its insolent hatred and grievance. She seems more interested in understanding him and his motives than the reverse. When he starts speaking explicitly about dying, she feels forsaken since he does not involve her in his suicide plans. She asks, "But our love, is it not Tristan *and* Isolde?" Only after two reminders does he start singing, accompanied by the melody that will later follow Isolde in her *Liebestod*: "Thus might we die . . . together, ever one, without end, never waking, never fearing, namelessly enveloped in love!"

Tristan's self-centred vacillations also appear in relation to Kurwenal. His companion saved his life after the battle with Melot by carrying him to Tristan's ancestral castle. Now he has sent a messenger to plead help from Isolde. While Tristan is waiting impatiently, his treatment of Kurwenal parallels his vacillations between optimism and pessimism concerning Isolde's return. In the third act's first scene, Kurwenal reveals his project of bringing Isolde to cure Tristan. Tristan's response expresses his gratitude but also his notion that Kurwenal has no will of his own. He should rather regard Tristan's interests as more important than his own moral standards.

> My Kurwenal, dearest friend! . . .
> He that I hated, you hated too.
> Him that I worshipped, you worshipped too.
> To the good King Mark, when I served him well,

you were truer than Gold!
When I had to betray that noble lord,
how glad you were to betray him too!
Never your own self, mine alone,
you suffer with me when I suffer:

Later, Tristan is hallucinating that Isolde is approaching. He orders Kurwenal: "Go and keep watch, you foolish wretch!" After a while, Isolde's ship is indeed arriving but gets briefly out of sight. Tristan immediately turns suspicious: "You too a traitor! Wretched man!" When Kurwenal finally announces that the ship is visible, Tristan again shifts his attitude: "Kurwenal! Most faithful of friends! All my goods and possessions, I bequeath this day!" With reservation that Tristan is in a desperate condition, he clearly regards Kurwenal from a narcissistic standpoint. When he is optimistic, Kurwenal is wonderful. When things look bad, the friend is stupid and treacherous.

We will now turn to Tristan's rage and guilt. Such emotions become evident vis-à-vis Isolde, though they hide beneath his idealizations. Let us first recapitulate: when Tristan was sent to war in Ireland, he beheaded Isolde's betrothed, Morold, and sent the head to her. However, Morold had wounded Tristan during the battle. When Tristan woke up to see Isolde, he was thus looking into the eyes of a woman he had desecrated. These events are related in the first act by Isolde to her confidante Brangäne: Tristan "gazed into my eyes. His wretchedness tormented me!" Instead of killing him, Isolde healed his wound and sent him home, so that his look should not "trouble" her anymore. What was the nature of that trouble? Was it only passion she wanted to reject, or was guilt involved? Was she only appalled that her fiancé had been murdered? We are left to speculate on other motives for saving Tristan than her instant infatuation.

Now to Tristan: his look at Isolde, was it only one of love? Could he but feel guilty and terrified when he lay in the hands of his "collateral" victim? As we reflect on the scene at the Irish sickbed, we understand better why Tristan chose Isolde to assume the role of companion in death. When they met, he was helpless in front of a woman whom he had devastated and humiliated. Out of this emerged a love relationship whose ingredients of healing and care were evident from the start. Isolde became the maternal healer who unconditionally sacrificed herself for the helpless and wounded child Tristan. Her other position became strangely short-lived; a humiliated woman bereaved of her fiancé. Scruton (2004) speaks of the parallel between Isolde and Tristan and a mother's total commitment to her child. This leaves out the lovers' unconscious guilt linked to transgression (Melon, 1983); the murder of Morold. It also leaves out that Tristan arranges a scene with Isolde in which a baby drags his helpless mother into a joint death. Evidently, this is another cause of his guilt.

The idea that the slaughter of Morold casts its shadow on the lovers is supported by an event towards the end of the opera. Isolde is approaching the wounded Tristan. He staggers towards her, exclaiming: "With bleeding wound I once battled with Morold. With bleeding wound I now pursue Isolde!" He tears the dressing from his wound, cherishing the blood streaming from it – and dies. This scene links the Irish sickbed to the Breton deathbed in the final act. What does Tristan mean by saying that he will pursue Isolde with his bleeding wound? His association to Morold inspires several interpretations. One is that the union with Isolde conceals his assassination of her, since he says he will "pursue" her; the German original "*erjagen*" means hunt or chase. A second interpretation concerns his guilt of killing Morold. He will now atone for it by committing suicide in front of Isolde. Her devastated words of farewell contain many accusations. She calls him a spiteful man who has punished her by not dying with her. Further, she no longer has any possibility of lamenting her suffering to him. In short, she is completely abandoned.

My interpretation is akin to that of Zuckerman (1964). He describes the lovers as being not in love with each other but with love itself. Their quest is

> for the obstacles that prolong passion – ultimately for the final obstacle, death, which is paradoxically the only permanent fulfilment … Tristan apotheosizes the unhealthiest Eros – the boundless desire for a suicidal union with the Infinite, objectified in a human love impossible of fulfilment.
>
> (p. 24)

If we agree with Bergmann (1995) that "love consists of many feelings: the joy of union, the fear of separation, the longing for the absent love object, and the joy of reunion" (p. 10), then Tristan emphasizes and idealizes the longing for the absent object. In Melon's words (1983), his relationship with Isolde is characterized by "the sweetness of unhappiness, the voluptuousness of pain, the pleasure in tears, the sobs replacing orgasm, and the sublime satisfaction of falling into death's abyss" (p. 61).

Such interpretations in no way detract from our being deeply moved by the fate of two unhappy, unknowing and unyielding characters heading towards destruction, the roots of which they do not understand. In this, they are tragic and poignant human beings like Oedipus, Hamlet, Rigoletto and many other characters. They deserve our respect and recognition in that they struggle with the same *Ur*-ailments as we all do. In Tristan, we recognize the yearning for basking *Ur*-eternally in a mother's complete devotion to our needs and wishes. Wagner invites us to "taste" these fantasies – and to realize their impossibility. This is, per se, a deeply moving experience. The singularly most poignant part is Tristan's self-analysis in the third act. There, he seeks to connect his lifelong despair with the loss of his parents in infancy.

## Approaching the primal repressions

In the third and final act of the opera, Tristan is lying wounded outside the castle of his forefathers. Kurwenal promises he will soon become well, but Tristan thoughtfully explains that he has been somewhere else, where no sunrays were to be seen:

> I was where I had been before I was,
> and where I am destined to go:
> in the wide realm of the Night of the world.
> But one certain knowledge is ours there:
> divine, eternal, utter oblivion (*Urvergessen*).

The prefix *Ur-* reappears in connection with a place where Tristan once was and to which he will return one day. One can only have an *Ahnung*, a premonition, of it he says. Paradoxically, it is connected both with certainty and oblivion. That which is *urvergessen*, forgotten forever, still attracts him. This attraction is countered by a *sehnsüchtige Mahnung*, a yearning exhortation, to once again see Isolde. Where is that place where he once was and is destined to go? The word *Urvergessen* provides an answer; it is not a physical place but a metaphor of a primordial state of mind. He yearns to attain it, yet he cannot but dimly recognize it.

How are we to describe this state of mind, which Tristan tries to grasp? I read it as a literary portrait of primal repression, *die Urverdrängung*. By this concept, Freud referred to "a first phase of repression, which consists in the psychical (ideational) representative of the instinct being denied entrance into the conscious. With this a fixation is established" (1915b, p. 148). Such an impulse was never conscious since it had not yet received any "cathexis from the Pcs [Preconscious] ... therefore [it] cannot have that cathexis withdrawn from it" (1915c, p. 181). Before coining the concept, Freud had established the links between infantile memories, fixations and character formation: "our 'character' is based on the memory-traces of our impressions; and, moreover, the impressions which have had the greatest effect on us – those of our earliest youth – are precisely the ones which scarcely ever become conscious" (1900, p. 539). Traumatic experiences may be involved in character formation, operating "in a deferred fashion as though they were fresh experiences" (1896, p. 167). Thus, primal repression may especially affect experiences that occur early in life and/or have a traumatic character. In a second step, repression might fan out beyond the singular experience by attracting to itself "everything with which it can establish a connection" (1915b, p. 148).

However, the concept harbours an inconsistency (Maze & Henry, 1996): if the impulses that primal repression works against were never conscious, how does the psyche "know" how to *Ur*-repress them? Freud's definition implies, according to Maze and Henry, that "the repressed must be known in order to remain unknown, and this seems a logical impossibility' (p. 1087). In addition, Freud claims that such never-known yet repressed impulses influence us strongly and permanently. I call this the paradox of the *living fossil*. Tristan has been at an *urvergessen* place. Thus, his experience is fossilized. Yet, he knows he was there before and it still influences him. Thus, the experience is alive.

Tristan's connecting *das Urvergessen* with *Ahnung* may help us solve the paradox. This everyday word is related to intuition, premonition and divination. *Ahnung* implies a vague and indistinct translation of an affect, impulse or memory. Such vagueness is implied in phrases such as "I cannot tell you that; what you would ask you can never know", used repeatedly in the opera. As long as such *Ahnungen* persist, piece of mind is reigning; but the more Tristan will "translate" into comprehensible language the impulses behind repression, the more he will experience anxiety. We are reminded of Freud's view of repression as a "failure of translation . . . the motive for it is always a release of unpleasure which would be generated by a translation" (1892–99/1950, p. 235). *Das Urvergessen* must thus remain lost in translation to guarantee his calm. Evidently, the self-analysis encounters momentous obstacles.

## Defining the trauma

Kurwenal informs Tristan about the plans of bringing Isolde to him. Tristan rejoices – but a plaintive shepherd's tune is signalling that Isolde's ship is out of sight. The tune pushes his self-analysis further on by evoking the loss of the parents in his infancy.

> Must I understand you thus,
> you ancient, solemn tune
> with your plaintive tones?
> Through the evening air it came, fearfully,
> as once it brought news to the child of his father's death.
> Through the grey light of morning, ever more fearful,
> as the son became aware of his mother's lot.
> As he begat me and died, so, dying, she bore me.

Tristan's *Ahnungen* become filled in by what he thinks are memories of losing the parents. The tune helps him in lifting the primal repression, but only to an incomplete extent. He has always known about his parents' death. Now he connects it with his lifelong depression and yearning and concludes that his fate is to be born to yearn. Even worse, he is "yearning to die" but is not allowed the solace of "dying from yearning". His primal repressions cannot be dissolved by an impulse made conscious and then handled by the ego. The only peace of mind possible is the one brought by "the far away physician" Isolde: through death.

Other emotions now emerge beneath Tristan's wish of dying with Isolde. He mentions Isolde's potion. When he drank it, she named it a "draught of reconciliation" for his murder of Morold. He sings of his hope of being healed by it, that is, of being reconciled with his guilt of the murder. Instead, the potion's "searing magic" was unleashed; he will "never die but inherit eternal torment". At this point, he accuses Isolde of her behaviour by the Irish sickbed. She healed his battle wound only to open it up again "with his sword". She opened up an emotional wound in him: to fall in love and yearn eternally for her. In despair he asks which balsam might bring relief. At this dramatic climax, Tristan suddenly realizes his own role in the draught's gruesome effects:

I, I myself, I prepared it!
From my father's distress and mother's anguish,
from tears of love everlasting,
from laughing and weeping, happiness and hurts,
I found the poisonous draught! . . .
I enjoyed it! Be accursed, fearful draught!

It is not the chemical properties of "*der furchtbare Trank*" that caused Tristan's emotional catastrophe. Rather, his infantile trauma is responsible for a lifelong unbearable inner situation. For a moment, he does not think that the losses of his parents directly caused his torments: he has "brewed" the draught out of his father's distress and mother's anguish. He has thus assigned "new meaning to memory traces" (Faimberg, 2005, p. 2) in a *nachträglich* (Freud, 1918) or après-coup action. The question we must approach is this: if the parental losses per se did not cause his torments, what did? In other words, which memory traces are involved in his infantile trauma, now causing gruesome suffering? Could memories other than of losing his parents have been involved?

I will approach this question in a roundabout way, by looking at how the aftermath of the trauma has continued in Tristan's life. I suggest that his idea of "brewing the draught" out of his father's distress and mother's anguish refers to projective identifications about parents he never knew. He has been searching, perhaps all his life, for human beings whom he could involve in these projections. He found them in Ireland. I suggest Morold and Isolde unconsciously represent the lost parental couple. Once he has subjected them to projective identifications of his longing, rage and guilt he fails to understand his infatuation with Isolde – indeed to understand her as a separate person. If his infatuation were of the kind that might lead him on to loving her, he would have wanted her to survive. Similarly, if he had wished her to compensate for the loss of his mother, he would not have wanted her to die. His rage at the primal object thus becomes apparent. The ensuing guilt is obvious when he hallucinates that Isolde wants to drink reconciliation with him. Reconciliation for what? The only reconciliation plausible is related to his death wishes against Morold *and* Isolde.

Tristan's rage and guilt against Isolde become obvious as she reappears towards the end. He insists she join him in death – only to break his promise. He sings of the blood from the Morold battle with which he shall pursue Isolde. He exults: "Let the world perish before my rejoicing haste!" In front of such a massive attack on the world, Tristan's analysis of his *Urvergessen* or primal repressions comes to a halt. His sorrow and depression are difficult enough to bring out from their repressed state, since they confront him with bottomless despair. His rage and guilt, however, must remain repressed since they clash with the ego-ideal of this likeable and admired youngster. Only one solution remains to guarantee the maintenance of the primal repressions: suicide. When Isolde follows him in death after the *Liebestod,* his attack on the primal objects is completed.

## The real loss: the devastated container

What constitutes Tristan's infantile trauma? He thinks it is his parents' deaths per se; however, he cannot have cathected, or invested feelings and thoughts in, parents he never knew. Similarly, his longing for the maternal womb is built on a fantasy, not on a real memory or even an *Ahnung.* I interpret it as his effort at filling in a void he experienced as a child – but the void stemmed from the insufficient containment by his caregivers. The memory traces that contribute to his misery do not pertain directly to losing his parents – because such traces do not exist. Rather, they refer to a child reading un-nameable sorrow and helplessness in the faces of the people around him. When Tristan bursts out, "For what fate was I then born? . . . To yearn – and to die!", I suggest he refers to his caretakers. Helpless and grief-stricken, they were standing by the cot asking for what fate this child was born.

My speculation about the failing containment is based on the few facts we have about Tristan's infancy. When he was born, his uncle Marke lost a sister and a brother-in-law. A childless man himself, he took care of his nephew. Later, he lost his wife. It seems that he lavished love on the baby while not coming to grips with the darker side of the child's personality. As the secret love affair unfolds, Marke cannot understand Tristan's treachery. They have loved each other tenderly, so why does Tristan dishonour him? Only the love potion, the existence of which Marke learns about later, provides an explanation he can believe in.

I suggest that the experiences out of which Tristan's yearning emerged were not related to his dead parents but to the people of his childhood, especially Marke. Tristan read his uncle's sorrow, dread and inability to sustain and address his painful feelings, that is, to contain them. Thus, Tristan's experiences were never assimilated in an interactive process (Muller, 1996) with his uncle. Due to the silence between the two, his experiences of the muted containment remained *urvergessen* or primally repressed. Tristan remained fixated to icons of a face, a scent, a tone of voice. He attributes them to his "father's distress and mother's anguish", while I suggest they were modelled on Marke's sad face. When the young man met Isolde she substituted for his idealized fantasy-mother's face, which, in its turn, had functioned as a compensation for Marke's distressed face. Perhaps the king was unaware of how deeply the losses had affected him – or he could not communicate it to Tristan. This left him unable to contain the boy, which marked the beginning of his catastrophe. Accordingly, I suggest Tristan's betrayal was an unconscious revenge for Marke's failing containment. In contrast, killing Morold and the joint suicide with Isolde issued from his rage against the fantasized parental couple, a rage aggravated due to the insufficient containment.

This reconstruction points to a link between primal repression and failed containment. I expressed similar ideas regarding Beate and her depressed mother Nadya in Chapter 5. I thus take an object relations view on primal repression, as suggested by Cohen (1985). In his understanding, traumatic events that "left the individual overwhelmed and helpless . . . are lived through but not experienced as part of the self". This leads to "an absence of structure and representable experience in a region of the self. This absence is primal repression" (p. 178). Unwittingly, Marke could not help baby Tristan feel understood and addressed about his parents' demise. Thus, Tristan was left overwhelmed and helpless with a situation, in which "structure is absent . . . no representations of need-satisfying interactions . . . provide the basis for symbolic interaction with the world and for goal-directed behaviour" (ibid). If such an infant "is not made to feel safe, protected" then primal repression will form "black holes" in psychic space (Grotstein, 2003, p. 104). Tristan interprets such holes as a result of his parents' demise. He yearns to fill it up, and Morold and Isolde become the perfect companions in this illusory project. A third victim in the drama is Marke, whose life is shattered.

Cohen and Grotstein, and also Green (1998), point to new and important ways of understanding primal repression. I agree with their focus on the object relations. My essential objection, as I also argued in connection with Beate, is that the hole is a sign – though it is primitive, iconic and scary. Tristan has a word for this kind of signs: *Ahnungen* or premonitions. He is governed by representations that he cannot recall but which influence him anyway. This results in the triple catastrophe.

It would be advantageous to study primal repression *in statu nascendi*, in parent–infant-therapies. This is the aim of the next chapter, where we will return to Beate and also introduce eight-month-old Tom. I will investigate if some recalcitrant symptoms in a child may reflect a dawning primal repression. If so, it would not only prove to be a clinically important mechanism but also help us formulate one aim of parent–infant treatments; to prevent such repressions from fossilizing into rigid character structures and symptoms. Finally, it might help explain adult patients' non-verbal communications and idiosyncratic behaviours.

# Chapter 8

# Classical concepts revisited I
## Primal repression

Do classical psychoanalytic concepts have a place in the theory of parent–infant treatments? The next chapters will approach this question by investigating three central concepts: primal repression, infantile sexuality and transference. In this chapter, we will look at primal repressions in the case of Beate (Chapter 5) and touch briefly on Tristan (Chapter 7). We will also introduce a new baby, eight-month-old Tom, and his mother Nina. I will compare Tom and Beate to illustrate that when an infant starts therapy reasonably early, we have a good chance of dissolving contradictory and compelling representations. As the baby gets older, our chances diminish. I will argue that this is due to the establishing of primal repressions.

Eight-month-old Tom and his mother Nina were caught up in unsuccessful weaning. Joint therapy managed to change his primal representations from 'Mum is my slave and I'm a slave to my own cravings' to 'Mum is my pal and I'm a happy chap'. The second dyad, Beate and her mother Nadya, was also enmeshed in weaning problems. As we recall, therapy started at 16 months and elucidated their roots in Nadya's postnatal depression. Despite substantial progress some primal representations had begun to petrify, and when we ended at three and a half years Beate was still influenced by them to some extent.

Freud introduced the concept of primal repression to explain the paradox that "the impressions which have had the greatest effect on us – those of our earliest youth – are precisely the ones which scarcely ever become conscious" (1900, p. 539). He was aware of problems with the concept (1915b) and today it has largely disappeared from theoretical discourse. I, however, suggest we retain it to understand the fate of primal representations. To make the concept useful one condition must be fulfilled, though; we must redress its definition and abandon Freud's hydraulic metaphors. Instead, we should return to his semiotic vision of the internal world.

## Case 1: eight-month-old Tom

Nina, a mother aged 40, enters the consulting-room with her eight-month-old son Tom. I get a strange impression that she is holding him as if she were his crutch. She feels insecure as a mother: "I don't know how much to give Tom, when to breastfeed him and such things. When I say no to him, I feel sort of thick-skinned and cruel. But when I say yes to him, I get exhausted." She and Tom cannot let go of each other and she holds his hand most of the time. When she lets him go, he frets and she feels "totally grey in the head". Tom wavers between plaintive efforts at crawling and proud smiles when he manages to stand up for a few seconds.

The conflict of "saying no and yes, letting go and keeping him close" is her everyday predicament, Nina says. She feels little support from her husband. She also relates that she is about to wean Tom. Evidently, mother and son have mixed feelings about weaning and having two separate lives. We decide to start joint mother–son therapy two to three sessions per week.

## Tom: Vignette I – Ambivalence in mother and son

In the second session Tom is lying on the carpet. Suddenly he discovers that he is on his own – though his mother is right behind him. He starts screaming and mother wants to embrace him but hesitates because, as she says, "I do this too often with him".

| | |
|---|---|
| *Analyst to Tom:* | You are sad, Tom. But you're angry, too. 'Damned Mum, why don't you pick me up!'<br>[He continues crying and mother does not know what to do.] |
| *A to T:* | You're expressing yourself very clearly, Tom. You're squealing like a pig. It's hard for you to feel that way, and it's hard for Mum to listen to you.<br>[He's looking at some object in the room.] |
| *A to T:* | Now, you caught sight of something funny. |
| *A to Mother:* | How are you, Nina? |
| *M crying:* | I have so many feelings inside. |
| *A to both:* | So there are two crying people here.<br>[Tom continues crying.] |
| *A to T:* | Mum needs to speak about her feelings. Meanwhile you are so angry, lying there on the carpet. |
| *M:* | It'll take a long time to tell you about my feelings!<br>[Mother picks up Tom who is looking reproachfully at me.] |
| *A to T:* | You are angry with *Mum* who didn't pick you up at once. You are angry with *me* because you feel this is my fault. |
| *M:* | [This is unusual. I know he is supposed to have such feelings.] I quench them, though. On such occasions, I breastfeed him. But actually, I think it's time to stop.<br>[Tom continues screaming and in the end, his mother nurses him. While he is screaming I note his accusatory look at us.] |

This vignette shows Tom's and mother's ambivalence at separating. Mother overlooks that Tom is not only a pitiable chap on the carpet. He is also an angry inter-actor who poses contradictory demands on her. He indicates that she should pick him up, but when Nina obeys he wants to get down on the floor again. We are reminded of Karen and her mother in Chapter 4; a muddling of the unconscious layers of two personalities, and a muddling of messages concerning separation and autonomy: 'Let me go, I want to be on my own – don't you ever desert me'. This ambivalence also applies to mother. She longs desperately to be on her own – and desponds what will happen once this becomes fulfilled.

## Tom: Vignette 2 – Indiana Jones

This vignette occurs two months into treatment. Upon arrival, Mum goes to the loo while Tom is waving happily at me from the waiting room. As they enter, Nina mentions Tom's "inherent joy", which she noticed since his birth. Nowadays he is showing it more, she adds.

Sitting in her lap, Tom indicates that he wants to get down on the carpet. He starts investigating the room.

| | |
|---|---|
| *A to T:* | You're out exploring the territory, eh? A real Indiana Jones! Now you're looking at the camera. You never noticed it before. |
| *T:* | Da da da. |
| | [Tom's babbling has a vital and joyful quality. He invites mother to a little walk. All is well until he stumbles and starts whining. Then he regains his physical and emotional balance and starts banging at the door of a little cupboard. It contains my private things and is locked. The mother dislikes this and thinks I am too strict. I tell Tom the door is locked but his toy-box is open. He catches sight of a frog there and starts playing with it. He seems to forget Mum. Then he whines again but looks out the window at a tree.] |
| *A to T:* | You're whining at Mum – and letting her go. You're looking at her, but you're also looking at the tree. Mum told me once your first word was "tee". |
| *M:* | Yeah, he says "tee" but people wonder why he can't say "Mum" and "Dad". |
| *A to M:* | Are you disappointed? |
| *M:* | Not really . . . |
| | [Nina's response seems defensive. I think she deplores that "Mum" was not Tom's first word. As the boy gets fascinated by the frog again, I explore her disappointment once more.] |
| *A:* | The frog seems more interesting than Mum. How does that feel to you, Nina? |
| *M laughs:* | Imagine a mother being substituted by a frog! By the way, I didn't breastfeed him for the last two nights. What a relief! I am puncturing |

the myths from that parenting website. They argue that one must carry babies all the time, otherwise they'll feel insecure. But you said all children are different . . .

[Nina is referring to a parenting website conveying that babies should be kept in a shawl and be breast-fed as long as they wish. This is supposed to ensure their harmonious development.]

*A to T:*  Mum punctured her myths and so did you, Tom. It isn't true to you any longer that happiness is only possible at the breast. When you were a tiny baby, you thought so, but not now any longer.

[Tom whines but his attention is soon captured by a steel handle on the cupboard. He tries to open it but fails.]

*A to T:*  You want to get into that cupboard but you can't. You get angry, that's easy to understand. It's like when you want Mum's breasts. She's locking them up for you. Then you might get angry and sad and feel like a real failure. That's hard on you.

[Tom wavers between whining on the carpet and getting up and investigating my wrist-watch. He stands in front of Mum on the brink of kneading her face. He switches mood, claps his hand cheerfully in front of her and gets due recognition for his skills. During yet another mood switch, his mother complains:]

*M to A:*  I just don't not know what he wants from me when he is whining!

[Meanwhile, Tom begins to explore the room. He discovers some heavy folders, which he tries to move in vain. He keeps up his spirits, plays with the frog and returns poking at my wrist-watch while looking at me confidently. He is fascinated by the steel watch bracelet and compares it with the steel handle of a door leading out to a balcony.]

## Comments to the vignettes with Tom

The two excerpts indicate an important shift in Tom's behaviour and, as I assume, in his representations. In the first vignette he treats mother as his subordinate and himself as a willy-nilly slave-driver. When his wishes are unfulfilled, he behaves like the slave of a mother who capriciously dismisses them. His primal representations run pell-mell: 'Mum is offering her breast and I am comforted'; 'Mum is rejecting me and I feel devastated'; 'Mum is taking me back and I am triumphing'; 'Mum is taking me back but I feel unhappy and guilty because I've been fussing with her.' These contradictions represent his confused and vacillating wishes. No wonder that mother does not know what he wants.

In vignette 2, new representations appear: 'Playing with a frog or a wrist-watch is more interesting than complaining to Mum'; 'I want Mum to admire my conquests'; 'Ordering Mum about becomes boring. The world beyond is more interesting'; 'When my conquests fail it's good to return to Mum for consolation, but I don't want to stay with her forever.' Many of these representations invoke a third object beyond the dyad, as when he touches my wrist-watch while looking into my eyes. His interest in the camera, the steel handle and the frog also imply a focus on a third object. These devices had been there all the time, but he was not ready to discover them until this session.

To sum up, Tom began treatment clinging to mother and anxiously going in search away from her [Hermann, 1976 (1936)]. I described to him the representations behind these vacillations: "You're angry with Mum who didn't pick you up when you fell" and "You're angry with me because it was my fault." In parallel I analyzed the mother's representations: "You think a baby must be carried around constantly to feel secure. I wonder why you think that way." "You think I am cruel with my locked cupboard. I acknowledge your critique, but I also wonder why one would be cruel in setting up limits to a child".

The analysis lasted some 40 sessions over six months. Tom's improvement was mainly due to three factors: (1) containment of his anxious clinging to and separating from mother, (2) containment of Nina's anguish in letting him go and taking pride in his individuation and (3) my representing the "Name of the Father" helping him better accept *symboligenic castration*, a concept discussed in Frida's case (Chapter 3). Let us now look at a second case, whose outcome was not equally beneficial; some representations in the child seemed recalcitrant to treatment.

## Case 2: 16-month-old Beate

During our first meeting (see "vignette 1: grabbing the breast" in Chapter 5), Beate is running in and out of my consulting-room to get hold of toys she never plays with. She gets more anxious and finishes by grabbing the breasts of her sighing mother Nadya. However, Mum's breasts cannot comfort her. She switches to scrambling for a doll, grabbing for raisins in Mum's bag and tucking her hand into Mum's mouth. Her anxiety seems to scramble about inside her, like raisins in a package.

I ask myself which representations correspond to Beate's unruly behaviour, but it is hard to find out. Her formal signifiers (Anzieu, 1990) seem to lack a vision of a reliable container. Mum's breasts do not provide comfort and neither do my words, the therapeutic frame, the raisins nor Mum's mouth. I imagine Beate's representations run something like, 'I am scared – but nobody's there'; 'My feelings scramble about like raisins in a box – yet the box is empty'. They evoke Beate's loneliness and constant beleaguering of mother. Nadya implies that problems started when Beate "got her own will". This is a gloomy verdict; at a time when Beate should develop more elaborate representations and exchange them with mother, their interaction havocked. Nadya's depression impaired her capacity to pay attention, empathize and feel affection for Beate.

The deadlock dissolved during treatment and Nadya began feeling love for her daughter. Beate was weaned smoothly but developed a fear of holes, later also of ghosts and monsters. We could refer these symptoms as well as her breast-grabbing to an original traumatic situation, in which her anxieties were not adequately contained by the depressed mother. Beate clung to the breast of today in order to escape anxiety pertaining to an earlier version of the breast connected with her mother's postnatal depression. While the holes represented experiences with a deficient container, the ghosts portrayed the emotionally absent mother who had turned into a persecutor (Bion, 1965). In another terminology, Nadya had not been able to assist in Beate's affect regulation (Fonagy et al., 2002). The result was, as with many infants of depressed mothers, an increase of negative mood (Tronick, 2007b).

Despite therapeutic progress, Beate's restlessness and sometimes taxing temperament did not vanish completely. A comparison with Tom's case points to a difference. Evidently all dyads are different, which makes parallels uncertain. Nevertheless, I submit the two cases to illustrate a recurrent clinical experience; towards the first birthday the infant psyche becomes more unalterable, unimpressionable and rigid. As I see it, this was one reason why therapy yielded less remarkable results in Beate's case than in Tom's. In Chapter 2, I linked this with a decreasing semiotic fluidity as the child's linguistic faculties develop. Now I will link it with the term under scrutiny in this chapter: primal repression.

## Primal repression and repression proper

The enigma of primal repression resides essentially in four factors: (1) the human mind becomes "fossilized" in infancy, (2) these deposits exert a continuous influence into adult life, (3) they are inaccessible to recall during psychoanalytic investigation and (4) they can only be understood in their reconstructed versions. Primal repression can thus be described as the paradox of the *living fossil*, an expression I introduced in the chapter on Tristan. This enigma occupied Freud from early on. He thought human character is based especially on those memory-traces that "scarcely ever become conscious" (1900, p. 539). When he later developed his repression concept he re-approached the enigma and coined the concept of primal repression, *die Urverdrängung*. It is "a first phase of repression, which consists in the psychical (ideational) representative of the instinct being denied entrance into the conscious. With this a *fixation* is established" (1915b, p. 148). As I reported in Chapter 7, he referred to impulses that had never been conscious.

Freud's formulations pose a problem. How does the psyche "know" how to *Ur*-repress impulses that were never conscious? Freud answers that they are held back by an "anticathexis" (1915c, p. 181), which establishes and continues the repression. However, that concept says nothing about the representations involved. The mechanistic metaphor of anticathexis refers to a "permanent expenditure [of energy] of a primal repression and . . . guarantees the permanence of that repression . . . [and indeed] is the sole mechanism of primal repression" (idem). Maze and Henry (1996) claim the Preconscious must know what it is about to repress. Like a fire-detector, it must discern some smoke of the germinating impulse to quench it. This argument applies to repression proper or ordinary repression. When Tom's mother moans that he insists on her breast, she is half aware of her vexation. This sets forth defensive operations, such as her guilty promise to carry him around to make him feel secure. Her argument seems based on a reaction-formation towards her anger, of which her Preconscious has glimpsed some "smoke".

In primal repression, we have a different picture. Supposedly, it handles unconscious impulses that *never* received any cathexis from the Preconscious. If we continue the metaphor we will face a problem; how can a fire-alarm detect smoke if its inlets are closed? The critical argument of Maze and Henry is pertinent: "The repressed must be known in order to remain unknown, and this seems a logical impossibility" (1996, p. 1087). The counter-argument, that a beginning of the impulse might be allowed, does not work because "although the infant had imagined a situation that would gratify some specific instinctual impulse, it had never admitted to itself that it had had such an image" (p. 1092). We might counter their critique with an argument by Cavell (2001). She suggests that consciousness is not an all-or-nothing phenomenon but "a process with a number of stages, only the last of which is fully explicit" (p. 73). If so, we must ask what characterizes these stages. Let us wait a little before we approach it.

Balestriere (2003) also recognizes the logical problem with primal repression. To her, it is an archaic defence, which preserves the impulse in its original state and prevents it from developing. This coincides with Freud's simile of an instinct as "successive eruptions of lava". Its very first eruption remains unchanged and undergoes "no development at all" (1915a, p. 131). This is an evocative metaphor, but it hardly explains how the instinct is prevented from developing.

In my view, the critique of Maze and Henry is logically sound but does not do justice to an infant's mental functioning. When they claim that an infant might never admit that it had an image of impulse gratification, they attribute too much cognitive functioning to a baby. On the other hand, Freud's and Cavell's metaphors of lava eruptions and stages bypass that the mind works with representations – not geological matter or time-tables. Freud suggested the term *thing-presentations* for these early representations. According to Ellman (Britton, Chused, Ellman & Likierman, 2006), it helps us explain the primal repression mechanism, in which the child represents his unnamed anxieties "in concrete terms (thing representations)" (p. 281). Thing-presentations stand in an oppositional relation to word-presentations, but in my view this bipolar division is unnecessarily restricted. First, a representation may be described in many more ways than whether it is linked to a word or not. Second, Freud (1915c) states that a presentation does not become conscious until the thing- and word-presentations are welded together. Accordingly, a non-verbal infant would be living in a permanently unconscious state of mind. However, it is plain to see that a baby has conscious representations of the mother without possessing any words for her. Thus, as I suggested already in chapters 1 and 2, we need other terms to describe these primitive representations. My solution to this challenge was to suggest the term primal representations. We shall now look at how this affects our view on primal repressions.

## The two repressions defined in semiotic terms

To counter the conceptual problems with primal repression, Freud took recourse to the abstruse idea of anti-cathexis. Alternatively, he suggested that it is released by "an excessive degree of excitation and the breaking through of the protective shield against stimuli" (1925–26, p. 94). These mechanistic metaphors have led many modern analysts to dispose of the concept. I, however, think it says something important about how the young mind handles "the earliest outbreaks of anxiety, which are of a very intense kind" (idem) – and also why a baby may need therapeutic help. I will suggest another way of understanding primal repression. First, I will briefly address some of Freud's views of repression proper to finally arrive at one which he formulated in semiotic terms. I will then transfer that view to primal repression.

In one of his models of repression proper, Freud suggests that its function is to minimize the load of unpleasant *affects* of an impulse. Certain infantile impulses would, if they were fulfilled, yield unpleasure. "The essence" of repression (1900, p. 604) consists of preventing such an affect from emerging. This idea resembles our fire-detector metaphor; the "secondary system" (idem) or the Preconscious discerns the impending impulse, scents the danger if it were to be fulfilled and therefore represses it. Freud refers mostly to lustful impulses but we also repress aggressive impulses. To illustrate, Tom not only desired his mother but was also angry and disappointed with her. His clinging and mood swings could be seen as vain attempts at repressing these affects.

In another view, Freud thought repression prevents *traumatic experiences* from becoming conscious. Childhood traumas may operate "in a deferred fashion as though they were fresh experiences" (1896, p. 166) but they do so unconsciously. Tom was in the midst of incipient traumatization, so we do not know what might have happened had he and Nina not been in therapy. We might speculate that he would have had to deal with suppressed anger and a stalemated relationship with his mother. In contrast, Beate's present symptoms seemed related to a very early trauma. However, it was not repressed in the dynamic sense and could thus not be retrieved through analysis. In other words, the two models of repression proper presented so far do not solve our fire detector problem: how can *never*-known impulses trigger activities, which retain them in an un-known yet psychologically active mode?

I will now posit that our fire-detector metaphor is inapplicable to primal representations such as the ones Beate were harbouring. Further, I suggest primal repression helps us explain what sometimes happens to such early representations. The condition is that we abandon the idea that it refers to never-conscious impulses. In my view, primal repression refers to impulses that were *conscious from the beginning but signified in an archaic mode*. They were then *retained in that form*. Primal repression thus works to preserve such represent-ations as primitive and unchanged. Grotstein probably has something similar in mind when he suggests that it is a barrier developing "at the time when the infant evolves from using prelexical, nonsymbolic imagery to the symbolic, lexical use of verbal language" (2003, p. 104).

We now understand better our metaphor for primal repression; the "living fossil". "Fossil" refers to representations that are archaic, vestigial and faintly outlined. "Living" indicates that they are active. Whereas impulses that escape this fate will develop in continuous re-translations, it is otherwise for the ones that succumb to primal repression; it bestows a sign of, say, a mother's voice or face, with a one-and-only meaning or interpretant which then remains unchanged. To exemplify, Beate reacted in a repetitive manner to her mother. It was of little help when Nadya comforted and spoke with her; an original "mask" remained in Beate's mind that signified her earliest experiences of mother's depressed face, voice and demeanour. In parallel, Beate seemed like a spooky icon. She smiled constantly – but did not appear happy. She was on the move all the time – but did not convey the joie de vivre of a harmonious child. To illustrate with an adult example, Tristan cannot see the real Isolde. He sees a mask – her beautiful and divine yet fossilized face – which must remain untouched by the ravages; not only of time but also of his internal objects emerging in the wake of inadequate containment.

To follow my view of primal repression we must first make a detour to Freud's third conception of repression proper, the one I call the semiotic. In this view, repression is "a failure of translation" (1892–99/1950, p. 235) of an impulse. It prevents the presentation from being translated into words "which shall remain attached to the object" (1915c, p. 202). Thus, if an impulse were expressed plainly or "translated" correctly, it would generate unpleasure. Ordinary repression, or repression proper, will prevent this from happening. Let us look at an example.

During the analysis, Tom's mother Nina resists my suggestion that her friendliness with him is sometimes feigned. One day Tom is in a bad mood. Suddenly, he sticks his nose into her mouth.

| | |
|---|---|
| *Analyst to mother:* | I wonder why you think he is doing this nose thing. |
| *M to A, with strained and artificial laughter:* | This is his way to contact me . . . I've heard kids do this up to three years of age! |

Clearly, her comment covers up or mis-translates her vexation and helplessness with Tom's intrusion. This is an instance of ordinary repression. Analysis will help her get in contact with repressed feelings and express them more openly. Tom's nose in Nina's mouth also mis-translates *his* anger, longing for contact and helplessness in sorting out his contradictory urges. His primal representations are muddled: 'Complaining Mum – bad Tom'; 'Helpless Tom – helpless Mum'; 'I want to get inside Mum's mouth to love her – to harm her.' Tom needs a responsive object to help him develop such representations to higher semiotic levels. However, when people around have too much anxiety to address tormenting emotions their distressed faces, feigned smiles, resigned sighs or evasive gazes will be engraved in the child's memory. The long-term result of such a milieu may be the creation of primal repressions – unless therapy is instituted early. Nina was overburdened with marital problems, unclear visions of how to raise an autonomous baby and problems in acknowledging her anger with Tom and allowing him to separate from her. During therapy, these visions changed. Similarly, Tom's self-representations developed from a clinging boy to an intrepid Indiana Jones.

In many of my presented cases, therapy was instituted early. This helped the mothers tackle their repressions proper, that is, they became able to translate more accurately their affects vis-à-vis their children and partners. Their babies were helped to sort out their primal representations and express them in a clearer way. On the other hand, what might happen when an infantile representation remains untransformed because the anxiety linked to it was not contained within the parent–infant interaction – and therapy was not instituted on the spot? My answer is that these are the very situations in which primal repressions are prone to develop.

## Recollection of trauma

Beate's phobias and restlessness were connected with her mother's depression and its pertaining deficient containment. If we agree that she suffered from trauma, we might ask to what extent she might recall it and how it would affect her personality development. Gaensbauer (1995) investigates if children retain such memories and if they will have enduring effects. He argues that children can indeed describe pre-verbal events. In support, he submits experiments by Rovee-Collier and Hayne (1987), which indicate that infants recall agonizing events. In his clinical work, he has noticed that children's games sometimes indicate memories and effects of a trauma whose reality the parents have confirmed to him afterwards. Truly, we do not know if such traumas may yield "specific psychic representation" (Gaensbauer, 1995, p. 125), but we may conclude that "memories in the preverbal period are neither prerepresentational in any absolute sense nor unavailable to conscious awareness" (p. 146). His child patients could "develop internal representations of their traumas" and transform and express them "in symbolic terms" (idem).

Do Gaensbauer's findings support that Beate recalls her mother's postnatal depression and/or is able to represent it symbolically? I would answer no. The reason is probably that she has not been subjected to a singular overwhelming trauma. She has rather suffered from a "cumulative trauma" (Khan, 1963) that was built up due to breaches in the mother's function as "protective shield" (Khan, 1964, p. 272) or container. This might have led some of Beate's ego functions to be "accelerated in growth and exploited in defensive action" (p. 274), such as her athletic but anxiety-ridden skills when running about in my office, throwing balls and groping for objects that she never played with.

In a recent paper, Gaensbauer (2011) invokes research on the mirror neuron system to explain traumatic repetitions. I would especially bring out one property of this system. It is well known that mirror neurons in person A fire when A sees person B performing a motor act. It is less known that they also fire if B is *simulating an action in her mind* (Decety, 2002). These neuronal structures are thus sensitive to the other's internal state. They help children become "increasingly aware of the resonance between their own bodily actions and those of others" (Gaensbauer, 2011, p. 95) and of the connections between their own and others' emotions. Reddy (2008) even denies that there is a complete separation between ourselves and the other. To her, action – and I would add emotion – is one singular phenomenon "between the doer, the planner, the imaginer, and the observer, but supported by a common neural substrate" (p. 58).

The mirror neuron system assists in building up shared states of mind. Its negative side is that when a child experiences a trauma, it will capture not just the action itself but also the "goals and motivation behind the action, including the subjective state of the person(s) being observed" (Gaensbauer, 2011, p. 98). The child will create a "holistic, affectively charged, and multimodally integrated schema of the observed action rather than a simple behavioural replication" (idem). As Decety (2010) sums up, an infant can "perceive and respond to another's affective state". This serves

> as an instrument for social learning, reinforcing the significance of the social exchange, which then becomes associated with the infant's own emotional experience. Consequently, infants come to experience emotions as shared states and learn to differentiate their own states partly by witnessing the resonant responses that they elicit in others.
>
> (p. 261)

What happens if one party is depressed, like Beate's mother? We might expect the infant to resonate with her depression and become sad. However, Beate was restless and fussy. To explain this, I recall a study by Cohn and Tronick (1989). They divided depressed mothers' behaviours into two categories: disengaged and intrusive. Nadya seemed to belong to the first group. Babies of such mothers fail to connect because of the mother's lack of response and repair. They become angry and then "dysregulated, fussy, and cry" (Tronick, 2007a, p. 285).

Whether the mirror neuron system between Beate and her mother was unbalanced or not eludes our psychoanalytic instrument of investigation. In return, Winnicott's concept "mirroring" (1971) fits well to describe their interaction. Ordinarily, when a baby is looking at her mother's face, she sees herself due to the mother's mirroring. Other babies "have a long experience of not getting back what they are giving. They look and they do not see themselves". "The mother's face is not then a mirror" and the child's "creative capacity begins to atrophy". Consequently, such children "look around for other ways of getting something of themselves back from the environment" . . . Perception replaces what "might have been the beginning of a significant exchange with the world" (p. 112–113). Negri (2007) describes that such a child will experience the mother "as a person concerned with herself – rejecting and hostile to her relationship with her baby. This experience strengthens the infant's sense of isolation" (p. 100). I believe this applies to Beate's experiences.

## Primal representations and primal repressions

Throughout the book I have emphasized, most clearly with Tristan and Beate, that the effects of a trauma must not only be assessed by what actually happened to the child. We must also consider the containment of the trauma. Every parent contains the child under the influence of projections, but depression can overwhelm his/her ability to interpret the child's signals in a flexible way. For example, a mother may tend to think of her baby's behaviour as a rejection. Tom's mother Nina said she wanted more freedom from him; yet she felt hurt when he was marching away on the carpet. Ambivalence coloured her containment and made her project diverging messages onto Tom: "Go on your own – don't leave me." This was why she must be his "crutch"; to support his adventures and yet convey that he could not do it on his own.

In Aulagnier's (2001) words, a mother's interpretation of her baby will always be distorted and subject to a "primary violence". Mother's ideas of the child are, to a great extent, motivated by *her* rather than the child's desire. She is bound to relate to him as to a "shadow" (p. 75). Aulagnier's term for this mechanism, "violence of interpretation", sounds pejorative or gloomy but is actually vital for his ego development. It helps set aside the pleasure principle and promote the institution of the symbolic order. Since "desire arrives signified otherwise than it was at the start" (Lacan, 1998, p. 148), the mother must inevitably use primary violence to understand her baby's messages. In Nina's terms, she needs to find out "just what he wants".

However, we have a problem if a mother fears her unconscious ambivalence vis-à-vis the baby and tries to conceal it, as did Nina and Nadya. In Aulagnier's terms, primary violence will then yield to secondary violence. The latter term refers to messages that are excessive and de-structuring. They force the child to "conform to a pre-established model [of thinking] imposed by the mother" (2001, p. 88). From now on, the mother–child discourse will follow a "*diktat*" (p. 12). One example is Nadya's cliché that Beate's "own will" was the root to the problem. It implied that a child with an autonomous mind creates problems. Needless to say, this view stood in stark opposition to Nadya's conscious values of how to raise a child. The book contains many other diktats; Miranda's conviction that Karen was "so sad" or Nina's idea that Tom would only feel safe if carried in a shawl all the time.

Aulagnier's term "secondary violence" refers to psychotic milieus but is applicable also to the interactions we are discussing. In the cases just referred, therapy seemed to forestall further development of secondary violence or, in another terminology, intrusive projective identifications. But when maternal depression is not alleviated quickly enough, and the baby does not receive parallel help, the mother may land in ruminations such as, "You're hopeless, I can't get myself to loving you, I'm a hopeless mother and when you look at me it confirms that you think so as well". In such situations, exemplified with the case of Beate and Nadya, the infant will fixate on an icon of its mother's face, her scent or her tone of voice – but the baby cannot proceed to translate them into more elaborate sign types. Mother's apparition forms a semiotic jumble, which the baby cannot sort out. In response, the baby creates significations that are remote from ordinary sign types and controlled by anxiety. One example was Beate's spindly appearance, shrill sounds and restless behaviour. I did not understand what they meant. Was her smile happy or tense, her jumping about joyful or anxious, her breast-sucking calming or exciting? It took much analytic work to answer these questions.

## Beate: Vignette 1 – The fluff

Three months into treatment, Beate starts collecting fluff from my floor. This happens during a period when she gently strikes her mother's cheek and then suddenly hits her. While walking about collecting the fluff, she frowns at me as if reproaching me for my untidy office. I also note that she seems terrified of the particles she keeps collecting.

*Analyst to Beate:*   There is much fluff here. You want to pick it up and get rid of it. There are also many fluffy, scary thoughts inside you, perhaps that you're angry with Mum and me. But you cannot get rid of these thoughts. They frighten you.
          [Mum listens and gets an association:]
*Mother to A:*   This thing about the fluff . . . I like to keep my home clean. My husband makes a mess, but it's hard for me to tell him. You know, I am insincere with him and with Beate, too! I tell her to express what she feels and wants, but I don't dare do it myself!
*A:*   You feel you are sincere, Nadya – and I feel you are insincere as well, Beate. You gently stroke Mum and then you hit her.
          [At this point Beate pauses, looks at me, and then walks to the analytic couch. She hits it while saying "Dinn". She looks playful and relaxed. Nadya smiles warmly.]

In Chapter 5, I submitted another "Dinn" vignette; Beate was uttering the strange word from the armchair throne. In the fluff vignette, she has developed "Dinn" from a bizarre icon to a comprehensible sign expressing her joie de vivre. It is now an index with which she invites us to share her relief and anger. Beate's relief comes from my sincere address to her and Nadya's talking about her insincerity. Her anger comes from my pointing out that she is slapping Mum's face. We all smile as she expresses these emotions in a sublimated and creative way. The displacement is easy to understand; she is hitting the couch instead of Mum's face – or mine.

When I first met Beate her breast-grabbing aimed to modify, through interacting with a need-mediating breast, her wrath and disappointment. When these affects arose they were fluffy and poorly signified. They had remained in that form, because Nadya could not help her advance on the semiotic ladder to show affects more openly and sincerely. Now, as a result of analytic work, her significations have become clearer. The analytic frame helps Beate ascend the semiotic ladder. As I erect it, I convey that I am prepared to receive her feelings by telling her that I understand she is angry with me and her mother. In doing this, I suggest more elaborate signs for her enactments. She responds by giving clearer and more unequivocal signs herself. The transformation of "Dinn" is a case to the point. Another example is the fluff, which, after we had been talking about it, simply disappeared from the scene. In Bionian terms, this β-element was contained in the session and thus transformed into α-elements such as the "Dinn", the banging on the couch and her smile.

The mechanism of primal repression poses a "major question for psychoanalytic pathology" (Laplanche, 2007, p. 203) concerning infant and adult patients. It explains why "man is possessed by messages that he fails to translate" (idem). In my view, it does not work on never-cathected and unrepresented psychic processes, and it does not engender representations that are completely and eternally inaccessible to conscious elaboration (Freud, 1915c). Neither does it create holes (Cohen, 1985), haemorrhages (Green, 1998) or merely-inscribed messages (Laplanche, 2007). Rather, it works by maintaining primal significations in their original, fragmented and iconical form. The root of this mechanism is trauma and how it has been contained. Trauma may have been sudden and overwhelming – or an insidious and cumulative (Khan, 1963) exposure to "morally repugnant conditions" (Cohen, 1994, p. 710), such as parental unawareness or non-responsiveness to a child's overwhelming feelings.

Primal repression aims at protecting the psyche against renewed traumatization, but it may also prevent primal representations from further semiotic development. Therapy aims to set this development on track. It should preferably be instituted early for two reasons: the duration of negative containment should be diminished and the baby should be helped to weld non-lexical aspects of our interventions to his iconic signs before they have become stalemated. If not, the child risks being influenced by the living fossil of primal repression.

# Chapter 9

# Classical concepts revisited II
## Infantile sexuality

We will now focus on *infantile sexuality* as we investigate the place of psychoanalytic concepts in parent–infant therapies. One may of course ask if these concepts are ready for the dustbin – or if they are valuable tools for understanding the therapeutic process. I see one general and one specific reason for an effort at integrating them with analytic theory. Any treatment method not grounded in a coherent theory – and that also allows us to test its validity by applying it to new cases – will perish. Its inconsistencies and obscurities will push it towards oblivion. The specific reason for our theoretical approach is the enigmatic therapeutic process in baby treatments. Already with adult cases, we analysts grope our way to interpret symptoms and transferences. This hazy state of affairs pertains even more to infants, who neither understand our interventions literally nor respond to them in a comprehensible vocabulary. This makes the need for a solid theoretical footing all the more urgent.

We recall from Chapter 1 that from its beginning, analytic theory was based on speculations on the internal world of the baby. Freud used baby observations and speculations to understand how the mother helps the baby handle anxieties (1895/1950), how frustrations force the baby to abandon hallucinatory wish-fulfilment in favour of realistic thinking (1900, 1911) and how anxieties manifest in the infant and how s/he handles them (1920, 1925–26). Over the years, this focus has dissolved to end up in models of the "baby within the adult" rather than of real babies. Concepts such as the oral phase, primal repression and infantile transference (Falzeder, 2002) describe mechanisms in the *adult* or the *verbal child* but not in the *baby*. Theory has come to refer to a virtual, reconstructed infant rather than to a baby in treatment. In this chapter I will focus on another concept. I will paraphrase André Green's (1995) question, "Has sexuality anything to do with psychoanalysis?" and ask: has Freud's concept of infantile sexuality anything to do with infants?

Post-Freudian major theoreticians continued formulating many theories about infantile life. For example, Klein (1935, 1945, 1946, 1952) described infantile anxieties, Bion (1962a, 1965) modelled his theory of containment on the infant's mind and Meltzer accounted for the infant's perverse fantasy world (1966) and aesthetic conflict (Meltzer & Harris-Williams, 1988). Yet these authors did not base their theories on clinical baby work. As for analysts experienced in such work (for example, Cramer and Palacio Espasa, 1993; Fraiberg *et al.*, 1975; Lebovici and Stoléru, 2003; Norman, 2001), their findings have only to a modest extent been used for developing general psychoanalytic theory.

Among the major psychoanalytic authors, Winnicott is of course an exception. He created many concepts from his clinical experience of infants and mothers; the holding environment (1955), the transitional object (1953), the parent–infant relationship (1960), the primary maternal preoccupation (1956), etc. However, only the paper on the spatula game (1941) is singularly devoted to a clinical account of mother–infant work. The youngest patient in his book on therapeutic consultations (1971) was two years old. As for infantile sexuality, he almost never mentions it explicitly. When he (1960) seeks to "reconstruct the dynamics of infancy and of infantile dependence, and of the maternal care that meets this dependence" (p. 595), he refers to adult borderline patients. Similarly, the concept of holding does not entail infantile sexuality but rather the child's "total environmental provision" (p. 589) and the mother's physical holding, "which is a form of loving" (p. 592). No mentioning of infantile sexuality.

To sum up, I agree with two Danish authors that "Freud's epoch-making discovery [has not] been followed by theories that have the infant's sexual development as their object" (Zeuthen & Gammelgaard, 2010, p. 4). This is also true for French analysts despite their anchorage in Freudian theory. When Diatkine (2008) deplores that infantile sexuality has disappeared from psychoanalytic discourse, he refers to adults or verbal children, not to babies. Similarly, when Lebovici and Stoléru (2003) speak of fantasies in "connection with maternity [and which] depend on the developmental level and on infantile sexuality" (p. 257), they refer to the mother. The same position applies to their Swiss colleagues, Cramer and Palacio Espasa (1993).

In contrast, the literature by mother–infant therapists contains abundant presentations of babies. In general, their theoretical models are founded on attachment theory amalgamated with parts of analytic theory (Acquarone, 2004; Baradon *et al.*, 2005; Papousek, Schieche & Wurmser, 2008; Stern, 1995). Lieberman and Van Horn (2008) describe

> the infant's biological propensity to develop a hierarchy of preferential emotional relationships with a small number of attachment figures based on the expectation that they will provide reliable protection against external and internal dangers. In psychoanalytic theory, this innate motivation is understood as closely intertwined with and colored by other motivations, including self-assertion, sexuality and the need for mutual recognition.
>
> (p. 8)

We note that the authors refer to sexuality in parents, not in infants. Similarly, the Parent–Infant Psychotherapy group in London (Baradon *et al.*, 2005) does not include infantile sexuality among the key concepts in early development.

They view attachment as the "unique and powerful relationship ... it is the outcome of the response of the parent to the absolute dependency of the infant at the beginning, and of the baby's propensity to relate" (p. 6). Consequently, sexuality is not mentioned as a contributing factor to infant pathology.

If these clinicians had considered infantile sexuality as a clinically valid concept they would have empowered it with examples, discussed its position in theory and used it to comprehend pathological states in babies. We run up against a paradox; infant clinicians rarely mention it and if so, not in connection with the baby – whereas analysts discussing the concept rarely mention the clinical baby. Its shadowy conceptual status and its dearth among infant therapists might reflect a present-day tendency to disregard sexuality, in its psychoanalytic sense, to explain psychopathology (Fonagy, 2008; Green, 1995). Alternatively, we might negate that infantile sexuality has anything to do with babies. But, if the prefix "infantile" only refers to verbal children and adults, it would imply that a baby is devoid of infantile sexuality until she has left infancy. If so, why speak of *infantile* sexuality? On the other hand, if "infantile" refers to phenomena or fantasies in the baby, we ought to investigate how they emerge in well-functioning as well as distressed babies. To achieve this task, we need first to excavate the roots of the concept.

## Freud and infantile sexuality

Let us look at what Freud, the creator of the concept, was referring to. In one quotation, he obviously refers to verbal children:

> Psycho-analytic research has had to concern itself, too, with the sexual life of children, and this is because the memories and associations arising during the analysis of symptoms [in adults] regularly led back to the early years of childhood. What we inferred from these analyses was later confirmed point by point by direct observations of children.
>
> (1916–17, p. 310)

"Direct observations" refers to the three-year-old Little Hans (Freud, 1909). In other instances he suggested it covers events in infancy the sexual connotations of which emerge only later, in a deferred way or *nachträglich*. An example is *the Wolfman* (1918), whose deferred understanding (*nachträgliches Verständnis*, p. 58) of the parental coitus only emerged after babyhood.

We will, however, get another picture in Freud's magnum opus on infantile sexuality, *Three Essays on Sexuality*: "There seems no doubt that germs of sexual impulses are *already present in the new-born child*" (1905b, p. 176, italics added). He brings out thumb-sucking as a sexual activity modelled on the baby's recall of the pleasures of breastfeeding. The baby is "sinking back satiated from the breast and falling asleep with flushed cheeks and a blissful smile" (p. 182). Clearly, Freud refers to a sexually active baby whose lips "behave like an erotogenic zone ... no doubt stimulation by the warm flow of milk is the cause of the pleasurable sensation" (p. 181). According to this work, Freud's response to our question must have been affirmative; infantile sexuality germinates in the newborn, although its manifestations "are mostly a matter of interpretation" (1916–17, p. 313), they are "unobtrusive" and "always overlooked and misunderstood" (1901, p. 682).

Three decades later, Freud returns to infantile sexuality when he discusses danger and anxiety. He now adds that the ego regards infantile sexual demands as dangerous per se: "It is a curious thing that early contact with the demands of sexuality should have a similar effect on the ego to that produced by premature contact with the external world" (1925–26, p. 155). He relates this to the infant's helplessness, which he regards as a biological factor. Today's infant therapists can also study helplessness *in the session*. I suggest that, if Freud had therapeutic experiences with screaming babies and desperate mothers, he would have realized that (a) the baby's impulses emerge in an object relationship, (b) her helplessness is also related to the emotional character of this traffic and (c) emotional factors will also determine if she experiences sexuality as dangerous or pleasant. We will soon return to the characteristics of this traffic and study if infantile sexuality might explain mother–infant interaction pathologies or "baby worries". First, we need to compare it with another concept often used to describe these situations; that of attachment.

## Infantile sexuality and attachment

To Freud, the major ingredients in early psychological development were infantile sexuality, the self-preservative instinct and the "affectionate current". The latter, he said, "is formed on the basis of the interests of the self-preservative instinct" (1912b, p. 180). It is "directed to the members of the family and those who look after the child" (idem) and "comprises what remains over of the infantile efflorescence of sexuality" (Freud, 1905b, p. 207). "Affectionate current" might seem identical to "attachment", which implies the child's seeking "proximity to and contact with a specific figure . . . notably when he is frightened, tired or ill" (Bowlby, 1969, p. 371). However, Bowlby was explicit that attachment does not refer to "needs or drives" (p. 179), while Freud's affectionate current contains "contributions from the sexual instincts – components of erotic interest" (1912b, p. 180).

Modern theorists have expanded the import of the attachment concept. Fonagy (2001) emphasizes that the search for proximity is "later supplanted by the more psychological goal of a feeling of closeness to the caregiver . . . [T]he goal is . . . a state of being or feeling" (p. 8). What this implies in terms of fantasies in the child remains unclear, however. Another question is what "later" refers to. Freud generally held that there exists no "later"; sexuality is there from the beginning. In my view, we do most justice to the terms "attachment" and "infantile sexuality" if we let the former comprise the relationship with the real, protective and nourishing mother. In contrast, infantile sexuality springs from the relationship with a mother who ignites sexual fantasies in the baby. Evidently, the two influence each other; attachment is influenced by encounters with real others and by the sexual fantasies that accompany them. Vice versa, infantile sexuality may be affected by alterations in the qualities of attachment, as when a trauma such as child abuse ensues.

I will now invoke video-recorded normal deliveries to study the dawning of infantile sexuality and attachment. A group of Swedish researchers found that if a baby is placed on the mother's tummy immediately after delivery, breast-seeking behaviour is observable within 30 minutes (Widström et al., 2007, 2011). He will start crawling towards the mother's nipple, looking at it, but then turning towards her face when she starts speaking. What terms cover such behaviours? His crawling must express a biological instinct; he is seeking milk to survive. He is still all organism; a set of behaviours driven by reflexes and not a mind driven by psychological intentions. Thus, his crawling cannot yet be classified as attachment behaviour with its connotation of relationship seeking.

On the other hand, the baby's looking at its mother's face could hardly be called a part of nourishment-seeking behaviour; no milk will come from the face. We might use the term "purposeful intersubjectivity" (Trevarthen & Aitken, 2001, p. 3) and gather confirming observations from neonates (Kugiumutzakis et al., 2005) and young babies (Meltzoff & Moore, 1977) who imitate adult facial expressions while displaying interest in the interaction. Nevertheless, one might object that such behaviour merely indicates their instinctual looking at anything with a human-like voice or tongue. In neuroscience terms, we might ask if mirror neurons already play a role in the child's looking at and paying attention to the mother (Bertenthal & Longo, 2007; Gaensbauer, 2011; Lepage & Théoret, 2007). This topic was briefly broached in the previous chapter.

What about infantile sexuality; could the newborn's crawling towards the breast express this phenomenon? Any analyst would probably agree that the *mother's* experience while looking at her child might contain a sexual component, but to say the same thing about her *newborn* sounds counter-intuitive and far-fetched. To sum up, we assert that attachment and infantile sexuality are linked with the instinct of survival, but we do not understand the time-table.

## Skin-to-skin contact and infantile sexuality

To bring order to the time-table, let us recall a 40-year-old observation. A group of paediatricians (Klaus et al., 1972) demonstrated a short, early period during which skin-to-skin contact between mother and baby proved essential for a positive development of their relationship. During the first two postnatal hours, such contact triggers breastfeeding and induces the infant's temperature regulation to work in unison with that of the mother (Bystrova et al., 2007). It may even have positive effects one year later (Bystrova et al., 2009) on infant self-regulation and maternal interaction and interest. Other investigations on infants' capacities of perception have shown their sensual skills in olfactory learning (Romantshik, Porter, Tillmann & Varendi, 2007), including connecting odours with pleasure or unpleasure (Soussignan & Schaal, 2005) and discerning the mother's odour

(MacFarlane, 1975; Van Toller & Kendal-Reed, 1995). Similarly, the mother discerns the odour of her baby (Russell, Mendelson & Peeke, 1983) and his garments (Porter, Cernoch & McLaughlin, 1983). We thus have rich evidence that mother and infant quickly develop a multifarious sensuous perspicacity and that their early sensual contact has important psychological effects.

Researchers explain these behaviours as governed by hormonal alterations (Romantshik *et al.*, 2007; Uvnäs-Moberg, 2000). I suggest they also substantiate psychoanalytic speculations concerning the birth of infantile sexuality. The early sensuous contact between mother and child turns on infantile sexuality in both. They acquire a sense of touch and smell for each other. The flushed cheeks of the Freudian baby thus represent hormonally induced thermal vasodilatation *and* sexual pleasure.

In 2001, Fonagy spoke of sexuality as "a genetically controlled physiological response that emerges within attachment contexts that are mutually regulatory, intersubjective, or relational" (2001, p. 128). This formulation seems to downplay the ingredients of autoerotism and fantasmatic activity, that is, infantile sexuality (Widlöcher, 2002). Later, Fonagy and Target (2007) have come to regret the reduced emphasis in attachment theory on "infantile sexuality as the predominant explanation of psychological disturbance" (p. 418). Fonagy (2008) now empha-sizes two confluent currents for the development of infantile sexuality. Attachment provides its relational basis while the mother–infant interaction fuels its fantasies: "Attuned secure parenting generates the interpersonal context for an erotically imaginative intercourse, while its content arises out of the adaptive mother–infant *misattunement*" (p. 26, italics added). These formulations are more in line with how I understand the delivery room scene. However, they need to be explicated somewhat and I will presently return to the concept of misattunement.

## Infantile sexuality or sensuality?

The self-preservative instinct pushes the newborn to crawl towards the nipple. He sucks and is satiated. As hunger sets in again, he begins to have access to dim memory traces of familiar smells, tastes and sounds, ways of being held and a sense of safety. A primitive recall of pleasure is now added to his instinctual search for nourishment. But, here we must stop and ask: why do we call this pleasure *sexual* and not *sensual*? To answer, let us invoke Fonagy's (2008) formulations about how parenting generates the context for erotic fantasies while dyadic misattunements shape their contents. It seems reasonable that a baby needs attuned parenting to develop an ability to fantasize – although it is not evident why this should lead to erotic imaginations. Still more obscure is why their contents would be shaped by *mis*-attunements between the generations. As we shall see however, it is precisely these misattunements that provide the argument as to why the baby's pleasure is not merely sensual but also sexual.

The misattunements arise from the gap in the sexual development of the parents and the baby. The adults know things that the baby is ignorant of; his birth is the result of their sexual relationship. His place of birth was the place where his mother received and enjoyed his father. Her tummy is used by him for crawling towards the nipple but was also used by his father in tender caresses. Before he sucked her breasts they were fondled by the father. Thus the parents will handle the baby, not only with conscious notions of promoting attachment but also with unconscious feelings "derived from [their] own sexual life" (Freud, 1905b, p. 223). When they say, "My dearest, aren't you sweet, what lovely cheeks, come let me kiss you Baby", this is not only a language of attachment and commitment but also one of love and sexuality.

One might object that such language only reflects the parents' sexuality and not that of the baby. Indeed, although Freud was adamant that sexuality exists in the infant, when pressed for proof he gave a dismissive reply: "Enough can be seen in the children if one knows how to look" (1933, p. 121). One problem in proving sexual inclinations in the baby is that we think of infantile sexuality as a mere predecessor to adult genital sexuality. Widlöcher (2002) emphasizes that it is something more; it involves "psychic creativity" (p. 19), that is, fantasies and autoerotism. Laplanche (1999a, 2002) asks how these fantasies arise. He retains Freud's infantile sexuality concept and studies its link to observable mother–infant interactions. He disagrees with Freud that "a child has its sexual instincts and activities from the first; it comes into the world with them" (1910, p. 42). He suggests that a baby's sexuality is created in response to enigmatic messages that are transmitted verbally and nonverbally through the parents' ways of speaking, holding, caressing and admonishing the child.

## The enigmatic message: returning to Frida

The concept of enigmatic message was discussed in Chapter 2, as part of our investigation of primal representations in the infant. By now, we have assembled more clinical examples, which will add substance to our continued investigation. Let us resume contact with three-month-old Frida from Chapter 3. In the session reported, she was screaming incessantly. When she finally gave me a warm smile I exclaimed, in relief and spontaneous joy at the emotional détente, "Oh, what a smile, Frida. One is totally charmed!" A remarkable word; "charmed" would be more appropriate coming from a man courting a woman. Still, Frida's mother did not object but smiled warmly as she saw her girl calm down, and I did not consider my words as a breach of ethics but as an everyday way of talking to a baby.

"Charmed" consisted of two currents: my conscious effort at containing a screaming baby and an unconscious fantasy about adult sexual relations. The word confirmed Laplanche's (1989) thesis, that

> an adult faced with a child is particularly likely to be deviant and inclined to perform bungled or even symbolic actions because he is involved in a relationship with his other self, with the other he once was. The child in front of him brings out the child within him.
>
> (p. 103)

In such an instance of primal seduction, "an adult proffers to a child verbal, non-verbal and even behavioural signifiers which are pregnant with unconscious sexual significations" (Laplanche, 1989, p. 126). Note that Laplanche does not refer to perverse acts but to normal adult–child interactions. Furthermore, the seduction would fall flat if Frida was not ready to also interpret me at a level beyond the one I consciously intended. Thus, we might speak of four characters in the analytic field (Ferro, 1999); the analyst as a man and a boy, plus a sexually ignorant girl and one who had begun to intuit the enigmas beneath the adults' messages. Frida had already experienced touches, smells, smiles and sounds from her adult entourage. Perhaps she noted a difference in how I uttered "charmed" compared with my other words. A smile, a tone of voice or a gesture might deviate from my previous communications with her.

The response to this osmosis of smiles, inflections of voice, changes in temperature and facial colour, altered odours, etc., is the creation of fantasies in the baby, which we subsume under the concept of infantile sexuality. Stein (1998) suggests this subject is so difficult to investigate because it is "taboo and takes place early in life on a covert, inner level of fantasy transmission and bodily sensations" (p. 615). In mother–infant treatments we can collect observations, comments from the mother, communications from the baby, responses to interventions and reflections on our countertransference. Taken together, they add substance to our guesswork about the traffic of fantasies between mother and infant. This applies both to well-functioning and disordered babies. If Frida belonged to the former category, I will now subsume a case vignette of a little boy who was clearly in dire straits. Let us return to little Nic from Chapter 1 and see if his suffering could be described in similar terms.

## Breastfeeding and infantile sexuality

In the mother's mind, the breast is represented in a complex way. It is an organ for lactation – and one that is unconsciously imbued with erotic meanings stemming from her infancy and womanhood. When she takes care of, enjoys and struggles with her child, she cannot help but transmit messages whose sexual component is partly unconscious to her. They are also enigmatic to the child who cannot grasp their erotic undercurrents. As we shall see, it is precisely this incomprehensibility that promotes the baby's salubrious infantile sexuality. However, if conflicts around the unconscious sexual implications of breastfeeding gain the upper hand, the outcome is less favourable. Indeed, breastfeeding problems are common reasons for maternal complaints, often correlating with postnatal depression (Gagliardi, Petrozzi & Rusconi, 2010; McCarter-Spaulding & Horowitz, 2007) and maternal identity issues (Cooke, Schmied & Sheehan, 2007).

As we recall from Chapter 1, Tessie's two-week-old son Nic fretted while breastfeeding. Already the mother–baby sessions revealed her conflict between wanting to reject Nic and care for him tenderly. The wounded nipple had paved the way for this conflict to emerge as a breastfeeding problem. Its links with her unconscious sexuality were elaborated later in individual therapy. Tessie was unsatisfied in her marriage and beset by anorectic ruminations though she kept her weight at a healthy level. Later, connections between the anorexia and her sexual fantasies became evident; she unconsciously equated eating in public places with promiscuity. Her anorectic restraint (looking at candy but not eating it) was linked with masochistic fantasies of begging for erotic satisfaction under humiliating circumstances.

Tessie found it hard to accept her son's sucking, just because he enjoyed it. Unconsciously, she wanted it all for herself and felt he took it away from her. She told me in embarrassment: "On the delivery ward I felt like a queen. Everyone said I was wonderful. But when I returned home to take care of him, I felt so lonely." Such fantasies clashed with her high ethical standards. Her wishes of having it all seemed to relate to *her* infantile sexual desire for the breast. Here, Nic was her competitor. We may ask, to what extent did *he* have corresponding conflicts? I guessed his alarm at the breast was a response to her ambivalence. This hypothesis emerged when I observed him fretting at the right-hand side while nursing smoothly at the left-hand side. Nic seemed to have internalized this maternal ambivalence, which created clashing emotions in him. This internal antagonism kept up the nursing problem. The object of function, the attachment breast, was reliable enough. Nic got the milk he needed and gained weight satisfactorily. But the sexual breast of pleasurable fantasies was already a confusing object – partly satisfying and exciting, partly frightening and rejecting. Now, we could speak of infantile sexual conflicts in him as well.

The problem for another dyad, Tina and her mother Nathalie (Chapter 2), was that the breast was the sole remedy against the baby's terrible screams. As I observed how Tina avoided mother's eyes while lying in her lap, I suggested she had "two Mums". One appeared when she was smiling and looking into Mum's eyes. The other Mum was frightening and one that must be avoided. As I mentioned this, Nathalie came to think of the two names she had been vacillated between since the girl was born. Tina sounded "nice and cosy". Christina was "stern and old-fashioned" – yet contained a word with a gentle ring to it.

The two names also emerged as metaphors of Nathalie's personality. "Christina" referred to her anorectic, well-controlled, distanced and elegant aspect, whereas "Tina" referred to a cuddly and spontaneous aspect. It was difficult for her to retrieve the latter part within herself because she despised it. Her love for the girl was mixed with contempt in that the nickname Tina was "base and common". Her ambivalence was reflected in a fantasy in the delivery room; the newborn was too sweet to be called Tina.

Nathalie breastfed her girl: "I know it's good for her but I don't like doing it." What imprints did such an attitude cause in the baby? And when Tina started screaming and mother lifted her up, how did she react to a maternal outlook reflected in Nathalie's smiling comment: "I think she's cute when she's crying"? It was plain to see that Nathalie's attitude emerged from identifications with her mother, whom she described as self-centred and overly cheerful. What interests us here is which identifications it might engender in Tina. I suggest they were affected by the mother's doubly enigmatic messages. Their aggressive and loving undercurrents were intertwined beyond Nathalie's awareness. Thus, when the girl was looking into mother's face she could not feel certain if it was "friend or foe"; was Mum welcoming, warm and cosy – or cool, reserved and ironic? I interpreted Tina's screaming and gaze avoidance to indicate a disturbed development of her infantile sexuality. Primal seduction, in which mother's messages should be "pregnant with unconscious sexual significations" (Laplanche, 1989, p. 126) was complicated by Nathalie's ambivalence towards her mother and her daughter.

## *Anlehnung* or enigmatic message: Freud versus Laplanche

After we have recapitulated the two cases of breastfeeding problems and speculated on how they might reflect a disturbed development of the baby's infantile sexuality, we return to Freud. He asks how infant sexuality arises in general. To answer, he invents a peculiar term, *Anlehnung*. It implies that the sexual drive leans on "one of the functions serving the purpose of self-preservation" (1905b, p. 182). Although *Three Essays* contains short but vivid descriptions of a baby with a caressing mother, Freud did not emphasize that *Anlehnung* occurred within an object relationship. As Laplanche argues, this obscures our understanding of the birth of sexuality. He suggests that the baby's sexual fantasies arise in the communication between mother and child. When the mother, to quote Freud, "strokes [the infant], kisses him, rocks him and quite clearly treats him as a substitute for a complete sexual object" (1905b, p. 223), her endearments are enigmatic to the child. This is because the mother–baby relationship is asymmetrical and the import of mother's messages is partly hidden to herself as well. The messages will precipitate in the baby as unconscious thing-presentations or "source-objects" (Laplanche, 1999a, p. 129), which constitute the fountainhead of his/her drive.

Laplanche's explanation is plausible only after he has made an amendment of drive theory and claimed that the drive is a message. We recognize a definition by Grotstein (1980) quoted in Chapter 2; the drive is a "messenger of information" (p. 495). The Frenchman emphasizes that the drive does not only arise from the baby's relation to his body but also from his communications with other human beings. Freud had emphasized the former perspective when he defined the drive as "the psychical representative of an endosomatic, continuously flowing source of stimulation" (1905b, p. 168). To Laplanche (1999a), in contrast, "the source-objects of the drive" (p. 129) spring precisely from that which Freud portrayed as the mother's strokes and kisses.

To sum up and simplify slightly, to Freud the drive comes from within but to Laplanche it arrives from without. Babies cannot grasp the full import of the parents' messages; they receive them but do not know what to do with them.

In situations of frustration or excitation, they are reactivated in the form of traumatizing signifiers, which the baby must bind. If he fails, these signifiers or *Ding-Vorstellungen* [*représentations de chose* or thing-presentations] turn into *Vorstellungs-Dinge* [*représentations-choses* or presentation-things] or "designified signifiers". The French terms are invented by Laplanche (1999a, p. 97). *Ding-Vorstellungen* stems from Freud (1915c, p. 202), while *Vorstellungs-Dinge* is my translation of Laplanche's second term.

Nic and Tina seemed beset by *représentations-choses*. We might translate them into 'Ouch, take away, hurts, bad, panic, what does it want, terrible handling'. Both Tessie and Nathalie were loving, distressed and irritated mothers. This made it difficult for their babies to create *représentations de chose* of, for example, 'Mum's nice voice' or 'Mum's pleasant smell' or 'Mum gets annoyed when I scream'. Had such representations developed they would, in a later step, become repressed and contribute to the development of these babies' adult genital sexuality. However, since *représentations-choses* remain stunted due to the derailed interaction, they remain enigmatic to the child. In Chapter 6, I brought out some terms that signify such experiences, such as Freud's "*Wahrnehmungszeichen*" or "signs of perception" (1892–99/1950, p. 234). Laplanche places his *représentations-choses* on equal footing with Freud's term. They also correspond to situations when *primal representations* (Chapter 2) remain stunted in their development to end up in a primal repression, as described in Chapter 8. *Bion's β-element* (1962a) is another term describing similar phenomena. When the mother's messages convey nothing "but energy or excitation" (Laplanche, 1999b, p. 106), they become traumatizing. In Bion's terms, the mother cannot contain the child's β-elements and the child is traumatized – like Nic and Tina when I first met them. The point with parent–infant analysis is to help such babies transform their *représentations-choses* into more comprehensible and unequivocal signs. This may help develop their infantile sexuality.

## Clinical conclusions

"Has infantile sexuality anything to do with infants?" My answer is affirmative. I have sought to show the value of the concept when we seek to understand mother–infant disorders in clinical practice. My major example of how it might influence the adult world was my expression "charmed" in front of Frida. My main infant examples were how Nic's and Tina's breastfeeding problems disturbed the development of a sound infantile sexuality. True, I have speculated about these babies' sexuality. As stated earlier, Freud himself was cautious about the demonstrability of sexual manifestations in infants. When I use mother–infant practice to support my arguments, I evidently rely on interpretations. However, I would argue that this restriction applies to any systematic effort at understanding the emotions behind a baby's behaviour, whether in laboratories, infant treatments or adult psychoanalyses.

Some mothers experience nursing as disgusting, pleasurable or provoking. Conflicts around sharing, autonomy, pleasure and dependence may be coloured by maternal infantile sexual conflicts. This drags the baby into a sexual conflict of his own, such as how to enjoy its mother while yet sensing her ambivalence. Older babies ready for weaning cannot bear losing their only imaginable comforter, the breast. They cling to it when ambivalence appears in them or their mother. From the perspective of the baby's sexuality, mother's breast is both enticing, comforting and a frustrating hindrance for attaining separation and individuation. We followed such examples in the cases of Karen (Chapter 4) and Tom (Chapter 8).

I conclude that we have good reasons for investigating infantile sexuality in mother–infant disturbances or "baby worries" such as crying, insomnia, breast-feeding issues or maternal depression and anxiety. I suggest these conditions may involve the infantile sexuality of mother and child. The two are involved in an intercourse that is sexual, that is, in the psychoanalytic sense of the term. The mother's sexuality is fully developed, while it is but dawning in the baby. If we want to better understand infantile sexuality as it emerges in this asymmetrical relationship, mother–infant treatments offer rich material.

# Chapter 10

# Classical concepts revisited III
## Transference

In the two preceding chapters, we found infantile sexuality and primal repression to be valuable concepts for understanding – from a psychoanalytic perspective – a baby's normal and pathological development. We have now arrived at the concept of transference. We psychoanalysts investigate how unconscious and conscious parts of the patient's mind interact; with each other and with the corresponding parts of the analyst's mind. The patient's contributions to this interaction – especially those emanating from his Unconscious – we name *transference*. Our clinical method aims to investigate and resolve it as far as possible: "It is on that field [of transference] that the victory must be won" (Freud, 1912a, p. 108). Any method named psychoanalytic must thus account for how transference appears and how the therapist handles it. This is so whether we aim to resolve it more completely in classical psychoanalysis or to a lesser extent as in brief psychotherapy.

When a parent seeks help for baby worries s/he may exhibit, just like any other patient, transferences to the therapist (Fraiberg, 1980). Can we discern transference in the *baby* as well? I will discuss three possible answers: (1) no, it does not exist, (2) yes, it exists sometimes and is then a redundant phenomenon that should be left un-addressed by the analyst and (3) yes, it exists sometimes and when this occurs we need to address it through some kind of analytic intervention. If (1) is the case, we need to unravel the situations where we erroneously believe infant transference is at work. If (2) is right, if the infant's interactions with us are coloured by unconscious urges and affects, we must try to grasp how they are connected with the baby's symptoms. This is so though we refrain from addressing the baby's specific relationship with us. If (3) is the case, we must also ask how to address the baby's transference.

It has been claimed (Flink, 2001) that the infant is not actively involved in therapy since she does not understand verbal communications. According to this objection, which has been discussed throughout the book, our interventions to the parent would be incomprehensible to the baby being an outsider in treatment. Thus, no impetus would drive her towards creating unconscious images of the clinician. In classical terminology, no libidinal or destructive cathexis would be directed towards the therapist. In object relational language, she would not form any unconscious internal objects connected with him. In short, no transference would emerge.

The classical authors on parent–infant psychotherapy (Cramer & Palacio Espasa, 1993; Fraiberg *et al.*, 1975; Lebovici & Stoléru, 2003) view the baby as actively involved in therapy. She is the "patient who cannot talk" and therefore needs "articulate spokesmen" (Fraiberg, 1987, p. 102), that is, a therapist. Nevertheless, as my literature review soon will indicate, when it comes to transference – the unconscious dimension of a patient's relationship with the therapist – they mostly refer to that of the parent and not of the baby. Thus, they would probably vote for alternative (2) as outlined previously. They would acknowledge the existence of an unconscious part of the child's mind but then focus on how it is influenced by the parental "ghost in the nursery" (Fraiberg *et al.*, 1975). They would explicate that the "mother's internal reality, her unconscious, constitutes the first world offered to the baby" (Lebovici & Stoléru, 2003, p. 279) and that this sometimes leads to pathology in the baby. They would also argue that treatment aims at liberating the mother–infant relationship from "projective distortions" (Cramer & Palacio Espasa, 1993, p. 82). *Nota bene*; this term refers to the mother's projections towards the child or the therapist, not the child's projections towards the therapist.

In principle, the task of demonstrating *parental* transference in parent–infant psychotherapy does not differ from other therapies. It is all a matter of choosing the appropriate method of investigation. Human relationships were known to be influenced by unconscious factors long before Freud. His specific contribution was to discover its existence in the psychotherapeutic situation, to name it transference, to trace its infantile origins and to study its links with outcome. This became possible once he had devised an instrument for studying and handling it: the psychoanalytic method. As analysts, we allow ample possibilities for the patient to create projective distortions about us, we pay attention to them and reflect on their connection with his emotional suffering and then we transform our reflections into interventions addressed to him. This is what therapists do every day in their consulting-rooms. To discuss transference in connection with a *baby* in therapy is more complicated. Just like when we work with adults, we would need to allow her to create projective distortions about us, pay attention to them, envisage their connections with her suffering and talk to her about it. But – since she cannot tell us how she experiences us and her communications are less explicit and more difficult to interpret than adult verbal comments – how would such a thing be possible?

In the cases I am about to present I have used the MIP method as described throughout this book. I seek to build up a relationship with parent *and* baby and to pay equal attention to them. The adult's communications contribute to the field dynamics (Baranger & Baranger, 2009; Civitarese, 2008; Ferro & Basile, 2011) but the baby's non-verbal communications are important as well; not only because they contribute to the session atmosphere but also because they may represent her efforts to communicate with her mother and me. But – until now my descriptions of MIP have only addressed the need to relate to the baby and pay attention to her communications – they have not opted for any of my three answers on infant transference.

Over the years, I observed that a baby sometimes related to me in a way coloured by intense negative emotions. Sometimes, they were restricted to me while she maintained a trustful attitude to her parent. This gave rise to the hypothesis that her emotions vis-à-vis me might reflect transference. In other words, she might harbour unconscious urges that she had been struggling with on her own – and which until now had been disguised as functional symptoms such as sleep disorders or breastfeeding problems. I thought that perhaps she was now rerouting these urges towards me and that this explained why she feared me. If this hypothesis proved tenable, I further suggested that transference in the baby might be used as a concept for understanding her anxieties. Perhaps it might even be possible to assuage them in a similar way to how we do it with adult patients; through interventions addressing the transference. If so, the question was how this could be done with non-verbal infants.

I will approach the following questions, which issue from the three alternatives I formulated earlier: is transference relevant for describing an infant's relationship with the analyst? If the answer is "yes, but only in certain situations", what characterizes them? Do we need to address the parent and/or the infant about it? If we choose to address the baby, how does such a technique differ from other parent–infant therapies?

The chapter focuses on three cases. The first sets the ground for the theoretical discussion: During her first consultation Jennifer, a girl of one and a half years, suddenly became terrified of me while maintaining a trustful relationship with her parents in the consulting-room. This started my reflections on transference in babies. To investigate if similar phenomena may occur in younger babies, the second case is a seven-month-old boy, David, who avoided looking at me. In the third case of Vance, a boy of nine months, his fear of me appeared when his father felt uneasy with me. As this paternal transference was resolved, the boy calmed down. This was soon replaced by another kind of fear, which no longer seemed connected with his father's unease. It rather reflected some internalized problem in the boy. Vance's case started my reflections on "direct" and "indirect" transferences.

## Case 1: Jennifer, 18 months

I was contacted by the parents of Jennifer because of her lifelong insomnia. They told me that she probably had no nightmares but woke up several times in tears. A mild sleeping-drug had been of little help. Paediatric investigations could not detect any underlying medical problems. In the first session, the mother seemed sad but said, "I'm just exhausted". She was trustful and friendly though I did not get close to her. The father was seriously concerned about the baby and his wife's health. I noted a strange countertransference phenomenon; I was suddenly overcome by an unpleasant feeling towards him. This brief and incomprehensible experience felt like a foreign body in my psyche, since he seemed a friendly and concerned parent and I had no information contradicting these impressions. During the interview, I talked with the parents and conveyed my empathy with their dire straits. Now and then I turned to Jennifer:

*Analyst:*   Mum and Dad tell me that you don't sleep well. They are so worried. It must be hard for you not to sleep.

Jennifer looked at me earnestly and perhaps sadly. My impression contrasted with the parents' description of her as cheerful. They were at the end of their tether because of her insomnia. We continued talking about these matters while I now and then looked at Jennifer and commented on what her parents were telling me. Suddenly, a terror appeared on Jennifer's face while she kept staring at me. I was not able to pinpoint any interchange or event that might explain this dramatic change. She started screaming "Out, out" and ran to the door. The shocked parents tried in vain to console her.

Why did Jennifer suddenly become terrified of me? One might suggest it reflected a general fearfulness, but the parents had never seen such a character trait previously. Alternatively, it might spring from a general shyness or prudence. However, as a rule she was a cheerful girl. Since I found no events in the session to explain her terror, I hypothesized that it sprang from earlier experiences. At the beginning of the session she was able to retain them as unconscious representations but after a while they suddenly emerged and became connected with me. As analysts, we have daily experiences of a lack of coherence between how we behave with the patient and how she experiences us. Such instances we label transference manifestations. I thus asked if I could conceptualize Jennifer's fear similarly. If this proved correct, unconscious forces were active; not only in relationship with me but perhaps also in connection with her insomnia and my transient countertransference towards the father. The ensuing mother–baby treatment allowed time for investigating these questions. Unfortunately, the mother would resume work in a few months' time, which set a time limit for our investigation.

The second session, with mother and daughter only, began with Jennifer staring at me in panic and trying to escape into the waiting room. The mother was taken aback and had a hard time to make her stay. At this point, I had to decide which port of entry (Stern, 1995) to approach. One might consider that Jennifer's panic reflected her mother's unease in coming to me. If so, the girl was the target of the mother's projections. I might address these issues directly to the mother ("How did you feel coming here today?") or to the girl ("Perhaps Mum was a bit uneasy coming here today"). Another entry would be to speak with Jennifer about her fear of arriving at an unknown place ("It's not easy coming to a new place"). The two latter alternatives would imply addressing the girl though not speaking with her directly about how she might be experiencing me. Since I recalled her terrified look at me during our first consultation, I thought the "hot spot" was to speak with her about this fear though I did not know its origins.

*Analyst:*     You are quite afraid of me, Jennifer. You don't know why, and neither do I. But I know that it's terrible to be scared. You really want to get rid of that scare. I hope I can help you with it.

As I was speaking, Jennifer slowly calmed down. I asked the mother to tell me more of how she experienced the present situation. She spontaneously started speaking about the delivery. An emergency caesarean was necessary due to protracted labour. She felt the staff had dismissed her when she asked them for support. When Jennifer was three months, some breastfeeding problems with sore nipples emerged. While speaking of this, she seemed restrained. I pointed out the contrast between her painful experiences and the subdued account. She did not comment on this. All in all, my impression was that the mother's words did not impact on the girl whereas my attention to her panic made her slowly relax.

The third session Jennifer entered, once again in panic. A diarrhoea with an acrid smell soiled her pants. After the mother had changed her diaper and clothes, I addressed Jennifer.

*Analyst:*     Perhaps you wanted to get rid of your "scare" by making a poo, but now the smell became scary, too. It's really scary in here and you think I am scary, too.

Once again, I was addressing Jennifer about her fear of *me* – not of coming to a new place generally or of her carrying the mother's projected anxiety with me. Another observation supported, as I see it, that this port of entry was relevant. After I had touched a toy animal or a piece of furniture she refused to touch it. She wanted to sit down on a little chair but my mere looking at it made her shrink back. Had she been afraid generally of the toys because they were new to her, she would have shunned them constantly. However, she was playing with them until I touched or looked at them. From then on she kept shunning them.

Intertwined with these episodes, another climate was dawning in which Jennifer was cheerful, enterprising and cautiously contacting; she placed her own teddy bear on the dreaded chair and walked around, uncertain where to move the chair to. At such times she would look cheerfully at me. The contrast between her cheerfulness and fearfulness was stunning. In my interchange with her mother, I pointed out their different temperaments; Jennifer was cheerful and dominant while the mother was more shy and restrained. She seemed unfamiliar with and charmed by Jennifer's enthusiasm. She was very fond of her husband, a supportive and devoted father. She felt content with life, except for the girl's insomnia. Our conversations changed little in Jennifer's fear or insomnia. In contrast, therapeutic effects seemed to take place in my direct address with her.

After a few sessions, Jennifer began to relax. She became charmingly mischievous and humorous. For example, she jested about whether she or I was to decide if her teddy bear should sit on her chair. One might argue, in line with a critical comment voiced throughout the book, for example, in connection with Figure 1.1 of Chapter 1, that this positive development occurred because *the mother* became more relaxed with me. However, our relationship did not change much. In contrast, Jennifer developed a trust in me and paid close attention to my interventions. This is not to say that I bypassed the mother. I told her how I interpreted Jennifer's insomnia. It seemed that some fear had accumulated from early on, the roots of which we might never understand. Jennifer could only express it through her insomnia and now, I suggested, through her fear of me. The theoretical assumption was that unassimilated internal objects were governing her. Though my brief countertransference displeasure towards the father was neither clarified nor talked about, I silently interpreted it as an experience akin to Jennifer's fears. I refer especially to its quality of un-assimilation or lack of "alphabetization" (Ferro, 2006). In other words the father's face appeared to me, for a second, as a scary icon. I assumed it had characteristics similar to the girl's nightly terror. In countertransference terms, it represented my concordant identification (Racker, 1968) with Jennifer, a concept discussed in Chapters 1 and 6. Thus, I do *not* claim she woke up because she feared her father.

We thus never got to know which experiences, if any, had precipitated her nocturnal fears. The important thing was that they had not been adequately contained initially. I achieved therapeutic effects mainly by re-establishing the container–contained link. This enabled her to work through her fear of me. During our 24-session treatment it disappeared completely, while her insomnia was significantly reduced. Three years later I contacted the parents for permission to publish material. They consented and added that since three years of age, Jennifer has slept well throughout the entire night. They thought this was only partly due to psychoanalysis and mentioned an allergy to milk protein as contributing to the insomnia. They did not think she had had any fears, a statement in stark contrast to my clinical impressions. Their comments seemed to indicate a mixture of unresolved negative transference and gratitude.

I will now use the case to approach our initial questions on infant transference. First, I will study how the transference concept has been used generally in child analytic literature.

## The Freud–Klein controversy and the issue of infant transference

As Laplanche and Pontalis (1973) remark, the concept of transference is problematic. To some analysts, notably Kleinians, it connotes every phenomenon in the patient's relationship with the psychoanalyst. Other analysts use narrower definitions. Common to all is that they refer to situations in which unconscious wishes consisting of "infantile prototypes" (p. 455) are actualized in the analyst–analysand relationship. This definition still leaves important questions unanswered: first, does transference occur ubiquitously or only in the analytic situation? Thus, did Jennifer fear other people as well? Second, it is often claimed that transference is "unrealistic" (p. 456) as regards content and extent. But, perhaps this merely reflects the "unreality" of the analytic situation? Maybe Jennifer's fear was simply a reaction to my "spooky" or unfamiliar behaviour? Third, if her present fear was built on earlier terrifying experiences, how do we know about the links between past and present? Freud (1914) spoke of experiences, which "occurred in very early childhood and were not understood at the time but were subsequently understood and interpreted" (p. 149). He assumed that even if they might be understood après-coup in an analytic process, the patient could never recall them. If so, it would be impossible to excavate the roots of Jennifer's fear. Alternatively, it might indicate a traumatic neurosis, where the "factor of displacement" (Freud, 1916–17, p. 363) had not succeeded in assimilating the excitation. If so, we would need to investigate the sources of the trauma and how they precipitated today as transference.

Let us approach these questions in Jennifer's case. As for the first one, her parents claimed she was confident with other people and that her fear appeared only with me. Regarding the second question, I maintained a psychoanalytic attitude in which I was friendly, attentive and spontaneous rather than "spooky". This makes it hard to explain why I could not even look at one of my toys without her having panic attacks. Third, the parents denied any early trauma and only reported her insomnia. The only plausible explanation must be that an unresolved emotional problem was now displaced as a fear of me. Infantile prototypes were thus actualized in our relationship and the conditions were fulfilled for naming her fear a transference.

At this point, one might object that transference refers to a *sustained* colouring of an object relation rather than a temporary fear. This objection adheres to the Freud–Klein controversy in child analysis (Winberg Salomonsson, 1997). Anna Freud (1926) argued that transference cannot occur in small children since their inner lives and unconscious processes are insufficiently developed. She referred mainly to the transference neurosis, whose existence she doubted in small children. As for Melanie Klein, she mostly used the term "transference situation" (Petot, 1990, p. 139), which referred to all unconscious fantasies that are "rooted in the earliest stages of development and in the deep layers of the unconscious" (Klein, 1952, p. 55). The problem with differentiating such fantasies from realistic relations is that in the child's mind, "every external experience is interwoven with his phantasies" (p. 54). In Petot's words,

> when the child comes for analysis, its "real" relationships with real objects are already in a sense transference relationships . . . the attitude of the three-year-old to its parents is not determined by the reality of their attitude, but by an internal imago, an imaginary or distorted representation of the parents.
>
> (p. 142)

Petot refers to situations when internal objects, especially bad and destructive ones, are projected onto the therapist.

Klein's views have been modified by post-Kleinians (Spillius, 1983). For example, they have come to focus more on a detailed analysis of the patient–analyst interaction, with an increasing inclusion of the countertransference perspective. This is implied in the term "transference as the total situation" (Joseph, 1985). Similarly, Anna Freud (1965) modified her "former opinion that transference in childhood is restricted to single 'transference reactions' and does not develop to the complete status of a 'transference neurosis'" (p. 36). The Contemporary Freudian group now acknowledges "the earliest internal influences on the child's development . . . [and] the existence of transference phantasies, anxieties and resistances from the outset of the analysis", (Sandler & Sandler, 1994, p. 387) as well the impact of countertransference (Piene, Auestad, Lange & Leira, 1983) and negative transference (Anthony, 1986).

Whether we adhere to a contemporary Kleinian or Freudian view, one question remains: when in life does transference begin? If a one-day-old baby is screaming at the breast, does this express a negative mother transference? That sounds far-fetched. What about a baby screaming at the therapist? The minimal prerequisite for speaking of transference is that the baby has developed a relationship with the analyst. This condition was fulfilled in Jennifer's case. However, as Anna Freud would perhaps object, we could neither confirm nor dismiss transference in her case, because without free associations we would lack the necessary investigatory tool.

The solution to this dilemma is, in my opinion, to paraphrase Klein and suggest that *transference-like* phenomena operate "throughout life and influence all human relations (Klein, 1952, p. 48), whereas we may speak of *transference* only when we can investigate it accurately, in the analytic situation. This view coincides with that of Muir (1991). She restricts transference to "those aspects of the primary relationship that are current and unresolved, that also get taken out of the family and *projected into a therapeutic relationship*" (p. 66, italics added). Actually, we therapists set up a relationship with the patient with the specific aim of cultivating transference. We gather it by maintaining the frame and paying close attention to the patient's communications and to our counter-transference. Thus, transference is sucked into the analytic situation "like a vacuum-cleaner" (Cohen & Hahn, 2000, p. 2). The interplay between transference and countertransference stimulates regression and places the analysand of any age in a "formally childlike role" (Stone, 1961, p. 21).

To illustrate the two concepts: if a baby starts crying at a stranger on the bus one could, at the most, call this a transference-like phenomenon. In contrast, Jennifer's fear emerged in a psychoanalytic setting. Thus, it *might* reflect a transference, a conjecture I could investigate in a psychoanalytic process. Having now delimited the term transference to the analytic situation, we run up against another problem; to what extent is a child able to deploy fantasies onto the analyst? To a post-Kleinian like Meltzer (1967) the answer is evident: the "flux and fluidity" (p. 4) of children's internal object relations make them prone to transference. In contrast, Anna Freud claimed that since the child has its "past relationship or fantasy firmly fixed to the persons of the parents" (Sandler, Kennedy & Tyson, 1990, p. 92), she cannot cathect the analyst. However, if Anna Freud was right, why did Jennifer fear me? I conclude that her fear must result from a process by which she was displacing affects that were connected with her *experiences* of people around; in essence, her parents. The italics emphasize that I do not refer to her real parents but to the internal objects as they emerged in the container–contained relation with me. These affects were uncanny and possibly connected with her sleep disorder. My friendly yet neutral psychoanalytic attention made them surge anew but also promised their containment. This dual motor propelled her to behave like any patient in therapy; she transferred her anxiety to our relationship.

In contrast, I avoid the term transference neurosis since it historically refers to older patients. In Jennifer's case, I label her fear of me a *direct* and *stable* infant transference, in which she projected a bad internal object onto me. As long as I was the target of her projections, she feared me. Conversely, she projected onto her parents the good internal object, as when she ran to her mother for protection. The term "direct" refers to the fact that her transference did not pass via the mother's transference. There were no signs that her mother feared me. To sum up, Jennifer's fear signified an infant transference, which we managed to resolve through dialogues and play. Our work also made her mother more relaxed and understanding of Jennifer's temperament, but the bulk was done in direct communication with the girl.

To conclude, transference seemed a relevant term for describing Jennifer's fear. It occurred early in treatment when negative internal objects were projected onto me. Substantial results were achieved by containing the girl's fear. I will postpone the investigation of how my technique differed from other authors' methods until I have investigated how they view babies and transference. I will do this after having answered a new question emerging from Jennifer's case. She was 18 months old and spoke a few words. Might transference also occur in younger infants? I will approach this question by the case of a seven-month-old boy.

## Case 2: David, seven months

When David's mother Irene contacts me on the phone, she explains that she worries because her son has been avoiding her eyes since four months of age. The ensuing mother–infant therapy lasts five months, with sessions twice-weekly and then once-weekly. All in all, we will work together for 39 hours. The entire therapy is video-recorded upon maternal consent. The aim is to document the treatment for myself in order to study the analytic process.

When we meet for a consultation, Irene tells me that David was born by caesarean delivery due to a breech presentation: "Maybe it has affected him negatively, though I don't know how!" At two months old he got a viral infection and was hospitalized with her: "I hadn't understood how ill he was! It was terrible with all these tubes and machines." After some days they returned home and David was fine – but at four months he started avoiding her eyes while yet looking at the other family members.

During our first meeting, David is breastfeeding calmly while playing with his mother's hand. He never looks into her eyes but often gives *me* long happy smiles. Irene does not seem depressed but speaks of her pain, guilt and stress in caring for her children. Her husband, she says, does not understand the depth of David's problem. The next session, she talks about her premonitions during pregnancy. She had feared that her concerns about her elder child might harm the foetus: "That's why David was born with a frown on his forehead." While she is speaking, David avoids her eyes constantly. In despair she asks him, "What did I do wrong to you!?" Much of the ensuing therapy centres on her guilt, frustration and humiliation concerning these issues.

During a session in the third week, David is looking happily at me while avoiding Irene's eyes. It is humiliating to her and bewildering to me. I feel he is pushing me into becoming his favourite. I suggest to both of them some images that enter my mind; they seem like two magnets with the identical poles repelling each other. David looks attentively at my accompanying gestures. When I, out of frustration, suggest Irene be more active in capturing the boy's gaze, this only leads to his rejecting her even more. By the end of the session, I feel even more frustrated with his consistent avoidance of her.

| | |
|---|---|
| *Analyst to David:* | Well David, one could really feel angry with you when you don't look Mum in her eyes. |
| | [As a consequence of my unassimilated countertransference frustration, when saying the word "angry" I knock my hand gently on the little table between us. He gives a start and cries briefly.] |
| *A:* | David, you got scared of me. You see, I feel so little and weak when I cannot help you and Mum get in contact. That's why I knocked on the table and you got scared. |
| | [The boy calms down and I continue.] |
| *A to the mother:* | It is easy to sense your guilt when he's avoiding you. I tasted the guilt myself right now – and his reproach, too! |
| | [The next session the boy is clearly avoiding *my* eyes.] |
| *A to D:* | You don't want to look at me today. |
| *Mother:* | I got a lot of response from David since we were here the other day. If I said, "David, look here", he didn't turn to me. But other than that, he looked into my eyes. [Mother lifts him up and searches his eyes but he avoids her.] |
| *A to D (he is literally turning his back on me):* | You really want to decide if you're gonna look at me or not, don't you! |

| | |
|---|---|
| *M:* | Yeah, right! When we got home after the previous session he had a hard time falling asleep. Unusual! Was it his reaction to what happened here? Or was he tired? I don't know. |
| *A:* | I want to listen to you, Irene, but first I'd like to tell you something, David. You look away from me, perhaps because we haven't seen each other for so long, since last Thursday. |
| *D:* | Aaah. |
| *A:* | Aaah. Last time, I banged the table (he looks happily at me for some seconds) and you started. Now you are looking at me. Mum says you were in a bad mood after the last time we met. "Silly Björn" banged the table. Then Silly Björn was gone from you. Now that you come back to me with Mum, you are looking away from me. That's easy to understand. [He looks at me a lengthier amount of time.] |
| *M smiling to D:* | Was that it, David? |
| *A to D:* | Was it the same when you were little, David? (He looks happily into my eyes.) Mum had so many things to worry about . . . |
| *D:* | Hehe. |
| *A:* | Yes, and one might turn away the eyes when one is sore and disappointed. When one has turned away from that person, it becomes unpleasant to look her in the eyes. |
| *M smiling at D:* | Was that it, David, was that it? |

I submitted this case to investigate if phenomena similar to Jennifer's fear might occur in younger infants. One difference was obvious: her fear of me was persistent whereas David's avoidance was temporary. Was its impact strong enough to merit the label transference? One could object that it simply represented a "habitual mode of relating" (Sandler *et al.*, 1990, p. 80). However, David easily looked other people in their eyes – including me save for the session referred. One could also retort that it simply resulted from a countertransference enactment. This was true, but since he otherwise avoided his mother consistently, I drew yet another conclusion: he avoided me because I had come to *temporarily represent an internal object, which he otherwise projected onto his mother.* Similarly to Jennifer's case, I therefore label his gaze avoidance of me a *direct* negative transference. Unlike her case, it was brief and contrasted with a prevailing positive or even idealized transference characterized by David's constant smiling at me while avoiding his mother.

David's case illustrates that transference may also occur in young infants. His avoidance did not simply reflect a transference flaring up when I knocked the table. It seemed rather to be an off-shoot of deeper emotional problems. It falls outside our topic to account for how they were resolved in the analysis. Suffice to say that the turning point came when I discovered that not only did David avoid mother's eyes; she also avoided *his* eyes in that she did not let out her feelings through her gaze. I formulated this in simple words to David: "I think Mum is shy. She doesn't dare show her feelings." When I spoke like this, he looked briefly in my eyes. Mother confirmed that she was a shy person generally. These sessions led to a warming up of their contact, to an increase of eye contact and to her improved self-confidence. Treatment was terminated when he was 12 months old. Since then, I have received two messages from Irene that their relationship, as well as David himself, is developing well.

## Transference in infants: a literature review

It is now time to study other parent–infant clinicians' views on transference. First, we need to clarify the terminology. Psychoanalytic literature abounds with references to "infantile transference", ever since Abraham in 1909 (Falzeder, 2002, p. 88) referred to the resurgence of infantile-like attitudes in adult patients. This connotation is still valid today. The term refers to adults or verbal and autistic (Tustin, 1981) children. In order to differentiate, I will use the term "*infant transference*" for the phenomena discussed here.

Most major parent–infant clinicians agree that the core component of therapies is "to understand how the parents' experiences shape their perceptions of and feelings and behaviour to the infant, with the infant contributing to interactional difficulties through physical or temperamental characteristics that have a particular meaning for the parents" (Thomson-Salo, 2007, p. 962, italics added). They also agree that earlier experiences may colour the parents' relationship with the therapist, a phenomenon often labelled parent–therapist transference. In contrast, infant–therapist transference, as I describe it, is not mentioned.

When Selma Fraiberg (1987) examines transference in child analysis (Chapter 9) she does not exemplify with infant cases. Neither do the chapters on "the ghosts in the nursery" (4), a therapy with a five-month-old boy (5), the adolescent mother and her infant (6) and pathological defences in infancy (7) refer to transference in the baby. The concept refers to parents, as when a "therapist who conjures up the ghosts will be endowed in transference with the fearsome attributes of the ghost" (p. 121). Similarly, her followers (Lieberman & Van Horn, 2008) explore "how the parents' problems affect the parent's feelings and behaviours toward the infant" (p. 65). In contrast, infant transferences are not explored.

Daniel Stern (1995) studies the "infant's representations viewed clinically" (p. 99). His examples refer mainly to constellations such as an infant's micro-depression with a depressed mother (idem) or her being the family "re-animator" (p. 102). Stern addresses the importance of the "infant's representations as (imagined) port of entry" (p. 134) for therapeutic interventions. Nevertheless, there are no accounts of specific infant–therapist relationships and no mention is made of infant transference.

Winnicott (1941) considered therapeutic work possible with mothers and babies, due to "the fluidity of the infant's personality and the fact that feelings and unconscious processes are formed then" (p. 232). He used a "set situation"

(p. 229) where he and the mother refrained from contributing to the clinical interchange, "so that what happens can fairly be put down to the child's account" (p. 230). He did not, however, describe any specific relating on the infants' part towards him; neither when illustrating their behaviours in the set situation, nor when treating a little girl by encouraging her to express aggression towards himself.

The Parent–Infant group at the Anna Freud Centre (Baradon *et al.*, 2005) illustrates their work with therapist–baby dialogues, in which the baby is a "partner in the therapeutic process" (p. 79). The aim is to "scaffold [the baby's] communications . . . and represent them to her parents" (p. 75). The vignettes indicate that the therapist tries to attain *contact* with the baby rather than to resolve infant transferences. The concepts "transference" (p. 119) and "positive and negative transference matrix" (p. 29) refer to how the parents' relationships with their own parents appear in relation to the therapist or the baby. Baby–analyst transferences are not mentioned.

The Tavistock clinicians build more explicitly on Kleinian and Bionian theories. A volume edited by Emanuel and Bradley (2008) illustrates their work with under-fives. Among its abundant references to transference, none concerns the kind I am discussing. The editors describe the baby's propensity to projective identifications, by which they mean those directed to the parents. The clinician may also be affected by them and use them to "consider their impact on her own emotional state, a helpful gauge of her client's state of mind" (p. 5). We do not find any discussion of how they might influence the infant–therapist relationship and, consequently, the term transference does not occur in this context. The intervention process is described as the therapist's attempt to "make contact with the infant or child, observing his play and attempting to understand the meaning of his communications, while also engaging the parent" (p. 6). This is not a description of infant transference. The therapist should be "sparing in addressing" the transference, by which is meant, again, the one emanating in the parent (p. 6). The same use of transference in connection with parents, not babies, is obvious in another chapter (Miller, 2008). Miller's point is that we have a limited mandate to work with the transference: the one from the parent. Similarly to the editors' introduction, she views countertransference as a valuable tool for understanding the predicaments of mother and baby, but the baby-therapist relationship is not delineated.

Another volume from the Tavistock Clinic focuses on infant work (Pozzi-Monzo & Tydeman, 2007). One chapter by Paul and Thomson-Salo on work with babies in groups describes how

> infants transfer onto us and the other group members' feelings and ideas that derive from their caregivers. The therapists become significant to the infants before the mothers do and how infants initially behave with the two of us [the therapists] is transferred from how they are with their mother.
>
> (p. 145)

This would indicate instances of infant transference as I define it. For example, a seven-month-old boy has a conflictual relationship with his mother. Smilingly, he touches the therapist's hand and mouths his finger, whereupon mother starts playing with him. "Some infants relate positively to us from the first, as though they have left aside the difficulties with their parents" (idem). In contrast to my vignettes, however, Paul and Thomson-Salo seem not to aim to interpret or resolve the baby's transference. They rather use it as a springboard to enhance mother–baby contact.

It is probable that the contrast between Paul and Thomson-Salo and me in our use of the term transference has to do with preconceptions and techniques. If one thinks babies leave aside difficulties with their parents while relating positively to the therapist, this could be boiled down to a simplified formula of what goes on in the baby's mind: 'Mum is bad but you, Doctor, you're good. That's why I prefer being with you.' In my preconception, a baby having difficulties with its mother is prone to a negative transference, according to another simplified formula: 'Doctor, you're bad just like Mum, that is, as I unconsciously and partially experience her. That's why I shun your eyes. Doing that might even help me get more relaxed with Mum.' Which view one takes is related to one's preconceptions. It also has to do with how much attention the analyst is paying to the baby's relationship with him and how much he is allowing negative feelings to become directed at him. This issue is intimately related to countertransference, as seen in my knocking the table with David.

In other papers (Thomson-Salo, 2007; Thomson-Salo & Paul, 2001; Thomson-Salo et al., 1999), these Melbourne clinicians' views come closer to mine but, as we shall see, they are not identical. Their idea of "direct work with the infant" is to enable the parents to "see more easily that their fantasies of having totally damaged or killed off the infant are not reality" (Thomson-Salo et al., 1999, p. 59). One clinician, Ann Morgan, suggests that parental projections may affect the infant negatively, that the therapist should make contact with the baby to understand "the experience from inside the infant's world rather than looking from outside as if it were inexplicable" (Thomson-Salo & Paul, 2001, p. 15) and that this aims at offering "the infant an experience (rather than the promise of a relationship)" (p. 16). This is described in terms of a mutual infant–therapist fascination and as a link between the two, in which the baby is viewed "as a subject in her own right which then allows a gap to be created between mother and baby, a space which allows growth" (p. 14). This gap will become "a transitional space" (p. 16).

The reason that a gap previously did not exist in the baby is often that the parent has identified him with "some internal object in the parent's mind rather than [having built] an empathic relationship with the infant" (p. 18). Once the therapist has created the space, s/he may work with parental projections and also "with the infant so that the mother sees her differently . . . the therapist becomes a container for the hate and the toxic projections for which the infant was previously the receptacle" (idem). Though these publications seemingly match my definition of infant transference, I note a difference; a therapist who is making a link with a baby is not necessarily aiming at creating a setting in which her transference to him may flourish and be talked about. I completely agree that infants are "subjects entitled to an intervention in their own right" (Thomson-Salo, 2007, p. 961). The question is if this implies that one regards – or does not regard – the infant's communications from a transference perspective and if one aims at resolving such a transference. The answer is determined by the therapist's preconceptions, as I delineated above.

The final Anglo-Saxon clinician I will refer to is Stella Acquarone (2004). She considers it "a resistance on the part of the therapist not to confront the baby's primitive transference and the countertransference" (p. 164). It is, however, hard to find examples of such confrontations. Even in the case of an eight-month-old boy (p. 188) who is calm with his mother but wary of the therapist, Acquarone handles this by pedagogy to the mother about his feelings rather than by addressing him. Thus, the baby's transference remains uninvestigated.

Among French analysts, Bernard Golse asks if "babies know how to transfer" (2006, p. 135). His cautious response stems from the inherent problems in attributing transference mechanisms to children who are too young for après-coup experiences (Golse & Roussillon, 2010). In other words, babies are too young to be able to retrospectively construct images of earlier interactions. He notes that if transferences do exist, the negative seem more visible than the positive. Golse asks if our often intense countertransference towards babies proves their capacities for transference. In the end, he leaves this question unanswered. Possibly, these French authors' après-coup perspective renders it more difficult to detect infant transference. As I see it, the concept of internal object makes it easier to explicate that babies such as Jennifer or David are able to harbour dreadful, part-object-like and un-assimilated internal "ghosts" and transfer them onto the therapist.

Some French clinicians work with a more direct baby address than is common in the Anglo-Saxon world. The most well-known was Françoise Dolto (1985), mentioned in Chapter 1 and 3. She addressed the baby since she was convinced that "everything can be said to a baby about things that may promote his perception of reality" (p. 95). Nevertheless, she did not view the baby's relationship with her in terms of transference. Though she aimed to make herself available to "the individual's most archaic drives" (Ledoux, 2006), that is, to the patient's transference, she did not, as far as I have learnt from her writings, apply this stance to the infant's relationship with her. The same impressions apply to her present-time compatriot, Myriam Szejer (2011).

One French-speaking analyst, Annette Watillon (1993), explicitly considers the baby's transference to her. She claims that all parent–infant analysts "agree on the intensity and immediacy of the baby's transference on to the therapist" (p. 1044), a surprising statement in view of my literature survey. She views the baby's "interference" as "a vital aspect of therapies . . . Even a tiny baby will play its part in the issues involved in the treatment" (p. 1038). She regards the therapeutic encounter with child and parent as one of "dramatisation . . . [a]

re-presentation [which] will allow each protagonist to effect a more tolerable (because detoxified) re-introjection of the relevant objects" (p. 1041). The baby transfers in order to find a different outcome to the conflict. She suggests the therapist should "understand, verbalise and demonstrate *to the parents* what the child is thereby staging" (p. 1044, italics added). Thus, Watillon's openness to baby transference does not imply that she addresses the baby. The reason is, as she writes, that it might arouse parental jealousy and collude with her own "unsatisfied infantile parts which seek love and understanding" (idem).

The Swedish analyst Johan Norman (2004) reported on a six-month-old boy. At three months, the parents were informed that he might have a severe illness. Later, they received reassuring information but the mother still worried and the boy was whimpering constantly and sleeping badly. When Norman spoke of the baby–analyst relationship, he referred to Bion's K link (1962a) and to projective identifications. He suggested, somewhat cautiously, the term transference to cover the boy's notion of a containing relationship with him. In contrast, he did not seem to conceive of the boy's panic as having a specific transference import.

To conclude, all the clinicians referred would probably agree with Barrows (2003) that "the prime aim of infant mental health work is the promotion of the infant's psychological well-being" and that "direct work with the infant might offer one way forward" (p. 286). Most of them would also agree with his observation that, paradoxically, very little such work has been undertaken. In my opinion, the infant's specific relationship with the therapist has been investigated even less. Consequently, the literature contains very few references to infant transference. When it is indeed considered, the observation is followed up by the therapist's comment to the *parent*, not by working it through with the baby. I see no other explanation than the fact that these therapists do not view the *child's* communications as signifying a transference with its own specificity and course, one that needs to be verbalized with its creator; the child.

## Case 3: Vance, nine months

So far, I have brought out two cases exemplifying *direct* infant transferences. This evokes the question of whether or not *indirect* transferences exist. The final case will investigate this and, if the answer is in the affirmative, how the two forms are connected.

Vance's parents are busy professionals. Mother Arlene has been on maternity leave and now the father, Henry, will take his share. Father and son will go to Arlene's home country to stay with Vance's grandmother. Arlene will visit them regularly but they wonder if the boy will miss his mother. They consult with me at the Child Health Centre to get advice. I meet a gentle mother and a conscientious though somewhat restless father. The project of visiting the mother's home country has already been cancelled, they tell me. Its raison d'être was Henry's anxiety of being alone with the boy: "I am used to a faster tempo than that of a baby. They say I was a hyperactive child." He wants to sit by his computer while taking care of Vance, but he is also worried and somewhat ashamed of his plan. I suggest he and Vance see me for some sessions, "to perhaps discover what is special about Vance's tempo and how it differs from yours".

In the first father–infant session the boy is anxiously clinging in father's lap, avoiding my eyes.

| | |
|---|---|
| *Father:* | This is quite unusual! |
| *Analyst to F:* | How did you feel coming here today? |
| *F:* | No problems. I thought this was going to be exciting! |
| *A:* | Last time you talked about how difficult it is being alone with Vance. |
| *F:* | Yeah, but that's already much better now. Now I can see his day-to-day progress. |

The father does not acknowledge any anxiety of seeing me. Later in the session, he speaks more openly of his guilt of prioritizing his work and the project of separating Vance and Arlene by bringing him to his grandmother.

At the second session, one week later, the boy is anxious again. He uses a pacifier, whines a little, clings to Dad and avoids me. The father gets stressed.

| | |
|---|---|
| *F to Vance:* | Are you scared, Vance, just like Dad was when we arrived today? |
| *A:* | What were you afraid of when coming to me? |
| *F:* | I don't know! Maybe that you, the expert, will discover that I'm not a good father. |
| *A:* | And what would be wrong with you as a father? |
| *F:* | I couldn't tell you. But I have the feeling you know it all! |
| | [Evidently, today father is less defensive about his fears of me, that is, his transference. After a while, he speaks of his own infancy.] |
| *F:* | Mum used to say that already at the delivery ward, I was rooting in a corner of the bed as if trying to get away from it. |
| *A:* | She implied that you were hyperactive? |
| *F:* | Mmm. |
| *A:* | It's as if you were branded already then. Now you think I will brand you as a bad father. |
| *F:* | It's even worse. It's as if I'm asking myself, "What does this man know about me that I don't know about myself"?! |

Our work with the father's negative transference, and his memories of negative attributions by his mother, bears fruit. At the third session one week later, Vance is looking at me calmly from his father's lap. The father is joking:

| | |
|---|---|
| *F:* | Today I'm not scared, so Vance is calm. I was thinking at home that maybe you don't know everything after all! |

[In this third session, my contact with Vance is smiling and lively. He starts playing with some wood blocks, which he hands to Henry and me. Henry starts speaking about his adolescence.]

*F:*   When I was 12 or 13 years old, Mum and Dad quarrelled. They stayed married but I sort of lost contact with my father who buried himself in work. These were troubling times for me.

[At exactly this point, Vance starts whining and clinging to his father. He avoids looking at me. This time, father neither gets upset nor tries to divert Vance's attention. He reflects:]

*F:*   It's remarkable how sensitive he is. That's encouraging – and scary. What if he gets friends who are not nice to him; will that cause him pain?

*A:*   What about *you* being sensitive?

*F:*   Well, I was considered a hard guy, but inside I was not.

Vance calms down and resumes playing with us. Ten minutes later, Henry returns to the theme of his childhood. He used to listen to his father's stories about nature. Positive expectations and sorrow blend in this story. He wants to do similar things with Vance in the future. Once again, Vance whines for a while, avoids me and clings to his father.

As long as Henry held back the painful adolescent memories, the resulting mixture of unconscious affect and defence was somehow communicated to Vance. This incomprehensible paternal gestalt disrupted the container–contained link between them. Vance handled the change in atmosphere by projecting this gestalt onto me. I became his phobic object while the father's lap was a safe haven. When father relaxed, the boy was OK with me again. Thus, Vance's transference was *indirect* in that it followed his father's transference. After some weeks, Henry had developed a stable trust in me. Meanwhile, Vance started playing with us. Smilingly, he kept handing out wooden blocks and taking them back again.

During the fourth session, a change occurred. Vance started walking proudly towards the door while Henry and I were looking warmly at him. After one metre's walk he stopped on the spot, turned around and flung into his father's lap while crying inconsolably. I did not understand the reasons for his change. Some weeks later, I realized that I had no more slots open at the Child Health Centre. I suggested we continue therapy at my private office and Henry accepted. The first session there, Henry said he appreciated its personal milieu – but Vance soon started crying. He avoided my eyes while looking through the window. As I followed him, I noticed the withering leaves outside. In my countertransference, a sad thought emerged: "This is the first autumn day of the year." As I remained in a sombre mood of transience, brevity and solitude my thoughts meandered to visualizing a baby sent away to a foreign and faraway place. Now I began to focus on a "detail" that the parents had referred to earlier but we had not elaborated on. When Vance was seven months old they took him to Arlene's home country. Father and son remained there while she returned to Stockholm.

A:          I'm thinking about that trip when Vance was seven months old. We
            haven't talked about it actually.
F:          I don't want to think about it! It was not a good trip.
A:          Why not?
F:          This thing about the foreign language, it was a new setting for Vance.
            Everybody was nice to him but he missed Mum. Arlene and I haven't
            been honest to ourselves; when we came home after two weeks Vance
            was quiet and sad. Arlene was sad too, but we didn't dare talk about it.
A:          Perhaps Vance experienced the move to my office similarly to his move
            to Mum's home country, especially after she returned to Stockholm.

Some sessions later, Vance wants to be the intrepid explorer again. He looks
proudly at me, walks towards the door, gets panicky while staring at me and then
runs to Dad. Henry becomes amazed but not excessively worried.

F:          He has many feelings inside. I know he must go through them!
            [Similar situations of Vance leaving us a metre or two, getting into a
            panic, staring at me in fear and rushing to Dad, recur many times. On
            one such occasion, I address him:]
A to V:     Maybe you're afraid that I'll take you to Mum's country. You were there
            once with Dad.
            [Vance is looking earnestly at me.]
A to F:     Perhaps it's a good idea to tell Vance what happened there.
F to V:     At first, you and I were with Mum and Granny and the others. Remember
            the chickens we were looking at? Then Mum went home and you and I
            remained. You were sleeping with Granny and I visited you much, but
            not as much as I should have done. I didn't know better!

The boy calms down while listening to his father. According to our terms indirect
and direct transference, Vance's fear of me now matches the latter. It seemed to
spring from un-elaborated emotions linked with his separation from his mother
two months earlier. They were heralded in his panic by the door at the Child
Health Centre, but the move to my office gave them new impetus. This awakened
my concordant identification (Racker, 1968) in the countertransference, in
the form of my autumnal sadness. As I started addressing Henry about their
journey, he got in emotional contact with hitherto suppressed worries about it.
Due to the parents' guilt of the journey and the separation, the boy's reactions
were insufficiently contained. Vance's direct transference seemed rooted in a
projection of a nameless dread (Bion, 1962a) onto me. I thus came to represent
his uncontained separation trauma, perhaps mixed with a fear that I would separate
him from the parents again.

During this "second act" of the therapy, Vance's fear of me erupted now and
then. I confirmed to him that he was afraid of being sent away, of being left alone
without Mum and of remaining with me as a threatening figure. I also conveyed

that all his feelings were accepted by his father and me. The mother later took part in a session and confirmed that the boy had been quite different when he returned home with his father. She now addressed her bad feelings about it. After some weeks of work, Vance was able to look at me with candour and joy. His negative transference waned and therapy was ended after 22 sessions when he was 13 months old. The father asked for a follow-up when Vance was one and a half years old. He showed no fear or apprehension when meeting me and seemed to be a happy chap according to the father's reports from their home and the nursery.

## Final comments

Once we have conceptualized an infant's emotions vis-à-vis the analyst as transference, we must logically ask if it may occur in other situations. To answer, I have differentiated between transference-like phenomena and transference. I reserved the latter term for the analytic situation, which is specifically constructed to boost such reactions and to provide the instrument needed for investigating them. To be true, if an infant looks in terror at a stranger on the bus, it might occur because she is projecting an internal object to him – but we lack the tools for investigating it. In contrast, if a baby is crying during a Child Health Centre visit, we can ask mother how she is feeling about seeing us. Maybe she will indicate that she is anxious and thus, the baby's crying seems more comprehensible. The clinician must discern if such behaviour is part of a relationship disturbance or rather a transitory indirect reaction to the mother's anxiety.

As with all psychoanalytic concepts, "direct" and "indirect" infant transference simplify a complex clinical reality. Nevertheless, the following could be stated: the more we observe a direct negative infant transference, the more we need to address the baby. Jennifer's persistent fear demonstrates this. During Vance's indirect transference, it was more important to address the father about his fear of me. When a direct transference emerged connected with Vance's early separation, it was essential to address the boy about it. This conclusion was also substantiated by the randomized controlled trial (RCT) of MIP treatments that I will report in the next chapter. Half of the babies seemed negatively affected by the relational disturbance with their mothers. This subgroup improved more if treated with MIP instead of traditional Child Health Centre nurse care. Interviews with the analysts confirmed that they had sought to establish a relationship with these troubled babies and investigate its emotional nature. In terms of my terminology, they had focused on the infant transferences if and when they appeared.

I emphasize that far from all babies respond with a direct transference. One precondition for it to emerge is that the clinician focuses on the baby's relationship with him. Otherwise, her internal objects will not become projected onto him – or the clinician will not intuit that her crying and shunning represent such a mechanism. It merits another study to decide the import of other factors, such as the impact of the child's and/or the parent's disorder. I would guess that direct transferences will occur mainly among children who are on the verge of becoming enmeshed in "baby worries" with the parent. As it happened in Vance's case, therapy seemed to prevent this from occurring.

To sum up, I asked in the chapter's beginning if transference in babies exists at all, or perhaps only as a redundant phenomenon to be left un-addressed by the analyst. Alternatively, it might exist and needs to be addressed through analytic interventions; I have provided arguments and clinical illustrations suggesting that it sometimes exists. If we use a technique focusing on parental transference or on merely making contact with the baby, we might regard it as redundant and leave it unaddressed. However, if our technique opens up for a dialogue with both baby and mother, we sometimes run into clinical situations in which the infant develops a specific emotional relationship with us. Since it seems to ensue from the baby's projections of internal and often terrifying objects, it merits to be labelled transference and to be talked about with the baby. My argument is simply one of urgency; if a baby is staring at me in terror I must handle it like any other overwhelming situation; through containment and interventions.

Our clinical work should be adapted according to the transference types, which may shift during treatment. The two types – direct and indirect – may help us understand the baby's predicament and when and how to address her. These treatments provide new empirical material to an old debate in child analysis, that is, whether transference is rooted in early development and if it appears at all in children. I answer both issues in the affirmative; even infants may form transferences of different kinds.

# Chapter 11

# Mother–infant psychoanalytic treatment

## Does it work?

By now, some readers might have got the impression: "This MIP treatment seems interesting. All cases related in the book improved. Indeed, MIP must be quite efficacious!" It is of course easy to object to such conclusions: are my reports reliable? Have I not "forgotten" to report unsuccessful cases? Or, have I only reported on such areas in which improvement was evident while skipping the others? Have I checked that my impressions are valid? For example, what do I mean by stating that Beate was weaned "successfully"? Then, what about objectivity; perhaps the case vignettes overrate my achievements? Finally, let us assume that all *my* cases were true successes. What about other clinicians using the same method; would they reach similar results?

Such questions form the basis of a critique against the kind of single-case presentations that pervade this book. Its impeccable logic has led to the following argument: "Sure enough, psychotherapy might be interesting for anyone undertaking it, but its general efficacy remains scientifically un-proved." Consequently, one demands that we scrutinize psychotherapy via a scientific method called "the randomized controlled trial" or "RCT". Its logic is simple: within a strictly defined and controlled paradigm, participants are randomized to treatment A or B. One will not find that A is always successful whereas B is worthless, but perhaps that the probability (indicated by the "p-value") is high enough to make us conclude that A seems better than B concerning these measures, for this sample, and under these conditions with these therapists. If a few RCTs reach similar results we conclude that A, the "index method", is "evidence-based". The RCT has become the shibboleth separating efficacious and scientifically proven treatments from those that are declared to have no established efficacy. Today, politicians and administrators tend to increasingly support only the former methods.

If we want to compare drugs against, say, a headache, a "double-blind" RCT is logically impeccable. After all, who would take sugar-pills instead of Aspirin against such malaise? However, the RCT paradigm also opens up to many psychotherapists' critique. A double-blind procedure in our area is impossible, since a participant will know what kind of therapy she is taking part in. Second, how do we know that our measures cover the changes we wish to achieve, and how do we measure psychotherapeutic success? In a critical lecture Bruno

Falissard (2012) claimed that "the methodological purity of RCT is a myth" and that its paradigm is "a totem with a frail basement". This did not prevent him from emphasizing that we must submit therapies to such scrutiny – provided we interpret the results wisely.

Over the years, I have realized that psychoanalytic practice and RCT research have more in common than is immediately evident. In psychoanalysis, as I argued in Chapter 2, we move about in inferential circuits. We all learnt about classical logic in school: "All humans throughout history have died." The induction runs: all humans are mortal. The deduction runs: "Jim is human. So, he is mortal." The abduction is trickier: "Humans are mortal. Jim just died. So, he was human." However, when I check it out, I find a dead creature on the street. People call it Jim. It has a four-legged body with a tail and a mane. I must now change my abduction: "Jim is dead but does not look human. He was something else. I must find out what." I take a closer look and conclude: "Jim was a horse."

Let us apply the inferential circle to a clinical case. Baby Karen in Chapter 4 is crying. Her mother Miranda has an inductive idea that crying babies are always sad. When Karen is crying during the session, Miranda deduces that her daughter is sad again. I get another impression; Karen is angry. This is because I have another inductive idea than Miranda; crying babies may be sad, desperate, enraged, tired, hungry, etc. To find out, we probe deeper into the matter. Since I feel Karen is angry rather than sad, I tell her about it. In response, she roars and I conclude, "I refute Miranda's deduction that Karen is sad. She is angry". The next time she is crying I may conclude, "Now, Karen is angry again". However, this time I notice her sad look, which makes me correct my deduction by abductive reasoning. In the end, I will tell myself, "Sometimes when Karen roars she is angry, sometimes she is sad. I wish to find out what differentiates the two situations".

RCTs obey the same logic. One reads my case vignettes and notices favourable results. The induction runs, "Mother and babies with baby worries improve from MIP treatment". This gives rise to a hypothesis, which we might test in an RCT. However, this will not be as easy as in our Jim example. Instead, we use statistical methods to calculate the probability that our induction is correct, that patients generally improve from MIP. To this end, we create two groups who receive either MIP or therapy X. Then we compare the results between the two groups. Alternatively, we might think: "This child and his mother got better. This proves they attended MIP." But when we check it out on our RCT data sheet, we discover that they had attended X and not MIP! This raises new questions: "Some patients get better from X and others from MIP. Which factors differentiate success of either treatment? If we could find out beforehand, we might recommend every patient the treatment she is most liable to benefit from!" This would lead to a better understanding of therapeutic specificity (Orlinsky, Rönnestad & Willutzki, 2004); which treatment suits which patients the best on which kind of outcome measures?

These deliberations might lead us to agree with the resigned commentary by Hans Sachs in Richard Wagner's (1868) opera *die Meistersinger von Nürnberg*, act II:3. He is trying to grasp the riddle behind the beautiful singing style of Walther von Stolzing, the young hero:

I feel it and cannot understand it . . .
and if I grasp it wholly,
I cannot measure it!
But then, how should I grasp
what seemed to me immeasurable?

Sachs concludes his task is hopeless – whereas I conclude that an RCT might yield results that are relevant to therapists and help improve our practice. The condition is that the study is well-performed, that its measures reflect clinically important areas and, last but not least, that we interpret our results wisely. We will not be able to claim that therapy A is always superior to B. Instead, we may find that A is generally better – or that for some patients, A is better whereas for others B will stand the best chance. My Aspirin/sugar simile might provoke the opposition that "the medical model does not adequately explain the benefits of psychotherapy" (Wampold, 2001, p. 203). I agree, but I claim that a well-performed study might indeed help explain *some* aspects of psychotherapy benefits. To be true it cannot explain all effects, but this objection applies to single-case reports as well.

I take this position, in contrast to psychoanalysts who object that quantitative assessments can neither cover complex therapeutic outcomes nor elucidate the intricate ways by which results are achieved. Falissard (2012) adds that it is difficult to transpose the results of one psychotherapy RCT to another. I agree that the assignment procedure does not reflect everyday clinical reality; cases are assigned to treatment by chance, whereas an analyst recommends treatment only after careful consideration. But, if our RCT uses a wise combination of quantitative and qualitative assessments – and if we interpret its results wisely and cautiously – it may be relevant to psychoanalytic practice. What the RCT paradigm *cannot* do, however, is to illuminate details of the therapeutic process. For this we need to elaborate case vignettes and clinical theory, just like I have done throughout the book.

## Meta-analyses of parent–infant psychotherapy

I will briefly relate some major comparative studies on parent–infant psychotherapy. In a meta-analysis on treatments for postpartum depression, Dennis (2004) remarked on methodological problems, which made many studies' results difficult to ascertain. Singleton (2005) meta-analyzed 25 studies of parent–infant interventions. The treatment differences were small on infant mental health and development, whereas parent–infant relationship and parent ability often reached significant levels. She also analyzed moderator effects and found that study quality, therapist training and psychodynamic methods yielded better effect sizes for the index treatment. Unexpectedly, lengthy therapies seemed less effective, either because they were "no longer effective for older infants, the families that receive long term therapy could have more difficulties, or the effects of parent–infant interaction interventions do not last" (p. 96).

## Specific studies

### Mother–infant psychotherapy

In a Swiss study (Robert-Tissot *et al.*, 1996), mothers and infants were randomized to mother–infant psychotherapy (Fraiberg, 1987) or Interaction Guidance (IG; McDonough, 2004). Follow-ups were made post-treatment and after six and 12 months. Significant effects *independent* of treatment modality were found at six months on maternal sensitivity, infant behaviour and symptoms. Maternal representations did not improve significantly. The study's large age span (2–30 months) makes it hard to interpret the results. Furthermore, therapies were brief, six sessions on average. This puts a question mark on the differential effects; IG brought greater improvement on maternal sensitivity, while mother–infant therapy increased maternal self-esteem. The results were "consistent with expectations often expressed in psychotherapy outcome research: the effects common to both treatments are greater than their specific effects" (Robert-Tissot *et al.*, 1996, p. 111).

A Canadian study (Cohen *et al.*, 1999) compared Watch, Wait and Wonder therapy (WWW) with mother–infant therapy *ad modum* Fraiberg. The WWW therapists advised mothers to follow the infant's lead. This was supposed to improve parental competence more than if one interpreted the unconscious determinants to their child relation, as in the Fraiberg model. Treatments consisted of about 14 once-weekly sessions. Immediately post-treatment, WWW was more efficacious in improving attachments, Bayley mental scores and maternal satisfaction, but not sensitivity or responsiveness. Both therapies equally reduced mother-reported presenting problems and stress and also improved mother–child relationships. Follow-ups were made six months after terminations (Cohen, Lojkasek, Muir, Muir & Parker, 2002). For the "Fraiberg therapies", some improvements emerged only now. Its focus on insight had perhaps left the mothers distressed in the beginning of therapy.

A US study (Lieberman, Weston & Pawl, 1991) investigated 12-month-old children in a high-risk Latino immigrant sample. Securely attached children formed the "secure control group". Anxious children were randomized to mother–infant psychotherapy or an "anxious control group". Therapies lasted one year. At 24 months, significant effects favoured the therapy group on most items; its scores now reached those of the secure control group.

## Depressed mothers

Depressed mothers (O'Hara, Stuart, Gorman & Wenzel, 2000) were randomized to 12 sessions of interpersonal psychotherapy (Klerman, Weismann, Rounsaville & Chevron, 1984) or a waiting list control. The researchers used questionnaires and an initial diagnostic interview (Hamilton, 1967) followed up by telephone. Intent-to-treat analyses yielded effects for the therapy group except on infant symptoms, perhaps because mothers had reported little dissatisfaction in this area and therapies did not focus on their relationship with the baby.

A group in Cambridge, UK (Cooper, Murray, Wilson & Romaniuk, 2003; Murray, Cooper, Wilson & Romaniuk, 2003) investigated if therapy for depressed mothers might improve dyadic relationships and child development. They were randomized to cognitive-behavioural therapy, psychodynamic mother–infant therapy, non-directive counselling (Holden, Sagovsky & Cox, 1989) or routine primary care. The three active treatment groups received ten sessions at home when the baby was 8–18 weeks. The active treatment groups lowered their depression scores immediately post-treatment, while only the mother–infant therapy group improved on the clinical interviews. Follow-ups at a child age of nine months, one and a half years and five years showed limited effects on mother-reported relationship problems, and the psychodynamic group even reported more behavioural problems post-treatment. Sensitivity only improved among mothers at social risk who received counselling. Thus, most outcomes failed to show any benefit of the active treatments.

In another study (Clark, Tluczek & Wenzel, 2003), depressed mothers with babies were assigned to a mother–infant therapy group, interpersonal individual therapy or a waiting list control group. Therapies focused on depression and baby relationships. Follow-ups were made three months after treatment. Both therapies improved maternal depression, perception of the infant, positive affect and verbalization. Though the active treatments often included the baby they did not show effects on infant interactive contributions.

## Conclusions and implications for the RCT on MIP

Psychotherapies yielded effects mostly on mothers' wellbeing. Effects on the infant were not always thoroughly investigated and, if found, they were weaker. Most studies did not use assessment interviews. When designing the RCT, I concluded that interviews are less reliable than objective assessments, but on the other hand they give a first-hand view of the relationship and the genesis of symptoms. The interviewer can also use qualitative assessments for analyzing differential treatment effects. I thus decided to use interviews for assessing diagnoses, qualitative categories and outcomes.

Concerning the age range, since MIP was developed for pre-verbal children we only included infants below one and a half years of age. As concerns the mothers, therapy might affect not only depression but also other kinds of psychopathology and stress. I therefore included questionnaires on global psychopathology, stress and depression. To avoid incomplete dropout-analyses, we decided on so-called intent-to-treat analyses. This statistical method includes cases that leave the study before termination. Every therapy mode thus has to bear the brunt of its drop-out cases (Chakraborty & Gu, 2009).

Which method should we use to compare with MIP? One might argue in different directions; since MIP is a well-described method one should compare it with one of similar standard and theoretical clarity. For various reasons, however, such a design was unfortunately not feasible. Another argument implies that since MIP is a new method, we should first compare it with the usual mode of taking care of baby worries. Comparisons with "treatments-as-usual" have been criticized (Kendall, Holmbeck & Verduin, 2004). For ethical reasons, they must have an acceptable quality. I knew this was the case with standard Swedish Child Health Centre care; it has a long and proud tradition including training nurses to pay attention to psychological distress in parents and infants. Kendall and co-workers also argue that one must ascertain which factors in the respective treatments contribute to differences in effects. For this purpose, I used interviews where mothers could tell me about their treatments and what they felt about them. I compared these with psychoanalyst interviews to understand the therapeutic specificity of MIP. Practical circumstances prevented me from conducting similar interviews with the nurses.

Other considerations regarding the design sprang from my clinical experience. I guessed that the assignment procedure might create emotional reactions, which I must contain during the interview. This was ethically mandatory and would also lessen the drop-out rate. Second, outcome instruments should comprise verbal communications and non-verbal interactive behaviour. This was a consequence of my focus on the different semiotic levels of communications and symptoms. Third, babies and mothers should also be described and categorized qualitatively.

## The RCT of MIP: a summary

The RCT set out from the Mother–Infant Psychoanalysis Project of Stockholm (MIPPS), which began in 2001 when a group of analysts started meeting for supervision and developing MIP practice and theory under the aegis of its inventor, Johan Norman. After his death in 2005, seven analysts continued as a peer-supervision group. During the years of the RCT, I left the group to uphold an "outsider" perspective. The RCT was designed to compare their treatments with regular Swedish Child Health Centre (CHC) care. The study issued from the Division of Child and Adolescent Psychiatry at Karolinska Institutet with Per-Anders Rydelius, Rolf Sandell and Andrzej Werbart as supervisors. Professor Rydelius is a child psychiatrist and head of this Child Psychiatry Division while Sandell and Werbart are professors in psychology at the Linköping and Stockholm Universities, respectively, and also psychoanalysts.

Our quantitative instruments will be described cursorily, since they were detailed in the RCT reports (Salomonsson & Sandell, 2011a, 2011b). All expert-rated measures were checked for reliability by testing intra-class correlations (ICC) or inter-coder agreements. These figures, which always reached acceptable levels, can be found in the reports. Other instruments were devised or amended for the RCT. I will describe them in depth and illustrate with clinical examples: (a) an interview format quantifying the impact of the mother's past and present experiences, (b) ideal types (Wachholz & Stuhr, 1999) of mothers and babies, (c) maternal suitability for psychoanalysis and (d) the analyst's adherence to the MIP method. Finally, I will submit some recommendations for future researchers setting up RCTs on similar samples. I will also relate how the RCT led me and the analysts to develop our practice. This discussion will form a bridge to an upcoming volume on parent–infant consultations at Child Health Centres and how supervisions of nurses may improve their clinical acumen and courage.

## Recruitment

The study targeted mothers with "baby worries"; they were concerned about the baby's functioning, themselves *qua* mothers or about their child relationship. Together with their babies below one and a half years of age they were recruited from CHCs, the delivery ward at the Karolinska University Hospital and advertisements on parental internet sites. To meet inclusion criteria worries should be present for two weeks, and the mother should live in Stockholm and speak Swedish reasonably well. Exclusion criteria were maternal psychosis or substance abuse if future collaboration seemed improbable.

Initially, 214 mothers contacted me and were interviewed by telephone. A majority declined participation because their concerns had abated. Some mothers told me they had just "wanted to support research" but did not experience any "real problems". I interviewed the remaining 90 mothers with babies at my office. At the end of the interview ten mothers declined randomization; they felt their worries did not warrant a possible assignment to MIP. The remaining 80 dyads were randomized upon maternal informed consent. I took care to enable mothers to vent any feelings about the assignment. Immediately after the interviews, four cases dropped out without providing data and one was in treatment at project termination. The statistical intent-to-treat analyses could thus use 75 cases out of 80.

In brief, the sample was socially low-risk and psychiatrically medium-risk. The typical mother was a 33-year old primipara with a post-A level education and living with the child's father. She had a history of depression, anxiety or eating disorder. The typical baby was delivered vaginally at full-term, though caesareans were unexpectedly frequent. The baby was now five months old and no serious somatic illness had been diagnosed.

## Instruments

### Self-rated measures

#### MOTHER-REPORT QUESTIONNAIRES

Maternal distress was rated on three self-report questionnaires; the Edinburgh Postnatal Depression Scale (EPDS; Cox *et al.*, 1987), the Swedish Parental Stress Questionnaire (SPSQ; Östberg, Hagekull & Wettergren, 1997) and the Symptom Check List-90 on general psychological distress (SCL-90; Derogatis, 1994; Fridell, Cesarec, Johansson & Malling Thorsen, 2002). The EPDS is validated on Swedish samples (Wickberg & Hwang, 1997). It has ten items on three-step scales. The SPSQ is a Swedish modified version of the Parenting Stress Index (Abidin, 1990) with 34 items rated on five-step scales. The SCL-90 subsumes symptoms into a mean score, the General Severity Index (GSI). Internal consistencies on all questionnaires were satisfactory.

To assess the infant's social and emotional functioning, mothers used a Swedish translation of the Ages and Stages Questionnaire: Social-Emotional (ASQ:SE; Squires, Bricker, Heo & Twombly, 2002). We used mean scores to enable comparisons across different infant age groups. The range was 0–13.4, where 0 was optimal. In a separate study (Salomonsson & Sleed, 2010) we investigated its inter-correlations with our other instruments. Its scores were closely associated with self-reported maternal distress rather than, as we had expected, with ratings of the dyads' interactions or relationships. It thus seemed that mothers' psychological distress, at least in this clinical sample, influenced how they rated their infants' functioning.

### Expert-rated measures

#### MOTHER–INFANT RELATIONSHIP

I used the Parent–Infant Relationship Global Assessment Scale (PIR-GAS; ZERO-TO-THREE, 2005) to make a global judgment of "overall relationship functioning, without regard to whether relationship impairments arise from the infant, the caregiver, or the unique fit between the two" (Boris, Zeanah, Larrieu, Scheeringa & Heller, 1998, p. 296). The PIR-GAS is part of a larger diagnostic instrument, the DC 0–3:R with five axes. Axis I assesses primary diagnoses such as regulatory, sleep or feeding disorders. Axis II covers the relational dimension by the Relational Problems Checklist (RPCL) and the PIR-GAS. Axis III concerns medical and developmental disorders, and Axis IV psychosocial stress factors. Axis V taps the child's emotional and developmental functioning. I assessed mothers and babies on all axes but V – but as an outcome instrument I only used the PIR-GAS, since it is the only quantitative instrument within this diagnostic system. PIR-GAS scores may range from 0 to 99, from "documented maltreatment" to "well-adapted". I made ratings from the video-taped intake interviews without knowing the questionnaire scores or the interaction ratings. Inter-rater reliabilities, as checked by an independent parent–infant psychologist outside "the psychoanalytic world", were excellent.

## MOTHER–INFANT INTERACTION

Ten-minute video-recordings were assessed by two independent and un-informed clinicians with substantial infant experience. They were trained and certified by the constructor of the Emotional Availability Scales (EAS; Biringen, Robinson & Emde, 1998). The dimensions are maternal sensitivity, structuring, non-intrusiveness and non-hostility, plus infant responsiveness and involvement. In line with the recent edition (Biringen, 2009) I transformed all scores to range from 0 to 1, with 1 implying optimal behaviour. Non-hostility was omitted due to low inter-rater reliability. ICCs for the remaining subscales were acceptable.

## THE ANALYSTS' TREATMENT ADHERENCE

We needed to certify that the therapists actually provided the kind of treatment they were supposed to. For the CHC group, I had to restrict myself to asking mothers at the follow-up interviews what kind of treatments they had received and their thoughts about it. I knew that the MIP analysts met weekly for super-vision and for maintaining treatment adherence. Thus, their mode of working was rather homogenous. To quantify adherence and investigate the treatment processes, I interviewed each analyst and mother after treatment had ended. I set up nine items regarding contact and containment of the child, reliance on interpretative interventions, awareness of negative maternal transference and ability to uphold a working alliance. I rated the items on a scale of 1 to 4 (optimal) and the maximum score was 36. I did not check with another rater for reliability. Instead, I compared scores between each mother and analyst to get information on therapies from two sources instead of only one. On the other hand one might object that ratings by a sole rater can be biased. Research methodology always implies compromises.

## THE MOTHER'S SUITABILITY FOR PSYCHOANALYSIS

Mothers differed in their motivation to work in psychoanalysis; if they were psychologically oriented or attributed experiences to external factors, if they focused on symptom relief or understanding and if they seemed patient or eager to obtain instant results. I condensed these impressions into one ordinal variable on a four-point scale, from "dubious" to "excellent" suitability. We hypothesized that it would positively predict mainly mother-related outcomes.

## THE INTERVIEW OF THE MOTHER'S EXPERIENCE (I-ME)

The intake interview lasted two hours with the baby present, including an interaction recording and a randomization procedure. I assessed how the mother experienced her past and present life, *qua* daughter to her parents, spouse and mother. Other items focused on the child's behaviour. My semi-structured interviews were psychoanalytically oriented, collecting the mother's verbal statements and spontaneous emotional expressions. I thought the baby's presence would influence mothers to express themselves more spontaneously.

Some mothers worried about their marital or family relationships. Others told of trauma or psychiatric disorders in childhood and young adulthood. Many had been treated for depression, anxiety or anorexia. When speaking of their pregnancy, some expressed indifference or anxiety. Others told of terrible deliveries. Mothers also worried about child feeding and sleeping problems or about their marriage. I assumed such experiences might predict the dyad's development and therefore devised a method for quantifying them.

I set up four major aspects, which several studies have shown to predict the dyad's development (for details, see Salomonsson & Sandell, 2012): maternal psychological well-being, mothering, support and the baby's well-being. For each aspect, five items were set up. "Maternal well-being" covered anxiety pre- and post-delivery and at present, as well as the mother's guilt and self-esteem. "Mothering" referred to her experiences of delivery and breastfeeding, if her feelings for the baby seemed integrated, if she described her baby as a person in his own right and was insightful about her history's influence on their relationship. "Support" included her confidence in me, the CHC staff, the baby's father and her parents. "Baby's well-being" referred to somatic health, sleep, appetite, mood and the relationship with its mother. I formulated each item as a positive statement, and then assessed on a four-point scale whether my impressions fit with them or not. A mean score, the I-ME score, was calculated. Our hypothesis was that it would add information beyond questionnaires and video assessments. Specifically, we thought the mothers' experiences would tell us something about the dyad's future development. Since some cases received psychotherapy and others did not, we hypothesized that I-ME scores would differentially predict dyadic interactions among these two subgroups.

## THE MATERNAL AND INFANT IDEAL TYPES

There were other differences between dyads that I could not subsume under the I-ME score. I refer to those impressions we clinicians gather during daily work. Some mothers stood out as anxious, helpless and filled with less mature expectations as to what kind of help they wanted. Others seemed more reflective and guessed they were adding something negative to their relationship with the baby, though without understanding how. Therapists learn to respect the individuality of each patient – yet clinical experience teaches us that some patients resemble each other. This is a kind of inductive reasoning, a way of sorting experiences into classes. "Good" and "bad" internal objects would be a similar case in point. *Nota bene*, unless such inductions are followed up by deductions and abductions they remain unproved conclusions, delusions or just prejudices.

I gathered my impressions of mothers and babies into "ideal types" (Wachholz & Stuhr, 1999). This concept was introduced by the sociologist Max Weber (1904) and implies an effort to put together typical instances of phenomena in the world of ideas. If I use the example "British gentleman", we realize that "ideal" has nothing to do with "perfectionism", moral superiority or statistical averages. Ideal types rather imply clustering one's impressions on a *qualitative* basis and to support the clusters on similarities along several dimensions. An ideal type is based on "certain elements common to most cases of the given phenomena" (Wikipedia, 2012). To some extent, the method has been used in psychotherapy research (Leuzinger-Bohleber, Stuhr, Ruger & Beutel, 2003; Lindner, 2006; Philips, Werbart, Wennberg & Schubert, 2007).

# Results

## Pre-treatment data

Table 11.1 illustrates the sample's psychological distress and dyadic dysfunctioning. For several instruments norm data were available, as indicated by a–g in the table. When we compared these figures with our sample, we concluded that our mean pre-treatment scores were at clinical levels across most dimensions.

## Treatment data

The number of cases lost at follow-up was equal in the two treatment groups, about ten per cent. This indicates that CHC mothers were *not* generally more disappointed than the MIP mothers with their assignment. This was also supported by the fact that pre-treatment data were generally more optimal in the CHC group. The low attrition rates satisfied our ethical concerns (Kendall *et al.*, 2004) and increased the study's face validity.

In the introduction to this book I accounted for Swedish CHC care routines, with regular nurse calls and paediatrician check-ups including efforts at detecting maternal depression. At the follow-up interviews, I learnt that brief therapies had been instituted for one third of mothers in the CHC group: cognitive behavioural or psychodynamic therapy, brief mother–infant therapy or supportive contacts, never exceeding five sessions.

The MIP mothers continued with CHC care as well. In addition they were treated by analysts (never by me). They received a median of 23 MIP sessions, two to three times weekly. The mean adherence scores of 29 indicated that the analysts had adhered to MIP reasonably well. The analysts with the highest scores had been in good contact with the baby and described him with insight and in

*Table 11.1* Pre-treatment data. Prevalence (%) or mean scores with standard deviations (SD)

| Measure | MIP | CHCC | Reference data |
|---|---|---|---|
| EPDS | 12.24 (4.64) | 11.51 (4.80) | 5.65[a], 6.92[b] |
| ASQ:SE | 2.03 (1.15) | 1.90 (1.17) | 0.87[c] |
| PIR-GAS | 68.0 (11.4) | 69.6 (12.9) | |
| SPSQ | 3.01 (0.49) | 2.92 (0.60) | 2.5[d] |
| GSI | 0.99 (0.61) | 0.96 (0.50) | 0.45[e], 0.34[f] |
| EAS Mother: sensitivity | 0.56 (.14) | 0.60 (.14) | |
| EAS Mother: structuring | 0.67 (.15) | 0.71 (.14) | |
| EAS Mother: non-intrusiveness | 0.82 (.16) | 0.78 (.20) | |
| EAS Infant: responsiveness | 0.60 (.18) | 0.67 (.19) | |
| EAS Infant: involvement | 0.59 (.20) | 0.64 (.22) | |
| DC 0–3:R, Axis 1 diagnosis | 19% | 8% | 18[g] |
| DC 0–3:R, Axis 2 RPCL notation | 81% | 86% | 8.5[g] |
| DC 0–3:R, Axis 3 diagnosis | 16% | 3%* | |
| DC 0–3:R, Axis 4 stressors | 62% | 87%* | |

Note. MIP = Mother–Infant Psychoanalytic treatment. CHCC = Child Health Centre Care. EPDS = the Edinburgh Postnatal Depression Scale. ASQ:SE = the Ages and Stages Questionnaire: Social-Emotional. PIR-GAS = the Parent–Infant Relationship Global Assessment Scale. SPSQ = the Swedish Parental Stress Questionnaire. GSI = the General Severity Index of the Symptom Check List-90. EAS = the Emotional Availability Scales. DC 0–3:R = the Diagnostic Classification ZERO-TO-THREE, Revised Edition. RPCL = the Relationship Problems Checklist.

*p < 0.05 (between-groups)
n = 38 for MIP and 37 for CHCC, except for the EAS (n = 33 and 30)
[a](Seimyr, Edhborg, Lundh & Sjögren, 2004)
[b](Wickberg & Hwang, 1997)
[c](Squires, Bricker & Twombly, 2004) (mean scores/item of "no-risk" infants < 1 year)
[d](Östberg et al., 1997)
[e](Fridell et al., 2002)
[f](Börjesson, Ruppert & Bågedahl-Strindlund, 2005)
[g](Skovgaard et al., 2008)

detail. They preferred a high frequency of sessions, since this would facilitate containment. On the other hand, they were flexible if frequency had to be adjusted according to the mother's life situation. Non-optimal scores often implied an insufficient working alliance with the mother or the analyst's failure to perceive her negative transference.

## Outcomes

Follow-up interviews were made six months after the intake interviews. Table 11.2 shows that MIP effects were more advantageous on the EPDS, the EAS sensitivity,

Table 11.2 Mixed-model analyses comparing treatment effects of MIP and CHC care

| Outcomes | F | p | Cohen's d | Becker's D |
|---|---|---|---|---|
| EPDS | 5.894 | 0.018 | 0.39 | 0.57 |
| ASQ:SE | 1.255 | 0.266 | 0.20 | 0.25 |
| PIR-GAS | 8.210 | 0.006 | 0.58 | 0.84 |
| SPSQ | 3.901 | 0.052 | 0.14 | 0.37 |
| GSI | 2.038 | 0.158 | 0.25 | 0.11 |
| Sensitivity | 4.872 | 0.031 | 0.42 | 0.67 |
| Structuring | 1.718 | 0.195 | 0.15 | 0.36 |
| Non-intrus. | 0.039 | 0.844 | 0.27 | 0.02 |
| Responsive. | 2.701 | 0.105 | 0.17 | 0.47 |
| Involve. | 0.444 | 0.508 | 0.10 | 0.22 |

Acronyms: See Table 1.

the PIR-GAS and nearly significant on the SPSQ. Effect sizes were small to moderate. Compared with other studies (Lieberman et al., 1991; Murray et al., 2003), our CHC group was far from a "no-treatment" control group; many nurses focused on psychological issues and, as said, one third of the mothers received additional psychological support. This might partly conceal a difference in efficacy between MIP and CHC and thus dampen the "real" effect sizes of MIP.

We were also interested in finding out if duration or frequency of therapy influenced outcomes, not the least since Singleton (2005) had found longer therapies to yield less optimal results. In fact, neither duration nor frequency influenced efficacy. This does not allow us to conclude that brief treatments were equally efficacious in general. The interviews indicated that mothers with the lengthiest treatments had a history of severe depression or anxiety states. This added an extra load to their suffering and necessitated lengthier treatments.

## Qualitative assessments

The finding that a score of psychoanalytic sessions yielded better results than CHC visits confirmed reasonable expectations. MIP was devised to help distressed mothers and babies. It would have been surprising to find no differences between the two groups. Therapists are probably more interested in finding out, "Which method should I recommend in *this* case?" We wished to learn if certain kinds of mothers and babies should be recommended MIP or CHC care, respectively. We hypothesized that outcomes would be associated with the ideal types and/or by the mothers' suitability for psychoanalysis. These assumptions were based on findings that "pretreatment characteristics of patients are important dimensions that influence therapeutic response" (Blatt & Shahar, 2004, p. 426). Furthermore, since the patient is an "active client" (Bohart, 2006, p. 218) in the therapeutic relationship, her attitudes ought to influence outcomes. If these factors proved to be influential they might illuminate the therapy specificity (Orlinsky *et al.*, 2004) of MIP and CHC and help parent–infant clinicians to suggest therapy mode for the individual case.

## Suitability for psychoanalysis

Scores were similar in the MIP and CHC groups, on average 2.4, that is, a medium level. They only predicted the PIR-GAS scores in the MIP group and in the entire sample. The more suitable the mother had seemed, the better the relationship developed – regardless of treatment. This surprised us; my assessments of the mother's fitness for psychoanalysis had very little predictive value. This could simply indicate that my assessments were unreliable. However, assessments by two experienced colleagues on a quarter of the sample yielded similar results. My hypothesis is therefore that in dyadic therapy – during the postnatal period's special psychological climate, and with the two participants functioning at quite different developmental levels – a traditional assessment of the adult party's analytic suitability predicts only vaguely the results of therapy.

## The I-ME scores

The I-ME measured the load of the mother's experiences that might be relevant for the dyad's development. Psychotherapies, whether MIP or the brief treatments in the CHC group, aimed at influencing maternal distress and emotional availability. They might thus influence the extent to which the I-ME predicted the dyad's development. Consequently, our analyses differentiated between cases with or without therapy. In the therapy group, the I-ME showed no predictive capacity. Treatments had thus affected outcomes, which abolished the I-ME's ability to "foresee" development. In contrast, we found significant predictions in the no-therapy group; the I-ME was the only predictor of the mother's general emotional availability, whereas the GSI score was the only predictor of the infant's emotional availability. For exact figures, see Salomonsson and Sandell (2012). In brief, the mother's load of experiences predicted *her* behaviour with the child six months later – but her general level of psychic distress predicted how her *infant* would interact with her.

## Ideal types of mothers

Categorizing the mothers went on continuously during the interviews and afterwards, as I was looking at the video-recordings. I established and assessed the types without knowing the questionnaire scores and the external interaction ratings. Initially, I created five ideal types.

## The Chaotic mother

The eight Chaotic mothers felt overwhelmed by having become mothers. Their comments were sometimes incoherent and hard to follow, though without having psychotic qualities. Their ego-functions seemed to falter when strong feelings overpowered them. They reported that it was taxing to care for the baby and themselves. This decreased their ability to observe the baby's needs. The mother of 16-month-old Ken said, "His father and I have been, we are still, together, but we moved apart. It's been quite intensive. He's got a bigger flat. We moved there, but things worked out really bad. So I moved back, and he (pointing at Ken but referring to father) is still living there".

Feelings of helplessness were often handled by projective identifications. The mother of six-month-old Martine blamed the midwife for her problems. Projective mechanisms were also evident when she said, "It feels like she (pointing at Martine) destroyed things for me". Nevertheless, this mother realized that she played some part in their relationship problems: "At home, I give her things to play with herself . . . I am rejecting her. I try to kiss her but it's difficult . . . Sometimes I forget her. It's terrible."

Chaotic mothers' babies often had a DC 0–3:R Axis 1 diagnosis, mostly of dysregulation. In contrast, the mothers did not have more previous psychiatric contacts than the others. The baby's arrival had aggravated the mothers' pre-existing chaotic tendencies that resulted from oscillations between projective and introjective attitudes. Now they tended to affect the child, as when Martine's mother alternately loved and rejected her baby. Needless to say, this affected the child negatively. When the mother noticed this it increased her guilt feelings and, in the next run, her chaos. Among those assigned to MIP, their analysts confirmed such defence mechanisms. Martine's analyst reported that the mother alternated between seeking and rejecting help. Another problem was the mother's envy of the child, which decreased her empathy with Martine.

## The Depressed/Reserved mother

Many of these 20 mothers felt unable to love the baby. Four-month-old Bobby's mother had anorexia and bulimia during adolescence. Now she was depressed and obese: "I'm terrified my depression will affect Bobby and that he won't attach. Maybe he likes Dad better than me, because they see each other only in the morning and evening? Dad is better at comforting him. Is this due to Bobby's first weeks in life? After three weeks of pumping, weeping, crying, I started bottle-feeding." Her low self-esteem and guilt were salient: "This was going to be the finest time of my life. I wanted to be everything to him but I just blame myself!"

Some mothers evinced a "smiling depression". The mother of six-month-old Nicole said with an enigmatic smile that the midwife suggested putting the newborn on her tummy but she rejected it. She felt unable to "take the girl on board. I have been sad and irritated, though she is a nice girl". While absent-mindedly stroking Nicole she said "Yes, you are a nice girl . . . aren't you . . . " On the interaction video, Nicole turned away from Mum who was reading a novel. The MIP analyst had difficulties in reaching the mother: "She wanted advice but rejected me! She feared I'd say things she couldn't accept." The negative transference was linked to mother's infancy when she got a younger sister. Nicole was her second child and revived the jealousy of the mother, who projected a little sister image on the girl. She had guilt feelings and feared the analyst's critique. The analyst did not interpret this "ghost in the nursery" (Fraiberg *et al.*, 1975), since this might increase negative transference. The mother told me in the interview: "The analyst helped me get it off my chest. I got some kind of mirroring . . . Maybe she had a clearer agenda than I realized. I liked her . . . Well, I was annoyed with her, too. She really saw Nicole." In general, these mothers wavered between narcissistic defences and rejections and a curiosity about how they might be contributing to the baby worries. We expected them to have less optimal initial EPDS scores, but in fact they did not differ from other maternal types on any measure.

### The mother with an Uncertain Maternal Identity

These 23 mothers had focused on professional careers and felt unprepared for motherhood. The mother of five-month-old Ursula said: "I got to have a perfect job and husband before having a child. I started a new job one week before pregnancy. I denied it would interfere with it. When I came home with her I wanted to give her back and put her clothes in the locker. I don't like wheeling the pram. At work I was in charge but now it's like one big cloud of not knowing what to do! I guess there's always guilt when a woman doesn't think motherhood is fantastic." She found it hard to empathize with the baby: "I wanted to be a good girl and breastfeed, but she refused the breast and avoided me. Scientifically they never proved breastfeeding is the best. Anyway, I took her refusal as a personal defeat." The interaction video showed evident insensitivity: "Do you want that toy? Yes or no? Aha, it's no. You wanna use it later on? No? OK. Do you want to stand up or just do a poo?"

Interviews with the analysts revealed problems in establishing a psychoanalytic dialogue. Emotional restraint towards the analyst reflected the mother's relational problems with the child. Some analysts thought a high frequency would enable a deeper contact, but mothers often rejected such suggestions. This risked creating negative countertransference since the analyst identified with the baby's suffering. If a mother suspected such attitudes in the analyst, this evoked guilt. In short, negative spirals of transference–countertransference were hard to avoid.

To maintain self-esteem these mothers resorted to professional achievements, which conflicted with wishes of being good mothers; it was hard for them to slow down and allow dream-like thoughts to emerge. Efforts at identifying with their mothers as a benevolent encouraging maternal figure (Bibring, Dwyer, Huntington & Valenstein, 1961) clashed with the fact that these relationships were often unsatisfactory. Ursula's mother said: "I would never ask my Mum about Ursula's upbringing or my childhood. She never talks feelings."

## The Anxious/Unready mother

Many of these 22 mothers panicked at any baby symptom. The mother of two-month-old Mike said: "He gets these hysteri . . . I mean he gets upset and nothing works. He doesn't want the breast, he's inconsolable. I am afraid he'll stop breathing. It's really scary when I don't see him." Her baby worries intertwined with personal anxiety: "I was always nervous myself. I put the baby to sleep in the cot. Then I lie awake checking if he's breathing. So, to get calmer I put him on my chest."

Anxious mothers seemed unready for motherhood because their own wishes of being taken care of competed with those of caring for the baby. Mike's analyst thought the mother identified with his older sister; Mum feared the girl had felt deserted after Mike's birth. She tried to control the analyst's behaviour towards Mike, which led to countertransference vexation. Treatment focused on the mother's anxiety and the analyst did not get much contact with the boy. In general, we expected these mothers to have less optimal ASQ:SE ratings than the other types, since they expressed so many baby worries during interviews. However, this was not the case. Neither were there any serious infant disorders in this group, that is, no Axis 1 disorders.

## The mother Conflicting with her Partner

Three mothers were abandoned by the child's father, in a concrete or emotional sense. Nevertheless, they focused on and enjoyed caring for the child. The mother of two-month-old Georgina said: "For years, we longed for a child. But when Georgina came, my husband kind of disappeared. She was only one week old but he went to the pub with his pals! I felt so lonely . . ." These mothers seemed not to allow their resentment to affect the baby relationship. Their primary interest in joining the study was to understand their relation with the father rather than with the baby.

## Differential outcomes for the five maternal types

The proportions of the types were similar in the MIP and CHC groups. Figure 11.1 shows the average distributions. We compared my division of ideal types with those of two experienced psychoanalysts and reached a reasonably good inter-coder agreement. We then compared the five types in a one-way ANOVA test to investigate if any one stood out on any initial measure. A post-hoc Scheffé test pointed to differences between Anxious/Immature and Chaotic mothers on the I-ME ($p = .052$). Chaotic mothers had the most negative experiences among the five types.

*The Overarching Maternal Ideal Types (OMITs): the Participators and the Abandoned*

To increase group sizes, I then subsumed the five types under two Overarching Maternal Ideal Types (OMITs), which I named the "Participators" and the "Abandoned". Inter-coder agreement for these ratings was excellent. The Participators comprised the Chaotic, the Depressed/Reserved and the mothers with an Uncertain Identity. Despite their psychological distress, they showed a clear wish to participate in a psychoanalytic exploration. They also guessed they contributed to the present problems though without understanding how. The Abandoned comprised the Anxious/Unready and the Conflicting mothers. They felt forsaken and were less interested in psychological understanding but rather demanded expert advice on how to handle the child or the partner relation. As seen in Figure 11.1, the proportion Participators:Abandoned was about 2:1 in both treatment groups.

To find out if there were any differences between the two OMITs on their initial scores, we performed a series of ANOVAs. We hypothesized that since the Participators were more insight-oriented they would have more optimal scores. However, to our surprise they scored *less* optimally on the I-ME and the PIR-GAS (p = 0.008 and 0.015).

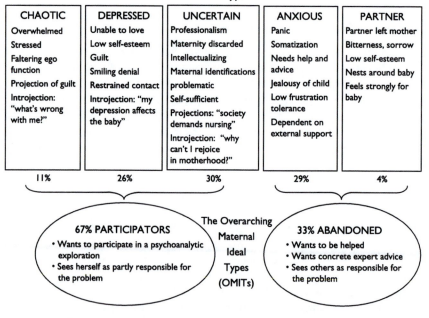

**The Ideal Types**

| CHAOTIC | DEPRESSED | UNCERTAIN | ANXIOUS | PARTNER |
|---|---|---|---|---|
| Overwhelmed | Unable to love | Professionalism | Panic | Partner left mother |
| Stressed | Low self-esteem | Maternity discarded | Somatization | Bitterness, sorrow |
| Faltering ego function | Guilt | Intellectualizing | Needs help and advice | Low self-esteem |
| Projection of guilt | Smiling denial | Maternal identifications problematic | Jealousy of child | Nests around baby |
| Introjection: "what's wrong with me?" | Restrained contact | Self-sufficient | Low frustration tolerance | Feels strongly for baby |
| | Introjection: "my depression affects the baby" | Projections: "society demands nursing" | Dependent on external support | |
| | | Introjection: "why can't I rejoice in motherhood?" | | |
| 11% | 26% | 30% | 29% | 4% |

**67% PARTICIPATORS**
• Wants to participate in a psychoanalytic exploration
• Sees herself as partly responsible for the problem

The Overarching Maternal Ideal Types (OMITs)

**33% ABANDONED**
• Wants to be helped
• Wants concrete expert advice
• Sees others as responsible for the problem

*Figure 11.1* The five original maternal types and the two Overarching Maternal Types (OMITs) with proportional frequencies.

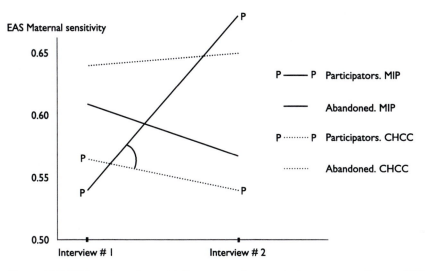

*Figure 11.2* EAS maternal sensitivity pre- and post-treatment according to MIP/ CHC care and OMITs.

## The Overarching Maternal Types' influence on outcomes

My main reason for categorizing the participants was to find out if MIP and CHC care would yield different results for the two OMITs. We found that Participators in MIP improved on EAS maternal sensitivity, whereas those in CHC decreased. This difference, indicated by $\alpha$ in Figure 11.2, was significant (p = 0.005). MIP Participators thus became more sensitive to the child's signals than their peers in CHC care. There was a reverse though non-significant effect for the Abandoned, who fared somewhat less well in MIP than in CHC care.

## Ideal types of infants

These types summarized my impressions of the baby plus the mothers' reports on his/her behaviour at home. I opted for a simple yet clinically relevant division; babies for whom I did and did not feel concern, respectively: the "Affected" and the "Unaffected" babies. Their distribution was about 50–50 in both treatment groups. Inter-coder agreement with the two external psychoanalysts was excellent.

### The Affected baby

This baby cried or reacted with negative emotions when the mother spoke of distressing topics. Alternatively, he arched away or avoided mother's gaze when she talked to him. Older babies looked unhappy and crawled away from Mum, indicating an avoidant attachment (Ainsworth *et al.*, 1978). Still older children seemed disorganized (Main & Solomon, 1986) by being overly active and jittery. Some defied their mother or slapped her face. A few exhibited a sexualized contact, as when weaned babies anxiously poked at their mother's breast.

Six-month-old Nicole, with her Depressed/Reserved mother described earlier, played by herself during the interview. When she failed to reach her toy, she did not turn to her mother for help. Maternal sensitivity and structuring were low, and so was Nicole's involvement of her mother. Due to her young age, she did not qualify for an Axis 1 diagnosis. The relationship was rated on the PIR-GAS as "disturbed" (50).

Four-month-old Bobby was also Affected; during the EAS recording his mother (reported under the Depressed/Reserved type) told him, "Nice shirt Mum's got, eh? You're a naughty boy, aren't you? Shall we jump?" Bobby started whining. She whispered in his ear and rubbed his back but he just whined more. She responded, "Blablabla". He whined still more. "Aha, you wanna take it easy!" He started avoiding her eyes. Despite his tension and frustration an Axis 1 diagnosis seemed premature. Since his behaviour was linked to mother's handling, their relationship was rated as "disturbed" (50) on the PIR-GAS.

In contrast, some older Affected babies qualified for an Axis 1 diagnosis. While the mother of nine-month-old Misha was telling me, "Life as a mother is not a bed of roses", he started climbing on her body. She commented, "Oh dear, aren't you an alert boy", adding that he was hanging around her skirts all the time. When he reached her breast she said, "Yeah, he started kissing my breasts . . . He is hard to calm down". I noted he was "all over the place". Mother also reported on his nightmares. Misha was diagnosed with a Regulation Disorder of Sensory Stimulation-Processing. I rated their PIR-GAS relationship as "significantly perturbed" (70).

### The Unaffected baby

These babies seemed calm even when their mothers were addressing painful topics. They might look gently and curiously at her or just go on playing peacefully. When their mothers caught their attention, they often responded with a smile. They were sleeping and eating well and were cheerful at home. Some were young and perhaps had not had time to develop symptoms. The mother of two-month-old Becky had an acute caesarean and they lost contact for four hours. This trauma was unresolved and she felt envious of the father's initial contact with Becky. This Anxious/Unready mother showered Becky with affection, sometimes on an intrusive note. The girl, however, cooed and seemed happy all along. On the PIR-GAS, in contrast, they received a rather low rating; distressed (60). This was because of the lack of joy in the mother's story: "I feel like a food-machine! Why is her contact with her father so much better? I think it's because they spent those first hours together without me."

Ten-month-old Eric also had an Anxious/Unready mother. She had contacted the project because of his sleeping difficulties, but her foremost worry was actually her husband's depression. While she reported on this, Eric was playing happily on the floor. He approached her, greeted her and she picked him up. The EAS video showed how he was involving her in play. They seemed to like being together. Evidently, she had created a free zone beyond her marital worries. The reason I did not rate their relationship as optimal but as "perturbed" (80) was the mother's tense and up-tempo way of talking about it.

## The infant types in relations to other measures and outcomes

Mothers with Affected babies reported significantly more baby problems (ASQ:SE; p = 0.002) and stress (SPSQ; p = 0.030) in comparison with mothers of Unaffected babies. They had less optimal relationships (PIR-GAS; p < 0.001), maternal sensitivity (p = 0.003) and structuring (p = 0.042). Affected babies were also less responsive (p = 0.002) and involving (p = 0.001). Thus, my clinical division of the babies corresponded well with many measures, which testified to the validity of the two types. When we compared the OMITs and the infant types, we found that Abandoned mothers more often had Unaffected babies, whereas Participator mothers more often had Affected babies.

We compared the results of MIP and CHC care for each infant type. The procedure was the same as with the OMITs. Significant effects were found on two measures for the Affected infants. MIP was superior in improving maternal sensitivity (p = 0.040), as indicated by α in Figure 11.3. Similarly, the PIR-GAS scores of Affected infants improved significantly more in the MIP group (p = 0.004). This is indicated by α in Figure 11.4.

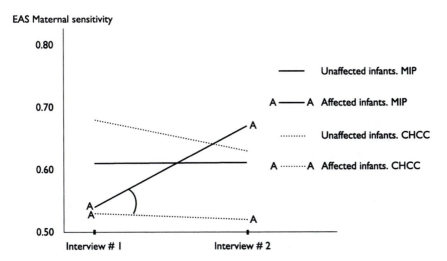

Figure 11.3 EAS maternal sensitivity pre- and post-treatment according to MIP/ CHC care and infant types.

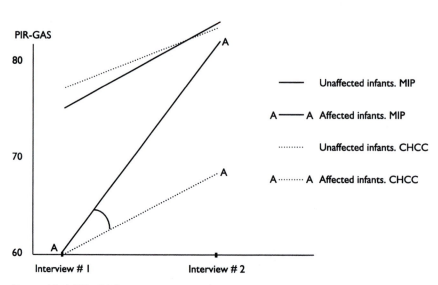

*Figure 11.4* PIR-GAS scores pre- and post-treatment according to MIP/CHC care and infant types.

## Discussion

Our design combined hermeneutic and positivistic approaches. The former focuses on "meaning, interpretation, and narration" (Luyten, Blatt & Corveleyn, 2006, p. 578). This is the perspective that pervades the case reports and theoretical discussions in this book. In contrast, our positivistic quasi-experimental approach contrasts with the "enumerative inductivism" (Fonagy, 1993, p. 577) of single-case reports. Fonagy refers critically to when therapists pile up various cases to prove the value of a therapy mode. It was in order to check such assumptions – that treatments amassed over the years by analysts in the MIPPS group showed good results – that we performed the RCT. Had we opted for a singularly hermeneutic approach we would have missed an opportunity of investigating which method is *generally* superior for treating baby worries. Had we opted for a positivistic design that only included quantitative measures we might have been able to answer that question – but we would have learnt little about differences between individual patients and therapists and about the therapeutic processes.

The first study aim was to quantify between-group outcome differences. The interviews fulfilled a second aim; to categorize the psychodynamics and symptoms. They were condensed into ideal types and maternal suitability for psychoanalysis, factors I thought might influence outcomes differentially in the two treatment modes. A third aim was to use interviews for predicting the dyads' future development. Fourth, I aimed to assemble these results into lessons that would be meaningful to clinicians and influence their daily practice. I hoped they would experience "a new empirical attitude . . . a habit of evaluating one's own theories in light of observed phenomena rather than selecting events with the – obviously preconscious – aim of propping up these theories" (Jimenez, 2007, p. 662). Finally, I aimed to disseminate our results among health care administrators deciding on treatment subsidies. In an era of an increasing variety of therapies, each one probably influencing individuals differentially, we need "to determine the proper place of psychoanalysis and psychoanalytic psychotherapies in the psychiatric armamentarium" (Busch, Milrod & Sandberg, 2009, p. 143). To fulfil these aims the RCT must have a sufficient sample size, describe patients and treatments adequately, provide therapies under controlled conditions, assess outcomes with adequate measures and statistical methods, assure participants of high ethical standards and not interfere with the nurses' and the therapists' practice.

It is always difficult to compare different study samples. Ours was a social low-risk sample whereas the sample of Lieberman *et al.* (1991) was high-risk. Half of our mothers had experienced psychiatric distress necessitating medication, therapy or hospitalization. Their psychiatric risk seemed higher than the Toronto sample (Cohen *et al.*, 1999). The Canadian mothers were mildly depressed, whereas our mothers' EPDS mean score was at the clinical level of 12 and a quarter of them had been treated for depressions. The measures on parental stress, general psychic distress and infant functioning also indicated that our mothers clearly experienced trouble with themselves and their babies.

### The I-ME interview instrument

Why did I devise an interview format? After all, I had already decided to use four questionnaires and external ratings of interactions and relationships! My answer is that the outcome measures missed one important point: how the mother *experienced* her life history and present life situation. I might have used an existing interview format, such as the Birmingham Interview for Maternal Mental Health (Brockington, Aucamp & Fraser, 2006), the Parent Attachment Interview (Bretherton, 2005) or the Working Model of the Child Interview (WMCI; Zeanah, Benoit & Barton, 1986). Some of them are well-validated, such as the WMCI (Vreeswijk, Maas & van Bakel, 2012). However, experience has taught me that a semi-structured interview with mother and baby present helps me get deeper into the matter. It enables me to assess symptoms and behaviours and their unconscious determinants. This helps me to understand the psychodynamics of the disturbance.

The I-ME score predicted the mothers' interactive contributions. Thus, their experiences were associated with how they behaved with the child. In contrast, it is unclear why the infants' contributions were predicted by the SCL-90. This measure focused on maternal distress symptoms, many of which were expressed non-verbally; for example, anxiety and irritation while being with the baby. Such symptoms might affect the child's emotional availability.

## Outcomes: MIP and CHC care compared

Psychoanalysts generally adhered to the MIP method, though I noted that negative maternal transferences were not always noted by the analyst and seldom brought up by the mother. MIP effects were found on self-reported maternal depression and stress, dyadic relationship qualities and maternal sensitivity. Comparisons with other studies must be cautious due to differences in samples, measures and therapies. In general, MIP matched other studies' results on maternal distress and dyadic interactions.

## Differential outcomes: the infants

Our aim with investigating therapy specificity was to find out if "certain treatments are more effective with certain kinds of patient" (Blatt & Shahar, 2004, p. 397). As for the choice of diagnostic system, we might have used Axis 1 of the DC 0–3:R and the DSM-IV for babies and mothers, respectively. However, our infants showed a large symptom variety and age span. Furthermore, some diagnoses are not applicable to our youngest babies. Our mothers corroborated Stern's (1995) observation that they saw themselves as "having a problem rather than an illness" (p. 3). We therefore classified them according to psychodynamics and relationship qualities. To this end, we chose the ideal types method. Such types constitute a "hypothesis about reality – and an unrealistic, utopian one, at that" (Wachholz & Stuhr, 1999, p. 331). Despite this "utopian" quality the two infant types differed on mother-reports and external ratings. Thus, their internal validity received support from other measures. Similarly, the high inter-rater reliabilities confirmed their face validity. These associations point to the value of combining qualitative and quantitative ratings. This procedure is often called triangulation (Elliott, Fischer & Rennie, 1999; Jick, 1979), in that the researcher applies several perspectives to the same phenomenon.

MIP seemed especially helpful for Affected babies on maternal EA sensitivity and dyadic relationships (PIR-GAS). Interviews indicated that the analysts' calm and attentive ways of speaking to such babies helped mothers relax and listen to their signals. I recall a mother who said, "Funny, but in the analysis I discovered that my boy is a person! I felt a bit embarrassed, as if I didn't know that already. Earlier, I didn't grasp any meaning behind his babbling, so I didn't pay much attention to it. Then one day after a session, I thought about my dog during my teens. I *knew* I understood him! People laughed when I said he was sad or angry, but I felt I could 'read' him. Analysis helped me discover something similar with my boy". Clearly, the analyst's baby focus enabled this mother to better understand her child's personality.

### Differential outcomes: the mothers

When I collected symptoms, experiences and unconscious attitudes beneath maternal worries I arrived at five types, later subsumed into two Overarching Maternal Ideal Types (OMITs). Abandoned mothers conveyed helplessness and desertion, while the Participators acknowledged some personal influence on the present problems. When inventing these types and classifying accordingly, I made no prognostic implications. Since each OMIT was equally represented in each treatment group, neither randomization nor interviewer bias seemed to have influenced categorizations. As for the overlap between OMITs and infant types reported above, it seems that the Abandoned mothers' main reasons for approaching the project were personal problems, whereas their babies were reasonably healthy.

In retrospect, it seems that the Abandoned and the Participator types resembled the "anaclitic" and "introjective" patient categories suggested by Blatt and co-workers (Blatt, 1992). Anaclitic individuals are "concerned about trust, closeness, and the dependability of others . . . [including] their capacity to receive and give love and affection" (Blatt, 2006, p. 507). Similarly, our Abandoned mothers feared "being abandoned and left unprotected and uncared for" (p. 501) and were sensitive to "interpersonal or relational dimensions of the treatment process" (Blatt & Shahar, 2004, p. 429). As Ingrid, an Abandoned mother, put it: "I think the analyst focused too much on my son. I needed to talk about *me*! I wished she had advised me out of her own experiences as a mother." She thus demanded active guidance by the analyst because, like anaclitic persons, she valued others "primarily for the immediate care, comfort, and satisfaction they provided" (Blatt, 2006, p. 501).

Introjective individuals seek to "achieve separation, control, independence, and self-definition, and to be acknowledged, respected, and admired" (Blatt, 2006, p. 508). Their conflicts involve "feelings of inadequacy, inferiority, worthlessness, guilt, and difficulty managing affect, especially anger" (idem). One recognizes such traits in the Participator mother of Martine, mentioned in the section "Chaotic mothers". She stated, "My contact with Martine became stronger during MIP. I still feel guilty sometimes, but I know I love her and she loves me. All this has to do with my own Mum. She had no skill in emotional matters!" She discovered Martine's emotional spectrum and could attribute changes in their relationship to topics addressed in analysis. For example, she understood that Martine's rejection of her had to do with her own ambivalence. This insight made her reduce negative projections on Martine.

Blatt's group found that psychoanalysis especially helped introjective patients to develop adaptive interpersonal capacities and to reduce maladaptive interpersonal tendencies. Supportive–expressive therapy (SEP) only helped reducing the latter and only among anaclitic patients. For this group SEP was more efficient on some measures than was psychoanalysis. This parallels our study; MIP is psychoanalytic in its aims and procedure, whereas the nurses' developmental guidance (Lojkasek *et al.*, 1994) has many supportive elements.

I am aware of the differences between our RCT and Blatt's study concerning outcome measures, the sample, the treatment mode, etc. Nevertheless, it was interesting to note that similarly to introjective patients, our Participator mothers did not develop object relational capacities, as measured by EA sensitivity, so well in CHC care. In the follow-up interviews, they felt the nurses sometimes responded with "meaningless" comments to their baby worries. This left them without a forum to ventilate these issues. It is known that individuals who gain the most from insight-oriented therapies are often self-reflective (Beutler *et al.*, 2004). They also tend to describe their problems in terms of interpersonal difficulties rather than symptoms (Horowitz, 1993 reported in Roth and Fonagy, 2005, p. 470). I got the impression that when Participator mothers witnessed the analyst–baby interaction, they used self-reflection and an interpersonal orientation to increase their sensitivity to the child. In contrast, CHC care left them with fewer possibilities to develop such capacities.

The reverse pattern, that Abandoned mothers developed their sensitivity less well in MIP compared with CHC care, was non-significant. Still, I got the impression that the analyst's baby-focus sometimes made them feel. They wished the analyst had shared advice and personal experiences with them. Outcomes for traumatized or bereaved patients may associate positively with a "wish for a sympathetic authority figure" (Jones, Cumming & Horowitz, 1988, p. 52). Evidently, the analysts did not always meet such expectations, which might have contributed to making these mothers somewhat less sensitive after MIP.

In contrast to the OMITs, we had a hypothesis about the suitability ratings: they would predict several maternal outcomes. However, they only predicted PIR-GAS outcomes. It is difficult to interpret this finding; perhaps suitability overlapped with maternal reflective functioning (RF; Fonagy, Steele, Steele, Moran & Higgitt, 1991). If so, it might contribute to the PIR-GAS score by assisting mothers to understand the baby when the baby was fussy or "impossible". This guess is based on other studies suggesting such links (Fonagy *et al.*, 1995; Schechter *et al.*, 2005; Slade, Belsky, Aber & Phelps, 1999).

In contrast, suitability failed to predict any mother-report questionnaire. Since we found that the Participators benefited more from MIP on maternal sensitivity, we investigated if other predictions were concealed by the Abandoned. However, despite a split analysis, suitability still predicted nothing but the PIR-GAS. Possibly, these meagre associations resulted from MIP's infant focus. Mothers who were suitable for individual therapy to get help with their own problems might find that MIP failed to meet such wishes.

### Research conclusions

Wagner's character Hans Sachs, quoted previously, regretted that he could not grasp the immeasurable. Nevertheless, the analyst's daily work consists in doing precisely this – though not with figures and diagrams. By combining this book's single case presentations with the RCT findings, my aim has been to contribute to improving other analysts' daily practice. To be true, we must recall that this RCT has limitations, just like every scientific study. Our results cannot automatically be extended to other samples. Mothers with other educational levels or with more severe psychopathologies might respond differently to MIP and CHC care; this conjecture should be investigated further. Concerning the study's procedure, it should be recalled that questionnaires were filled in after, not before, the interview. During the initial telephone contacts many mothers seemed wary of opening up to an unknown person, which is why I preferred that they first got acquainted with me and then filled in the questionnaires. The initial scores in the two groups were roughly equal; this, plus the equal drop-out rate in the two groups, indicated that when mothers filled in the questionnaires, their assignment did not influence them. There was an objectivity problem with the PIR-GAS ratings, since I made them and my allegiance must be considered to be in favour of MIP. We therefore chose a second rater who had no allegiance whatsoever to MIP. Our inter-rater reliability and allegiance calculations strongly indicated that ratings were not biased in any direction.

### Clinical conclusions

Like other RCTs showing short-time positive effects of parent–infant therapy (Cohen *et al.*, 1999; Cooper *et al.*, 2003; Lieberman *et al.*, 1991; O'Hara *et al.*, 2000; Robert-Tissot *et al.*, 1996), this study showed effects on self-reported maternal depression and stress, sensitivity and dyadic relationship qualities. Certain mothers and babies benefited from a more ambitious therapy. One should especially recommend MIP and similar therapies to mothers who intuit that the baby worries are not solely caused by other people such as their partner, or by non-psychological factors such as food allergies. The clinician should also be alert to the baby's suffering. Babies who seem negatively affected by the relationship should be given priority for psychotherapy; those who cry constantly, refuse the breast or do not let go of it, do not look mother into the eyes, cannot fall asleep or wake up repeatedly – in short, cases like the ones presented throughout the book's clinical section.

The study supports that in order to assess a parent–infant dyad we need a lengthy interview. It should include observations of mother and baby plus a thorough history of the mother's experiences. The I-ME study indicates that the clinician's intuition, observation and assessment of mother and child may yield important information. This may seem trivial. The reason I reiterate it is that modern health care increasingly relies on patient-report questionnaires to arrive at diagnosis and treatment. In fact, our ASQ:SE study (Salomonsson & Sleed, 2010) indicated that distressed mothers were not optimal raters on a questionnaire on baby distress. Questionnaires may thus yield an incomplete clinical picture.

As for choosing therapy mode, one should consider mother *and* baby, each with a right to make his/her voice heard. There are many challenges for the therapist, such as simultaneously focusing on mother, child and the countertransference. Another challenge is to assess the mother's wish and capacities for reaching psychological insight, as well as her wish to be given "tools" and advice for handling the problems. If the practitioner does not respect both sorts of wishes, s/he may lose the case due to unresolved maternal negative transference. Indeed, such transferences seem surprisingly common, probably because mothers with baby worries are taken by surprise. They had expected motherhood to be positive and enriching but now they find themselves anxious, depressed and incapable of handling formerly trivial challenges. Just as a "ghost in the nursery" (Fraiberg *et al.*, 1975) may appear as an uninvited guest in their life, the therapist may be felt to be an unexpected threat to their psychological equilibrium. So, we need to be vigilant on negative maternal transference. On the other hand, some factors that we psychoanalysts consider essential seem not to have the same influence as in adult therapy. I refer especially to session frequency; I think it is important to let the mother decide on this issue rather than to impose a "one-size-fits-all" therapy.

### Considerations for the future

The results of the RCT were calculated on a six-month follow-up basis. It will be interesting to know how they will bear out in the future, especially since very few long-term follow-up studies exist in this field. To this end, we have launched a follow-up study when the children have reached four and a half years of age. The study is not yet completed.

The differential results among Abandoned and Participator mothers inspired my clinical work to take new directions. The RCT showed that MIP was generally superior on some measures. We also found that certain mothers and babies benefited from a more supportive approach, whereas others gained more from an insight-oriented and anxiety-provoking therapy. Another observation was that many mothers, whether they were Participators or Abandoned, or treated in MIP or CHC, were still brittle and afraid of the future. I concluded that a parent–infant therapy should not automatically be regarded as a once-and-for-all treatment. Many parents need to know that they can get renewed support if and when new troubles emerge. This may happen when another child is born, when there is a divorce in the family, when the child or mother gets ill, etc.

It would thus be better, I concluded, to offer qualified psychotherapeutic resources to a Child Health Centre. I contacted the Mama Mia Child Health Centre in Stockholm. My idea was to be stationed next door to the nurse's office; this would raise less doubts and fears in mothers with baby worries. I would be able to help "on the spot" when a mother had hinted to the nurse that something was not OK with her or the baby. This mode of working necessitated supervising the nurses; to help them increase their psychological sensitivity and their skill and courage to raise such issues with the mother.

Since 2008, I have been developing a model of psychoanalytic consultations at the CHC. I have integrated the MIP technique with toddlers and mothers as well. The supervision model has also promoted the nurses' skills in handling baby worries. The next volume will relate how this model developed and provide clinical vignettes. The Swedish Inheritance Fund Commission recently provided the Stockholm Parent–Infant Psychoanalyst Group with a generous grant, which will enable this model to be implemented at several CHCs. The plan is to evaluate this project in a systematic way.

# Epilogue

NO WORRIES

She is
brimming:
her clogged honey
is last summer's.
There has been
a laying-down
of arms: hers feel
only the static
of a sofa.
In her, each
baby-suck
makes two kinds
of vacuum.

Backtrack, checking
for echoes; configure
the basic grammar
of the tongue
at the nipple,
of mamaland,
of its interpreters,
so that all the
sweet fluencies
will issue
like tones
picked up from
kindergartens at
calling-home time.

By now I fear the reader is replete with concepts, speculations, cases and feelings of dizziness and perhaps even dejection: "The enigma of infancy gets lost among all these abstract terms!" I have therefore submitted another portrait of the landscape we have been travelling through. The poem "No Worries" was written by Philip Hale, a friend and an Irish bard, as he got inspired by these issues in our conversations.

This book suggests that when baby worries are around, we need to study their "basic grammar" carefully. I acknowledge the complexities in grasping it and the uncertainties of our interpretations. Yet, I see important reasons for not giving up in our efforts and not abandoning our fantasy as we try to visualize what a crying or sleepless baby might feel. The first reason is one of urgency. The sight of a sobbing baby or an unhappy mother is hard to bear and urges us to take action. The second reason is that if we take psychoanalytic developmental theory seriously, infancy is at the root of much suffering later in life. This is not to say that life gets settled in infancy, but I do suggest that we take earnestly the ideas of the great psychoanalytic thinkers; the foundation of our personality and our *Weltanschauung* was laid while this "backtrack, checking for echoes" went on between us and our parents. The practice of parent–infant psychotherapy is therefore an important empirical field that awaits further exploration, and it may also inspire work with adult therapy patients. My hope is that such explorations will yield more insights into the roots of emotional disorders and psychiatric disturbances – and be of help for the many dyads of today that suffer from baby worries.

# References

Abidin, R. R. (1990). *Parenting Stress Index (PSI)—Manual*. Odessa, FL: Psychological Assessment Resources, Inc.

Acquarone, S. (2004). *Infant–parent psychotherapy*. London: Karnac Books.

Ahlberg, A. (1967). *Filosofins historia (The history of philosophy)*. Stockholm: Natur och Kultur.

Ainsworth, M. S., Blehar, M. C., Waters, E. and Wall, S. (1978). *Patterns of attachment: A psychological study of the strange situation*. Oxford: Lawrence Erlbaum.

Anthi, P. R. (1983). Reconstruction of preverbal experiences. *Journal of the American Psychoanalytic Association, 31*, 33–58.

Anthony, E. J. (1986). The contributions of child psychoanalysis to psychoanalysis. *Psychoanalytic Study of the Child, 41*, 61–87.

Anzieu, D. (Ed.). (1989). *Psychanalyse et language. Du corps à la parole (Psychoanalysis and language. From the body to the word)*. Paris: Dunod.

Anzieu, D. (Ed.). (1990). *Psychic envelopes (Les enveloppes psychiques)*. London: Karnac Books.

Apel, K.-O. (1995). *Charles S. Peirce: From pragmatism to pragmaticism* (J. M. Krois, Trans.). New Jersey: Humanities Press.

Arfouilloux, J.-C. (2000). *Guy Rosolato*. Paris: PUF.

Aulagnier, P. (2001). *The violence of interpretation. From pictogram to statement (La violence de l'interprétation: du pictogramme à l'énoncé, 1975. Paris: PUF)*. London: Routledge.

Bahrick, L. E. and Hollich, G. (2008). Intermodal perception. In M. M. Haith and J. B. Benson (Eds.), *Encyclopedia of infant and early childhood development* (Vol. 2, pp. 164–176). San Diego, CA: Academic Press.

Bailly, L. (2012). *A new approach to the traumatic phenomenon*. Paper presented at The Anna Freud Centre Colloquium, London.

Balestriere, L. (2003). *Freud et la question des origines (Freud and the question of origins)*. Bruxelles: De Boeck and Larcier.

Balint, M. (1949). Changing therapeutic aims and techniques in psycho-analysis. *International Journal of Psychoanalysis, 31*, 117–124.

Balint, M. (1952). *Primary love and psycho-analytic technique*. London: Maresfield Library.

Balkanyi, C. (1964). On verbalization. *International Journal of Psychoanalysis, 45*, 64–74.

Balter, L., Lothane, Z. and Spencer, J. H. (1980). On the analyzing instrument. *Psychoanalytic Quarterly, 49*, 475–503.

Baradon, T., Broughton, C., Gibbs, I., James, J., Joyce, A. and Woodhead, J. (2005). *The practice of psychoanalytic parent–infant psychotherapy: Claiming the baby*. London: Routledge.

Baranger, M. and Baranger, W. (Eds.). (2009). *The work of confluence. Listening and interpreting in the psychoanalytic field*. London: Karnac Books.

Barrows, P. (2003). Change in parent–infant psychotherapy. *Journal of Child Psychotherapy, 29*(3), 283–300.

Beebe, B., Jaffe, J., Lachmann, F., Feldstein, S., Crown, C. and Jasnow, M. (2000). System models in development and psychoanalysis: The case of vocal rhythm coordination and attachment. *Infant Mental Health Journal, 21*(1–2), 99–122.

Beebe, B., Knoblauch, S., Rustin, J., Sorter, D., Jacobs, T. J. and Pally, R. (2005). *Forms of intersubjectivity in infant research and adult treatment*. New York: Other Press.

Beebe, B. and Lachmann, F. M. (2002). *Infant research and adult treatment: Co-constructing interactions*. Hillsdale, NJ: Analytic Press.

Bergmann, M. S. (1995). On love and its enemies. *Psychoanalytic Review, 82*(1), 1–19.

Bertenthal, B. I. and Longo, M. R. (2007). Is there evidence of a mirror system from birth? *Developmental Science, 10*(5), 526–529.

Beutler, L. E., Malik, M., Alimohamed, S., Harwood, T. M., Talebi, H., Noble, S. and Wong, E. (2004). Therapist variables. In M. J. Lambert (Ed.), *Bergin and Garfield's handbook of psychotherapy and behaviour change* (5th ed., pp. 227–306). New York: John Wiley and Sons, Inc.

Bibring, G. L., Dwyer, T. F., Huntington, D. S. and Valenstein, A. F. (1961). A study of the psychological processes in pregnancy and of the earliest mother–child relationship: I. Some propositions and comments. *Psychoanalytic Study of the Child, 16*, 9–24.

Bion, W. R. (1962a). *Learning from experience*. London: Karnac Books.

Bion, W. R. (1962b). A theory of thinking. *International Journal of Psychoanalysis, 43*, 306–310.

Bion, W. R. (1963). *Elements of psychoanalysis*. London: Karnac Books.

Bion, W. R. (1965). *Transformations*. London: Karnac Books.

Bion, W. R. (1970). *Attention and interpretation*. London: Karnac Books.

Bion, W. R. (1987) *Clinical Seminars and Four Papers*. Abingdon: Fleetwood Press

Bion, W. R. (1997). *Taming wild thoughts*. London: Karnac Books.

Biringen, Z. (2009). *The universal language of love. Assessing relationships through the science of emotional availability (EA)*. Retrieved from www.emotionalavailability.com (accessed September 5 2013).

Biringen, Z., Robinson, J. L. C. and Emde, R. N. C. (1998). *Emotional availability scales* (3rd ed.). Colorado State University: Unpublished manual.

Blake, W. (1994). *William Blake. Selected Poetry*. Oxford: Oxford University Press.

Blatt, S. J. (1992). The differential effect of psychotherapy and psychoanalysis with anaclitic and introjective patients: The Menninger Psychotherapy Research Project revisited. *Journal of the American Psychoanalytic Association, 40*(3), 691–724.

Blatt, S. J. (2006). A fundamental polarity in psychoanalysis: Implications for personality development, psychopathology, and the therapeutic process. *Psychoanalytic Inquiry, 26*(4), 492–518.

Blatt, S. J. and Shahar, G. (2004). Psychoanalysis – with whom, for what, and how? Comparisons with psychotherapy. *Journal of the American Psychoanalytic Association, 52*(2), 393–447.

Bohart, A. C. (2006). The active client. In J. C. Norcross, L. E. Beutler and R. F. Levant (Eds.), *Evidence-based practices in mental health* (pp. 218–224). Washington DC: the American Psychological Association.

Bonaparte, M., Freud, A. and Kris, E. (Eds.). (1954). *The origins of psychoanalysis: Letters to Wilhelm Fliess, drafts and notes: 1877–1902.* New York: Basic Books.

Boris, N. W. M. D., Zeanah, C. H. M. D., Larrieu, J. A. P., Scheeringa, M. S. M. D. and Heller, S. S. P. (1998). Attachment disorders in infancy and early childhood: A preliminary investigation of diagnostic criteria. *American Journal of Psychiatry, 155*(2), 295–297.

Börjesson, K., Ruppert, S. and Bågedahl-Strindlund, M. (2005). A longitudinal study of psychiatric symptoms in primiparous women: Relation to personality disorders and sociodemographic factors. *Archives of Women's Mental Health, 8*(4), 232–242.

Bott Spillius, E. and Feldman, M. (1989). Introduction. In E. Bott Spillius and M. Feldman (Eds.), *Psychic equilibrium and psychic change. Selected papers of Betty Joseph London.* London: Tavistock.

Bowlby, J. (1969). *Attachment and loss.* London: Pimlico.

Bretherton, I. (2005). In pursuit of the internal working model construct and its relevance to attachment relationships. In K. E. Grossmann, K. Grossmann and E. Waters (Eds.), *Attachment from infancy to adulthood: The major longitudinal studies* (pp. 13–47). New York: The Guilford Press.

Britton, R., Chused, J., Ellman, S. and Likierman, M. (2006). Panel I: Contemporary views on stages versus positions. *Journal of Infant, Child and Adolescent Psychotherapy, 5*(3), 268–281.

Brockington, I., Aucamp, H. and Fraser, C. (2006). Severe disorders of the mother–infant relationship: Definitions and frequency. *Archives of Women's Mental Health, 9*(5), 243–251.

Bruner, J. (1990). *Acts of meaning.* Cambridge, MA: Harvard University Press.

Busch, F. N., Milrod, B. L. and Sandberg, L. S. (2009). A study demonstrating efficacy of a psychoanalytic psychotherapy for panic disorder: Implications for psychoanalytic research, theory, and practice. *Journal of the American Psychoanalytic Association, 57*(1), 131–148.

Bydlowski, M. (2001). Le regard intérieur de la femme enceinte, transparence psychique et représentation de l'objet interne (The interior look of the pregnant woman, psychological transparency and representation of the internal object). *Devenir, 13*(2), 41–52.

Bystrova, K., Matthiesen, A.-S., Vorontsov, I., Widström, A.-M., Ransjö-Arvidson, A.-B. and Uvnäs-Moberg, K. (2007). Maternal axillar and breast temperature after giving birth: Effects of delivery ward practices and relation to infant temperature. *Birth: Issues in Perinatal Care, 34*(4), 291–300.

Bystrova, K., Ivanova, V., Edhborg, M., Matthiesen, A.-S., Ransjö-Arvidson, A.-B., Mukhamedrakhimov, R. and Widström, A.-M. (2009). Early contact versus separation: Effects on mother–infant interaction one year later. *Birth: Issues in Perinatal Care, 36*(2), 97–109.

Calvocoressi, F. (2010). Touching the void: Observations of a very depressed mother in an inpatient unit. *Infant Observation, 13*(1), 37–44.

Camus, A. (1994). *Le premier homme (The First Man).* Paris: Gallimard.

Cavell, M. (2001). Seeing through Freud. *The Annual of Psychoanalysis, 29*, 67–82.

Chakraborty, H. and Gu, H. (2009). A mixed model approach for intent-to-treat analysis in longitudinal clinical trials with missing values. *RTI Press publication MR-0009-0903.*

Retrieved from www.rti.org/pubs/mr-0009-0904-chakraborty.pdf (accessed September 5 2013).

Chinen, A. B. (1987). Symbolic modes in object relations: A semiotic perspective. *Psychoanalysis and Contemporary Thought, 10*(3), 373–406.

Ciccone, A., Mellier, D., Athanassiou-Popesco, C., Carel, A., Dubinsky, A. and Guedeney, A. (2007). *Le bébé et le temps. Attention, rythme et subjectivation (The baby and time. Attention, rhythm and subjectivation)*. Paris: Dunod.

Civitarese, G. (2008). *The intimate room. Theory and technique of the analytic field* (P. Slotkin, Trans.). London: Routledge.

Clark, R., Tluczek, A. and Wenzel, A. (2003). Psychotherapy for postpartum depression: A preliminary report. *American Journal of Orthopsychiatry, 73*(4), 441–454.

Cohen, J. (1985). Trauma and repression. *Psychoanalytic Inquiry, 5*(1), 163–189.

Cohen, J. (1994). A view of the moral landscape of psychoanalysis. *Journal of the American Academy of Psychoanalysis, 22*(4), 699–725.

Cohen, M. and Hahn, A. (Eds.). (2000). *Exploring the work of Donald Meltzer*. London: Karnac Books.

Cohen, N. J., Lojkasek, M., Muir, E., Muir, R. and Parker, C. J. (2002). Six-month follow-up of two mother–infant psychotherapies: Convergence of therapeutic outcomes. *Infant Mental Health Journal, 23*(4), 361–380.

Cohen, N. J., Muir, E., Parker, C. J., Brown, M., Lojkasek, M., Muir, R. and Barwick, M. (1999). Watch, wait and wonder: Testing the effectiveness of a new approach to mother–infant psychotherapy. *Infant Mental Health Journal, 20*(4), 429–451.

Cohn, J. F. and Tronick, E. (1989). Specificity of infants' response to mothers' affective behaviour. *Journal of the American Academy of Child and Adolescent Psychiatry, 28*(2), 242–248.

Cooke, M., Schmied, V. and Sheehan, A. (2007). An exploration of the relationship between postnatal distress and maternal role attainment, breast feeding problems and breast feeding cessation in Australia. *Midwifery, 23*(1), 66–76.

Cooper, D. E. (Ed.). (1999). *Epistemology: The classic readings*. Oxford: Blackwell.

Cooper, P. J., Murray, L., Wilson, A. and Romaniuk, H. (2003). Controlled trial of the short- and long-term effect of psychological treatment of post-partum depression: 1. Impact on maternal mood. *British Journal of Psychiatry, 182*(5), 412–419.

Corradi Fiumara, G. (1995). *The metaphoric process. Connections between language and life*. London: Routledge.

Cox, J., Holden, J. and Sagovsky, R. (1987). Detection of postnatal depression: Development of the 10-item Edinburgh Postnatal Depression Scale. *British Journal of Psychiatry, 150*(6), 782–786.

Cramer, B. and Palacio Espasa, F. (1993). *La pratique des psychothérapies mères-bébés. Études cliniques et techniques (The practice of mother–infant psychotherapies. Clinical and technical studies)*. Paris: PUF.

D'Entremont, B. (1995). *One- to six-months-olds' attention and affective responding to adults' happy and sad expressions: The role of face and voice*. Ontario: Queen's University.

da Rocha Barros, E. M. and da Rocha Barros, E. L. (2011). Reflections on the clinical implications of symbolism. *International Journal of Psychoanalysis, 92*(4), 879–901.

DeCasper, A. J. and Fifer, W. P. (1980). Of human bonding: Newborns prefer their mothers' voices. *Science, 208*(4448), 1174–1176.

Decety, J. (2002). Is there such a thing as functional equivalence between imagined, observed, and executed action? In A. N. Meltzoff and W. Printz (Eds.), *The imitative mind: Development, evolution, and brain bases* (pp. 291–310). New York: Cambridge University Press.

Decety, J. (2010). The neurodevelopment of empathy in humans. *Developmental Neuroscience, 32*(4), 257–267.

Dennis, C.-L. E. (2004). Treatment of postpartum depression, part 2: A critical review of nonbiological interventions. *Journal of Clinical Psychiatry, 65*(9), 1252–1265.

Derogatis, L. R. (1994). *Symptom Checklist-90-R: Administration, scoring and procedures manual* (3rd revised ed.). Minneapolis, MN: National Computer Systems.

Diatkine, G. (2007). Lacan. *International Journal of Psychoanalysis, 88*(3), 643–660.

Diatkine, G. (2008). La disparition de la sexualité infantile dans la psychanalyse contemporaine (The disappearance of infantile sexuality in contemporary psychoanalysis). *Revue Francaise de Psychanalyse, 72*(3), 671–685.

Dolto, F. (1982). *Séminaires de psychanalyse d'enfant, vol. 1 (Seminars on child psychoanalysis, vol. 1)*. Paris: Editions du Seuil.

Dolto, F. (1985). *Séminaires de psychanalyse d'enfant, vol. 2 (Seminars on child psychoanalysis, vol. 2)*. Paris: Editions du Seuil.

DSM-IVTR. (2000). *Diagnostic and statistical manual of mental disorders* (4th ed. Text Revision). Washington, DC: American Psychiatric Association.

Eco, U. (1968). *La struttura assente (The absent structure)*. Milano: Bompiani ([1971] Den frånvarande strukturen. Lund: Cavefors.).

Elliott, R., Fischer, C. T. and Rennie, D. L. (1999). Evolving guidelines for publication of qualitative research studies in psychology and related fields. *British Journal of Clinical Psychology, 38*(3), 215–229.

Emanuel, L. (2006). Disruptive and distressed toddlers: The impact of undetected maternal depression on infants and young children. *Infant Observation, 9*(3), 249–259.

Emanuel, L. and Bradley, E. (Eds.). (2008). *"What can the matter be?" Therapeutic interventions with parents, infants, and young children*. London: Karnac Books.

Faimberg, H. (2005). Après-coup. *International Journal of Psychoanalysis, 86*(1), 1–6.

Falissard, B. (2012). *Treatment for the brain, treatment for the mind: the same "Evidence-Based Medicine" for both?* Paper presented at the 20th World Congress of the International Association for Child and Adolescent Psychiatry and Allied Professions, Paris.

Falzeder, E. (Ed.). (2002). *The complete correspondence of Sigmund Freud and Karl Abraham 1907–1925*. London: Karnac Books.

Feldman, R. (2007). Parent–infant synchrony and the construction of shared timing; physiological precursors, developmental outcomes, and risk conditions. *Journal of Child Psychology and Psychiatry and Allied Disciplines, 48*(3–4), 329–354.

Ferenczi, S. (1931). Child-analysis in the analysis of adults. *International Journal of Psychoanalysis, 12*, 468–482.

Ferenczi, S. (1933). Confusion of tongues between adult and the child. In *Final contributions to the problems and methods of psychoanalysis (1955)* (pp. 156–167). London: Maresfield.

Fernald, A. (2004). Hearing, listening and understanding: auditory development in infancy. In G. Bremner and A. Fogel (Eds.), *Blackwell handbook of infant development* (pp. 35–70). London: Blackwell.

Ferro, A. (1999). *The bi-personal field: Experiences in child analysis*. London: Routledge.

Ferro, A. (2006). Clinical implications of Bion's thought. *International Journal of Psychoanalysis, 87*(4), 989–1003.

Ferro, A. and Basile, R. (2004). The psychoanalyst as individual: Self-analysis and gradients of functioning. *Psychoanalytic Quartely, 73*, 659–682.

Ferro, A. and Basile, R. (Eds.). (2011). *The analytic field: A clinical concept.* London: Karnac Books.

Ferry, A. L., Hespos, S. J. and Waxman, S. R. (2010). Categorization in 3- and 4-month-old infants: An advantage of words over tones. *Child Development, 81*(2), 472–479.

Field, T. (2000). Infant massage therapy. In C. H. J. Zeanah (Ed.), *Handbook of infant mental health* (pp. 494–500). New York: The Guilford Press.

Flink, P.-O. (2001). On Norman's 'The psychoanalyst and the baby: A new look at work with infants'. *International Journal of Psychoanalysis, 82*(3), 805–807.

Fonagy, P. (1993). Psychoanalytical and empirical approaches. Can they be usefully integrated? *Journal of Royal Society of Medicine, 86*(10), 577–581.

Fonagy, P. (1996). Discussion of Peter Wolff's paper "Infant observation and psychoanalysis". *Journal of the American Psychoanalytic Association, 44*(2), 404–422.

Fonagy, P. (2001). *Attachment theory and psychoanalysis.* New York: Other Press.

Fonagy, P. (2008). A genuinely developmental theory of sexual enjoyment and its implications for psychoanalytic technique. *Journal of the American Psychoanalytic Association, 56*(1), 11–36.

Fonagy, P., Gergely, G., Jurist, E. L. and Target, M. (2002). *Affect regulation, mentalization, and the development of the self.* New York: Other Press.

Fonagy, P., Steele, M., Steele, H., Leigh, T., Kennedy, R., Mattoon, G. and Target, M. (1995). Attachment, the reflective self, and borderline states. In S. Goldberg and J. Kerr (Eds.), *Attachment research: The state of the art* (pp. 233–278). New York: The Analytic Press.

Fonagy, P., Steele, M., Steele, H., Moran, G. S. and Higgitt, A. (1991). The capacity for understanding mental states: The reflective self in parent and child and its significance for security of attachment. *Infant Mental Health Journal, 12*(3), 201–218.

Fonagy, P. and Target, M. (2007). The rooting of the mind in the body: New links between attachment theory and psychoanalytic thought. *Journal of the American Psychoanalytic Association, 55*(2), 411–456.

Fraiberg, S. (1980). *Clinical studies in infant mental health.* New York: Basic Books.

Fraiberg, S. (1982). Pathological defenses in infancy. *Psychoanalytic Quarterly, 51*(4), 612–635.

Fraiberg, S. (1987). *Selected writings of Selma Fraiberg.* Columbus, OH: Ohio State University Press.

Fraiberg, S., Adelson, E. and Shapiro, V. (1975). Ghosts in the nursery. A psychoanalytic approach to the problems of impaired infant–mother relationships. *Journal of the American Academy of Child Psychiatry, 14*(3), 387–421.

Freud, A. (1926). *Introduction to the technique of child analysis.* London: Imago Publishing Co.

Freud, A. (1965). *Normality and pathology in childhood: Assessments of development.* New York: International Universities Press.

Freud, S. (1895/1950). Project for a scientific psychology. In J. Strachey (Ed.), *The standard edition of the complete psychological works of Sigmund Freud, Vol. I* (SE) (pp. 281–391). London: Hogarth Press.

Freud, S. (1892–99/1950). Extracts from the Fliess papers. SE 1, pp. 175–282.

Freud, S. (1896). Further remarks on the neuro-psychoses of defence. SE 3, pp. 157–185.

Freud, S. (1900). The interpretation of dreams. SE 4–5.

Freud, S. (1901). On dreams. SE 5, pp. 629–686.

Freud, S. (1905a). Fragment of an analysis of a case of hysteria. SE 7, pp. 1–122.

Freud, S. (1905b). Three essays on sexuality. SE 7, pp. 123–246.

Freud, S. (1909). Analysis of a phobia in a five-year-old boy. SE 10, pp. 1–150.

Freud, S. (1909). Some general remarks on hysterical attacks. SE 9, pp. 227–234.

Freud, S. (1910). Five lectures on psycho-analysis. SE 11, pp. 1–56.

Freud, S. (1911). Formulations on the two principles of mental functioning. SE 12, pp. 213–226.

Freud, S. (1912a). The dynamics of transference. SE 12, pp. 97–108.

Freud, S. (1912b). On the universal tendency to debasement in the sphere of love (Contributions to the psychology of love II). SE 11, pp. 177–190.

Freud, S. (1913). The claims of psycho-analysis to scientific interest. SE 13, pp. 165–192.

Freud, S. (1914). Remembering, repeating and working-through. SE 12, pp. 145–156.

Freud, S. (1915a). Instincts and their vicissitudes. SE 14, pp. 109–140.

Freud, S. (1915b). Repression. SE 14, pp. 141–158.

Freud, S. (1915c). The Unconscious. SE 14, pp. 159–216.

Freud, S. (1916–17). Introductory lectures on psychoanalysis. SE 15–16.

Freud, S. (1917). Mourning and melancholia. SE 14, pp. 237–258.

Freud, S. (1918). From the history of an infantile neurosis. SE 17, pp. 1–124.

Freud, S. (1920). Beyond the pleasure principle. SE 18, pp. 1–64.

Freud, S. (1923). Two encyclopedia articles. SE 18, pp. 233–260.

Freud, S. (1925–26). Inhibitions, symptoms and anxiety. SE 20, pp. 87–178.

Freud, S. (1933). New introductory lectures on psychoanalysis. SE 22, pp. 1–182.

Fridell, M., Cesarec, Z., Johansson, M. and Malling Thorsen, S. (2002). *Svensk normering, standardisering och validering av symptomskalan SCL-90 (a Swedish standardization and validation of the SCL-90)*. Stockholm: Statens Institutionsstyrelse.

Gaensbauer, T. (1995). Trauma in the preverbal period. Symptoms, memories, and developmental impact. *Psychoanalytic Study of the Child, 50*, 122–149.

Gaensbauer, T. (2011). Embodied simulation, mirror neurons, and the reenactment of trauma in early childhood. *Neuropsychoanalysis, 13*(1), 91–107.

Gagliardi, L., Petrozzi, A. and Rusconi, F. (2010). Symptoms of maternal depression immediately after delivery predict unsuccessful breast feeding. *Archives of Disease in Childhood, 97*(4), 355–357.

Gammelgaard, J. (1998). Metaphors of listening. *Scandinavian Psychoanalytic Review, 21*(2), 151–167.

Gervain, J., Macagno, F., Cogoi, S., Peña, M. and Mehler, J. (2008). The neonate brain detects speech structure. *Proceedings of the National Academy of Sciences of the United States of America, 105*(37), 14222–14227.

Gervain, J. and Mehler, J. (2010). Speech perception and language acquisition in the first year of life. *Annual Review of Psychology, 61*, 191–218.

Gibello, B. (1989). Fantasme, langage, nature, trois ordres de réalité (Fantasy, language, nature, three orders of reality). In D. Anzieu (Ed.), *Psychanalyse et langage (Psychoanalysis and language)* (pp. 25–70). Paris: Dunod.

Goetzmann, L. and Schwegler, K. (2004). Semiotic aspects of the countertransference: Some observations on the concepts of the 'immediate object' and the 'interpretant' in the work of Charles S. Peirce. *International Journal of Psychoanalysis, 85*(6), 1423–1438.

Golse, B. (2006). *L'être-bébé (The baby – a Being)*. Paris: PUF.

Golse, B. and Roussillon, R. (2010). *La naissance de l'objet (The birth of the object)*. Paris: PUF.

Green, A. (1995). Has sexuality anything to do with psychoanalysis? *International Journal of Psychoanalysis, 76*(5), 871–883.

Green, A. (1998). The primordial mind and the work of the negative. *International Journal of Psychoanalysis, 79*, 649–665.

Green, A. (2004). Thirdness and psychoanalytic concepts. *Psychoanalytic Quarterly, 73*(1), 99–13.

Grotstein, J. (1980). A proposed revision of the psychoanalytic concept of primitive mental states: Part I. Introduction to a newer psychoanalytic metapsychology. *Contemporary Psychoanalysis, 16*, 479–546.

Grotstein, J. (1997). Integrating one-person and two-person psychologies: Autochthony and alterity in counterpoint. *Psychoanalytic Quarterly, 66*(3), 403–430.

Grotstein, J. (2003). Toward a name of her own: Commentary on Farhi. *Contemporary Psychoanalysis, 39*, 99–106.

Grotstein, J. (2008). *A beam of intense darkness. Wilfred Bion's legacy to psychoanalysis.* London: Karnac Books.

Guiraud, P. (1975). *Semiology* (G. Gross, Trans.). London: Routledge and Kegan Paul.

Hamilton, M. A. (1967). Development of a rating scale for primary depressive illness. *Journal of Social and Clinical Psychology, 6*(4), 278–296.

Hermann, I. (1976 [1936]). Clinging – going-in-search: A contrasting pair of instincts and their relation to sadism and masochism. *Psychoanalytic Quarterly, 45*(1), 5–36.

Hinshelwood, R. D. (1989). *A dictionary of Kleinian thought.* London: Free Association Books.

Holden, J. M., Sagovsky, R. and Cox, J. L. (1989). Counselling in a general practice setting: Controlled study of health visitor intervention in treatment of postnatal depression. *British Medical Journal, 298*(6668), 223–226.

Horowitz, M. J. (1993). Interpersonal problems, attachment styles and outcome in brief dynamic therapy. *Journal of Consulting and Clinical Psychology, 61*(4), 549–560.

Hundeide, K. (2007). When empathic care is obstructed: Excluding the child from the zone of intimacy. In S. Bråten (Ed.), *On being moved. From mirror neurons to empathy* (pp. 237–256). Amsterdam: John Benjamins Publishing Company.

Jick, T. D. (1979). Mixing qualitative and quantitative methods: Triangulation in action. *Qualitative Methodology, 24*(4), 602–611.

Jimenez, J. P. (2007). Can research influence clinical practice? *International Journal of Psychoanalysis, 88*(3), 661–679.

Jones, E. (1916). The theory of symbolism. In *Papers on psycho-analysis, 1948* (5th ed., pp. 87–144). London: Baillière, Tindall and Cox.

Jones, E. E., Cumming, J. D. and Horowitz, M. J. (1988). Another look at the nonspecific hypothesis of therapeutic effectiveness. *Journal of Consulting and Clinical Psychology, 56*(1), 48–55.

Joseph, B. (1985). Transference: The total situation. *International Journal of Psychoanalysis, 66*, 447–454.

Kant, I. (1996). *Critique of pure reason: Unified edition (1781, 1787)* (W. S. Pluhar, Trans.). Indianapolis, IN: Hackett.

Karmiloff, K. and Karmiloff-Smith, A. (2001). *Pathways to language.* Cambridge, MA: Harvard University Press.

Kendall, P. C., Holmbeck, G. and Verduin, T. (2004). Methodology, design, and evaluation in psychotherapy research. In M. J. Lambert (Ed.), *Bergin and Garfield's handbook of psychotherapy and behaviour change* (Vol. 5, pp. 16–43). New York: John Wiley and Sons Inc.

Kermode, F. (1985). Freud and interpretation. *International Review of Psychoanalysis, 12*(1), 3–12.

Khan, M. M. (1963). The concept of cumulative trauma. *Psychoanalytic Study of the Child, 18*, 286–306.

Khan, M. M. (1964). Ego distortion, cumulative trauma, and the role of reconstruction in the analytic situation. *International Journal of Psychoanalysis, 45*, 272–279.

Klaus, M., Jerauld, R., Kreger, N., McAlpine, W., Steffa, M. and Kennell, J. H. (1972). Maternal attachment: Importance of the first postpartum days. *New England Journal of Medicine, 286*(9), 460–463.

Klein, M. (1935). A contribution to the psychogenesis of manic-depressive states. In R. Money-Kyrle (Ed.), *The writings of Melanie Klein* (Vol. 1, pp. 262–289). London: Hogarth Press.

Klein, M. (1945). The Oedipus complex in the light of early anxieties. Vol. 1, pp. 370–419.

Klein, M. (1946). Notes on some schizoid mechanisms. Vol. 3, pp. 1–24.

Klein, M. (1952). The origins of transference. Vol. 3, pp. 48–56.

Klein, M. (1959). Our adult world and its roots in infancy. Vol. 3, pp. 247–263.

Klerman, G. L., Weismann, M. M., Rounsaville, B. J. and Chevron, E. S. (1984). *Interpersonal psychotherapy of depression*. New York: Basic Books.

Kloesel, C. and Houser, N. (Eds.). (1992). *The essential Peirce, vol. 1: 1867–1893*. Bloomington, IN: Indiana University Press.

Kloesel, C. and Houser, N. (Eds.). (1998). *The essential Peirce, vol. 2: 1893–1913*. Bloomington, IN: Indiana University Press.

Krentz, U. C. and Corina, D. P. (2008). Preference for language in early infancy: The human language bias is not speech specific. *Developmental Science 11*(1), 1–9.

Kugiumutzakis, G., Kokkinaki, T., Makrodimitraki, M. and Vitalaki, E. (2005). Emotions in early mimesis. In J. Nadel and D. Muir (Eds.), *Emotional development* (pp. 162–182). Oxford: Oxford University Press.

Kuhl, P. K. (2004). Early language acquisition: Cracking the speech code. *Nature Neuroscience, 5*(3), 831–843.

Køppe, S., Harder, S. and Væver, M. (2008). Vitality affects. *International Forum of Psychoanalysis, 17*(3), 169–179.

Lacan, J. (1966). *Écrits, Vol. 1*. Paris: Seuil.

Lacan, J. (1975). *Encore: Séminaires* (On feminine sexuality, the limits of love and knowledge: The Seminar of Jacques Lacan, Book XX, Encore) (Vol. 20). Paris: Dunod.

Lacan, J. (1998). La forclusion du Nom-du-Père (The foreclosure of the Name of the Father). In J.-A. Miller (Ed.), *Le séminaire vol. 5. Les formations de l'inconscient (The seminar, Vol. 5. Formations of the unconscious)* (pp. 143–159). Paris: Ed. du Seuil.

Lakoff, G. and Johnson, M. (1999). *Philosophy in the flesh*. New York: Basic Books.

Langer, S. (1942). *Philosophy in a new key* (3rd ed.). Cambridge, MA.: Harvard University Press.

Laplanche, J. (1989). *New foundations for psychoanalysis (Nouveaux fondements pour la psychanalyse, 1987)* (D. Macey, Trans.). Oxford: Basil Blackwell.

Laplanche, J. (1995). Seduction, persecution, revelation. *International Journal of Psychoanalysis, 76,* 663–682.

Laplanche, J. (1997). The theory of seduction and the problem of the other. *International Journal of Psychoanalysis, 78*(4), 653–666.

Laplanche, J. (1999a). *Essays on otherness.* London: Routledge.

Laplanche, J. (1999b). *The unconscious and the id.* London: Rebus Press.

Laplanche, J. (2002). Sexuality and attachment in metapsychology. In D. Widlöcher (Ed.), *Infantile sexuality and attachment* (pp. 37–63). New York: Other Press.

Laplanche, J. (2007). *Sexual. La sexualité élargie au sens Freudien ("Sexual". Sexuality enlarged in the Freudian sense).* Paris: PUF.

Laplanche, J. and Pontalis, J. B. (1973). *The language of psychoanalysis.* London: Hogarth Press.

Lebovici, S. and Stoléru, S. (2003). *Le nourisson, sa mère et le psychanalyste. Les interactions précoces (The baby, his mother and the psychoanalyst. Early interactions).* Paris: Bayard.

Ledoux, M. H. (2006). *Dictionnaire raisonné de l'oeuvre de F. Dolto (A commented dictionnary on the work of F. Dolto).* Paris: Payot and Rivages.

Lepage, J.-F. and Théoret, H. (2007). The mirror neuron system: Grasping others' actions from birth? *Developmental Science, 10*(5), 513–523.

Leuzinger-Bohleber, M., Stuhr, U., Ruger, B. and Beutel, M. (2003). How to study the quality of psychoanalytic treatments and their long-term effects on patients' well-being: A representative, multi-perspective follow-up study. *International Journal of Psychoanalysis, 84*(2), 263–290.

Levenson, E. (2005 [1983]). The ambiguity of change. An inquiry into the nature of psychoanalytic reality. In E. Levenson (Ed.), *The fallacy of understanding: The ambiguity of change.* Hillsdale, NJ: The Analytic Press.

Lichtenberg, J. (1983). *Psychoanalysis and infant research.* Hillsdale, NJ: Analytic Press.

Lieberman, A. F. and Van Horn, P. (2008). *Psychotherapy with infants and young children: Repairing the effects of stress and trauma on early attachment.* New York: The Guilford Press.

Lieberman, A. F., Weston, D. R. and Pawl, J. H. (1991). Preventive intervention and outcome with anxiously attached dyads. *Child Development, 62*(1), 199–209.

Lindner, E. (1912). *Richard Wagner über Tristan und Isolde (Richard Wagner on Tristan and Isolde).* Leipzig: Breitkopf and Härtel.

Lindner, R. (2006). Suicidality in men in psychodynamic psychotherapy. *Psychoanalytic Psychotherapy, 20*(3), 197–217.

Litowitz, B. E. (2012). Why this question? Commentary on Vivona. *Journal of the American Psychoanalytic Association, 60*(2), 267–274.

Lojkasek, M., Cohen, N. J. and Muir, E. (1994). Where is the infant in infant intervention? A review of the literature on changing troubled mother–infant relationships. *Psychotherapy: Theory, Research, Practice, Training, 31*(1), 208–220.

Luyten, P., Blatt, S. J. and Corveleyn, J. (2006). Minding the gap between positivism and hermeneutics in psychoanalytic research. *Journal of the American Psychoanalytic Association, 54*(2), 571–610.

MacFarlane, A. (1975). Olfaction in the development of social preferences in the human neonate. *Parent–infant interaction. CIBA-foundation symposium, 33.* Retrieved from http://onlinelibrary.wiley.com/doi/10.1002/9780470720158.ch7/summary (accessed August 20 2013).

Maiello, S. (1995). The sound object. *Journal of Child Psychotherapy, 21*(2), 23–42.

Main, M. and Solomon, J. (1986). Discovery of a new, insecure/disorganized/disoriented attachment pattern. In T. B. Brazelton and M. W. Yogman (Eds.), *Affective development in infancy* (pp. 95–124). Norwood, NJ.: Ablex.

Mark, E. (2001). Is the self of the infant preserved in the adult? *Medicine, Health Care and Philosophy, 4*(3), 347–353.

Markova, G. and Legerstee, M. (2006). Contingency, imitation, and affect sharing: Foundations of infants' social awareness. *Developmental Psychology, 42*(1), 132–141.

Marks, Z., Murphy, S. and Glowinski, H. (2001). *A compendium of Lacanian terms.* London: Free Association Books.

Maroda, K. (2000). Reflections on Benjamin Wolstein, personal analysis, and coparticipation. *Contemporary Psychoanalysis, 36*, 241–249.

Maroda, K. (2002). No place to hide: Affectivity, the unconscious, and the development of relational techniques. *Contemporary Psychoanalysis, 38*, 101–120.

Martindale, C. (1975). The grammar of altered states of consciousness: A semiotic reinterpretation of aspects of psychoanalytic theory. *Psychoanalysis and Contemporary Science, 4*, 331–354.

Maze, J. R. and Henry, R. M. (1996). Problems in the concept of repression and proposals for their resolution. *International Journal of Psychoanalysis, 77*(6), 1085–1100.

McCarter-Spaulding, D. and Horowitz, J. A. (2007). How does postpartum depression affect breastfeeding? *The American Journal of Maternal/Child Nursing, 32*(1), 10–17.

McDonough, S. (2004). Interaction guidance. Promoting and nurturing the caregiving relationship. In A. J. Sameroff, S. C. McDonough and K. L. Rosenblum (Ed.), *Treating parent–infant relationship problems* (pp. 79–96). New York: The Guilford Press.

Mehler, J., Jusczyk, P. W., Lambertz, G., Halsted, N., Bertoncini, J. and Amiel-Tison, C. (1988). A precursor of language acquisition in young infants. *Cognition, 29*(2), 144–178.

Melon, J. (1983). D'amour et de mort (On love and death). *Revue Belqique de psychanalyse, 3*, 51–72.

Meltzer, D. (1966). The relation of anal masturbation to projective identification. *International Journal of Psychoanalysis, 47*, 335–342.

Meltzer, D. (1967). *The psychoanalytic process.* Perthshire: Clunie Press.

Meltzer, D. (1992). *The claustrum.* Perthshire: Clunie Press.

Meltzer, D. and Harris-Williams, M. (1988). *The apprehension of beauty: The role of aesthetic conflict in development, violence and art.* Perthshire: Clunie Press.

Meltzoff, A. N. and Moore, M. K. (1977). Imitation of facial and manual gestures by human neonates. *Science, 198*(4312), 74–78.

Meltzoff, A. N. and Moore, M. K. (1994). Imitation, memory and the representations of persons. *Infant Behaviour and Development, 17*(1), 83–99.

Meltzoff, A. N. and Moore, M. K. (1997). Explaining facial imitation: A theoretical model. *Early Development and Parenting, 6*(3–4), 179–192.

Miller, L. (2008). The relation of infant observation to clinical practice in an under-fives clinical service. In L. Emanuel and E. Bradley (Eds.), *"What can the matter be?" Therapeutic interventions with parents, infants, and young children* (pp. 38–53). London: Karnac Books.

Misri, S. and K. Joe (2008). Perinatal mood disorders: An introduction. Perinatal and postpartum mood disorders. In S. Dowd Stone and A. Menken (Eds.), *Perinatal and postpartum mood disorders* (pp. 65–83). New York, Springer.

Mittag, A.-M. (2009). The Child Health Care of Stockholm. *Vårdguiden*. Retrieved from www.vardguiden.se/Sa-funkar-det/Halso-och-sjukvard/Narsjukvard/Barnhalsovard/ (accessed 5 September 2013).

Moore, B. E. and Fine, B. D. (1990). *Psychoanalytic terms and concepts* (as published in 2010, "PEP Consolidated Psychoanalytic Glossary", Eds. Tuckett and Levinson). New York: Yale University Press.

Muir, D., Lee, K., Hains, C. and Hains, S. (2005). Infant perception and production of emotions during face-to-face interactions with live and "virtual" adults. In J. Nadel and D. Muir (Eds.), *Emotional development* (pp. 207–234). Oxford: Oxford University Press.

Muir, E. (1991). Integrating individual and family therapy. In R. Szur and S. Miller (Eds.), *Extending horizons. Psychoanalytic psychotherapy with children, adolescents and families* (pp. 65–82). London: Karnac.

Muller, J. (1996). *Beyond the psychoanalytic dyad.* New York and London: Routledge.

Muller, J. and Brent, J. (2000). *Peirce, semiotics, and psychoanalysis.* Baltimore and London: The Johns Hopkins University Press.

Murray, L., Cooper, P. J., Wilson, A. and Romaniuk, H. (2003). Controlled trial of the short- and long-term effect of psychological treatment of post-partum depression. 2. Impact on the mother–child relationship and child outcome. *British Journal of Psychiatry, 182*(5), 420–427.

Nagy, E. and Molnar, P. (2004). Homo imitans or homo provocans? Human imprinting model of neonatal imitation. *Infant Behavior and Development, 27*(1), 54–63.

Nazzi, T., Bertoncini, J. and Mehler, J. (1998). Language discrimination by newborns: Toward an understanding of the role of rhythm. *Journal of Experimental Psychology: Human Perception and Performance, 24*(3), 756–766.

Negri, R. (2007). Therapeutic consultation: early detection of "alarm symptoms" in infants and treatment with parent–infant psychotherapy. In M. E. Pozzi-Monzo and B. Tydeman (Eds.), *Innovations in parent–infant psychotherapy* (pp. 95–116). London: Karnac Books.

Norman, J. (1994). The psychoanalyst's instrument: a mental space for impressions, affective resonance and thoughts. In *The analyst's mind: From listening to interpretation* (pp. 89–100). London: IPA Press.

Norman, J. (2001). The psychoanalyst and the baby: A new look at work with infants. *International Journal of Psychoanalysis, 82*(1), 83–100.

Norman, J. (2004). Transformations of early infantile experiences: A 6-month-old in psychoanalysis. *International Journal of Psychoanalysis, 85*(5), 1103–1122.

O'Hara, M. W., Stuart, S., Gorman, L. L. and Wenzel, A. (2000). Efficacy of interpersonal psychotherapy for postpartum depression. *Archives of General Psychiatry, 57*(11), 1039–1045.

Olds, D. D. (2000). A semiotic model of mind. *Journal of the American Psychoanalytic Association, 48*(2), 497–529.

Orlinsky, D. E., Rönnestad, M. H. and Willutzki, U. (2004). Fifty years of psychotherapy process-outcome research: Continuity and change. In M. J. Lambert (Ed.), *Bergin and Garfield's handbook of psychotherapy and behaviour change* (5th ed., pp. 307–390). New York: John Wiley and Sons, Inc.

Östberg, M., Hagekull, B. and Wettergren, S. (1997). A measure of parental stress in mothers with small children: dimensionality, stability and validity. *Scandinavian Journal of Psychology, 38*(3), 199–208.

Papousek, M., Schieche, M. and Wurmser, H. (Eds.). (2008). *Disorders of behavioural and emotional regulation in the first years of life.* Washington, DC: Zero to Three.

Peterfreund, E. (1978). Some critical comments on psychoanalytic conceptualizations of infancy. *International Journal of Psychoanalysis, 59,* 427–441.

Petot, J.-M. (1990). *Melanie Klein: Vol. 1: First discovery and first system (1919–1932)* (C. Trollope, Trans.). Madison, CT: International Universities Press.

Philips, B., Werbart, A., Wennberg, P. and Schubert, J. (2007). Young adults' ideas of cure prior to psychoanalytic psychotherapy. *Journal of Clinical Psychology, 63*(3), 213–232.

Piene, F., Auestad, A.-M., Lange, J. and Leira, T. (1983). Countertransference–transference seen from the point of view of child psychoanalysis. *Scandinavian Psychoanalytic Review, 6*(1), 43–57.

Porge, E. (2000). *Jacques Lacan, un psychanalyste (Jacques Lacan, a psychoanalyst).* Ramoville Saint-Anne: Eres.

Porter, R. H., Cernoch, J. M. and McLaughlin, J. F. (1983). Maternal recognition of neonates through olfactory cues. *Physiology and Behaviour, 30*(1), 151–154.

Pozzi-Monzo, M. E. and Tydeman, B. (Eds.). (2007). *Innovations in parent–infant psychotherapy.* London: Karnac Books.

Quinodoz, D. (1992). The psychoanalytic setting as the instrument of the container function. *International Journal of Psychoanalysis, 73*(4), 627–635.

Racker, H. (1957). The meanings and uses of countertransference. *Psychoanalytic Quarterly, 26*(3), 303–357.

Racker, H. (1968). *Transference and countertransference.* London: Karnac Books.

Reddy, V. (2008). *How infants know minds.* Cambridge, MA: Harvard University Press.

Robert-Tissot, C., Cramer, B., Stern, D. N., Serpa, S. R., Bachmann, J.-P., Palacio-Espasa, F. and Mendiguren, G. (1996). Outcome evaluation in brief mother–infant psychotherapies: Report on 75 cases. *Infant Mental Health Journal, 17*(2), 97–114.

Romantshik, O., Porter, R., Tillmann, V. and Varendi, H. (2007). Preliminary evidence of a sensitive period for olfactory learning by human newborns. *Acta Paediatrica, 96*(3), 372–376.

Rosenfeld, H. (1987). *Impasse and interpretation: Therapeutic and anti-therapeutic factors in the psychoanalytic treatment of psychotic, borderline, and neurotic patients.* London: Tavistock.

Rosolato, G. (1978). Symbol formation. *International Journal of Psychoanalysis, 59,* 303–313.

Rosolato, G. (1985). *Éléments de l'interprétation (Elements of interpretation).* Paris: Gallimard.

Roth, A. and Fonagy, P. (2005). *What works for whom: A critical review of psychotherapy research,* 2nd ed. New York: Guilford Publications.

Roussillon, R. (2011). *Primitive agony and symbolization.* London: IPA and Karnac.

Rovee-Collier, C. and Hayne, H. (1987). Reactivation of infant memory: Implications for cognitive sevelopment. In H. Reese (Ed.), *Advances in child development and behavior* (pp. 185–238). New York: Academic Press.

Russell, M. J., Mendelson, T. and Peeke, H. V. S. (1983). Mothers' identification of their infant's odors. *Ethology and Sociobiology, 4*(1), 29–31.

Salomonsson, B. (1989). Music and affects: Psychoanalytic viewpoints. *Scandinavian Psychoanalytic Review, 12*(2), 126–144.

Salomonsson, B. (1998). Between listening and expression: On desire, resonance and containment. *Scandinavian Psychoanalytic Review, 21*(2), 168–182.

Salomonsson, B. (2006). The impact of words on children with ADHD and DAMP. Consequences for psychoanalytic technique. *International Journal of Psychoanalysis, 87*(4), 1029–1047.

Salomonsson, B. (2007a). Semiotic transformations in psychoanalysis with infants and adults. *International Journal of Psychoanalysis, 88*(5), 1201–1221.

Salomonsson, B. (2007b). "Talk to me baby, tell me what's the matter now". Semiotic and developmental perspectives on communication in psychoanalytic infant treatment. *International Journal of Psychoanalysis, 88*(1), 127–146.

Salomonsson, B. (2009). Mother–infant work and its impact on psychoanalysis with adults. *Scandinavian Psychoanalytic Review, 32*(1), 3–13.

Salomonsson, B. (2011). The music of containment. Addressing the participants in mother–infant psychoanalytic treatment. *Infant Mental Health Journal, 32*(6), 599–612.

Salomonsson, B. (2012). Has infantile sexuality anything to do with infants? *International Journal of Psychoanalysis, 93*(3), 631–647.

Salomonsson, B. (2013a). An infant's experience of postnatal depression: Towards a psychoanalytic model. *Journal of Child Psychotherapy, 39*(2), 137–155.

Salomonsson, B. (2013b). Transferences in parent–infant psychoanalytic treatments. *International Journal of Psychoanalysis, 94*(4), 767–792.

Salomonsson, B. and Sandell, R. (2011a). A randomized controlled trial of mother–infant psychoanalytic treatment. 1. Outcomes on self-report questionnaires and external ratings. *Infant Mental Health Journal, 32*(2), 207–231.

Salomonsson, B. and Sandell, R. (2011b). A randomized controlled trial of mother–infant psychoanalytic treatment. 2. Predictive and moderating influences of quantitative treatment and patient factors. *Infant Mental Health Journal, 32*(3), 377–404.

Salomonsson, B. and Sandell, R. (2012). Maternal experiences and the mother–infant dyad's development: Introducing the Interview of Mother's Experiences (I-ME). *Journal of Reproductive and Infant Psychology, 30*(1), 21–50.

Salomonsson, B. and Sleed, M. (2010). The ASQ:SE. A validation study of a mother-report questionnaire on a clinical mother–infant sample. *Infant Mental Health Journal, 31*(4), 412–431.

Sandler, J., Kennedy, H. and Tyson, R. (1990). *The technique of child psychoanalysis. Discussions with Anna Freud.* London: Karnac Books.

Sandler, J. and Rosenblatt, B. (1962). The concept of the representational world. *The Psychoanalytic Study of the Child, 17*, 128–145.

Sandler, J. and Sandler, A.-M. (1994). Phantasy and its transformations: A contemporary Freudian view. *International Journal of Psychoanalysis, 75*, 387–394.

Sandler, J., Sandler, A.-M. and Davies, R. (Eds.). (2000). *Clinical and observational psychoanalytical research: Roots of a controversy.* London: Karnac Books.

Sandler, P. C. (2005). *The language of Bion. A dictionary of concepts.* London: Karnac Books.

Schechter, D. S., Coots, T., Zeanah, C. H., Davies, M., Coates, S. W., Trabka, K. A. and Myers, M. M. (2005). Maternal mental representations of the child in an inner-city clinical sample: Violence-related posttraumatic stress and reflective functioning. *Attachment and Human Development, 7*(3), 313–331.

Scruton, R. (2004). *Death-devoted heart: Sex and the sacred in Wagner's Tristan and Isolde.* Oxford: Oxford University Press.

Segal, H. (1957). Notes on symbol formation. In *The work of Hanna Segal* (pp. 49–68). Northvale, NJ: Aronson, 1981.

Segal, H. (1991). *Dream, phantasy and art*. London: Routledge.

Seimyr, L., Edhborg, M., Lundh, W. and Sjögren, B. (2004). In the shadow of maternal depressed mood: experiences of parenthood during the first year after childbirth. *Journal of Psychosomatic Obstetrics and Gynecology, 25*(1), 23–34.

Seligman, S. and Harrison, A. (2012). Infancy research, infant mental health, and adult psychotherapy: Mutual influences. *Infant Mental Health Journal, 33*(4), 339–349.

Sheriff, J. K. (1994). *Charles Peirce's guess at the riddle: Grounds for human significance*. Bloomington IN: Indiana University Press.

Silver, A. (1981). A psychosemiotic model: An interdisciplinary search for a common structural basis for psychoanalysis, symbol-formation, and the semiotic of Charles S. Peirce. In J. Grotstein (Ed.), *Do I dare disturb the universe? A memorial to W. R. Bion* (pp. 270–315). London: Karnac Books.

Silverman, R. and Lieberman, A. (1999). Negative maternal attributions, projective identification, and the intergenerational transmission of violent relational patterns. *Psychoanalytic Dialogues, 9*(2), 161–186.

Singleton, J. L. (2005). *Parent–infant interaction interventions: A meta-analysis*. Dissertation Abstracts International: Section B: The Sciences and Engineering.

Skelton, R. M. (2006). *The Edinburgh International Encyclopaedia of Psychoanalysis* (as published in 2010, "PEP Consolidated Psychoanalytic Glossary", Eds. Tuckett and Levinson). Edinburgh: Edinburgh University Press.

Skovgaard, A., Olsen, E., Christiansen, E., Houmann, T., Landorph, S. and Jörgensen, T. (2008). Predictors (0–10 months) of psychopathology at age 1½ years: A general population study in the Copenhagen Child Cohort CCC 2000. *Journal of Child Psychology and Psychiatry, 49*(5), 553–562.

Slade, A., Belsky, J., Aber, J. L. and Phelps, J. L. (1999). Mothers' representations of their relationships with their toddlers: links to adult attachment and observed mothering. *Developmental Psychology, 35*(3), 611–619.

Solms, M. and Turnbull, O. (2001). *The brain and the inner world. An introduction to the neuroscience of subjective experience*. New York: Other Press.

Soussignan, R. and Schaal, B. (2005). Emotional processes in human newborns: A functionalist perspective. In J. Nadel and D. Muir (Eds.), *Emotional development* (pp. 127–160). Oxford: Oxford University Press.

Spillius, E. B. (1983). Some developments from the work of Melanie Klein. *International Journal of Psychoanalysis, 64*, 321–332.

Spitz, R. (1965). *The first year of life*. New York: IUP.

Squires, J., Bricker, D., Heo, K. and Twombly, E. (2002). *Ages and Stages Questionnaires: Social-Emotional. A parent-completed, child-monitoring system for social-emotional behaviours*. Baltimore: Paul H Brookes Publishing.

Squires, J., Bricker, D. and Twombly, E. (2004). Parent-completed screening for social emotional problems in young children: The effects of risk/disability status and gender on performance. *Infant Mental Health Journal, 25*(1), 62–73.

Stein, R. (1998). The enigmatic dimension of sexual experience: The "otherness" of sexuality and primal seduction. *Psychoanalytic Quarterly, 67*(4), 594–625.

Steiner, J. (1993). *Psychic retreats*. London: Routledge.

Stern, D. N. (1985). *The interpersonal world of the infant*. New York: Basic Books.

Stern, D. N. (1988). The dialectic between the "interpersonal" and the "intrapsychic": With particular emphasis on the role of memory and representation. *Psychoanalytic Inquiry*, 8(4), 505–512.

Stern, D. N. (1995). *The motherhood constellation: A unified view of parent–infant psychotherapy*. London: Karnac Books.

Stern, D. N. (2004). *The present moment in psychotherapy and in everyday life*. New York: W.W. Norton and Company ltd.

Stern, D. N. (2008). The clinical relevance of infancy: A progress report. *Infant Mental Health Journal*, 29(3), 177–188.

Stern, D. N. (2010). *Forms of vitality: Exploring dynamic experience in psychology, the arts, psychotherapy, and development*. New York: Oxford University Press.

Stone, L. (1961). *The psychoanalytic situation*. New York: IUP.

Szejer, M. (2011). *Si les bébés pouvaient parler (If babies could talk)*. Paris: Bayard.

Thomson-Salo, F. (2007). Recognizing the infant as subject in infant–parent psychotherapy. *International Journal of Psychoanalysis*, 88(4), 961–979.

Thomson-Salo, F. and Paul, C. (2001). Some principles of infant–parent psychotherapy. Ann Morgan's contribution. *The Signal. The World Association for Infant Mental Health*, 9(1–2), 14–19.

Thomson-Salo, F., Paul, C., Morgan, A., Jones, S., Jordan, B., Meehan, M. and Morse, S. (1999). "Free to be playful": Therapeutic work with infants. *Infant Observation*, 31(1), 47–62.

Trevarthen, C. (2001). Intrinsic motives for companionship in understanding: Their origin, development, and significance for infant mental health. *Infant Mental Health Journal*, 22(1–2), 95–131.

Trevarthen, C. and Aitken, K. J. (2001). Infant intersubjectivity: research, theory, and clinical applications. *Journal of Child Psychology and Psychiatry and Allied Disciplines*, 42(1), 3–48.

Tronick, E. (2005). Why is connection with others so critical? The formation of dyadic states of consciousness and the expansion of individuals' states of consciousness: Coherence governed selection and the co-creation of meaning out of messy meaning making. In J. Nadel and D. Muir (Eds.), *Emotional development* (pp. 293–315). Oxford: Oxford University Press.

Tronick, E. (2007a). Depressed mothers and infants: Failure to form dyadic states of consciousness. In *The neurobehavioural and social-emotional development of infants and children* (pp. 274–292). New York City: W.W. Norton.

Tronick, E. (2007b). Infant moods and the chronicity of depressive symptoms: The cocreation of unique ways of being together for good or ill, Paper 2: The formation of negative moods in infants and children of depressed mothers. In E. Tronick (Ed.), *The neurobehavioural and social-emotional development of infants and children* (pp. 362–377). New York City: W. W. Norton.

Tronick, E., Als, H., Adamson, L., Wise, S. and Brazelton, T. B. (1978). The infant's response to entrapment between contradictory messages in face-to-face interaction. *Journal of the American Academy of Child and Adolescent Psychiatry*, 17(1), 1–13.

Tustin, F. (1981). *Autistic states in children*. London and Boston: Routledge.

Uvnäs-Moberg, K. (2000). *The oxytocin factor: Tapping the hormone of calm, love and healing*. Cambridge, MA: Perseus Book Group.

Van Buren, J. (1993). Mother–infant semiotics: Intuition and the development of human subjectivity. Klein/Lacan: Fantasy and meaning. *Journal of the American Academy of Psychoanalysis and Dynamic Psychiatry*, 21(4), 567–580.

Van Toller, S. and Kendal-Reed, M. (1995). A possible protocognitive role for odor in human infant development. *Brain and Cognition, 29*(3), 275–293.

Vivona, J. M. (2012). Is there a nonverbal period of development? *Journal of the American Psychoanalytic Association, 60*(2), 231–265.

Vouloumanos, A. and Werker, J. F. (2004). Tuned to the signal: The privileged status of speech for young infants. *Developmental Science, 7*(3), 270–276.

Vreeswijk, C. M. J. M., Maas, A. J. B. M. and van Bakel, H. J. A. (2012). Parental representations: A systematic review of the working model of the child interview. *Infant Mental Health Journal, 33*(1), 1–15.

Wachholz, S. and Stuhr, U. (1999). The concept of ideal types in psychoanalytic follow-up research. *Psychotherapy Research, 9*(3), 327–341.

Waddell, M. (2006). Infant observation in Britain: The Tavistock approach. *International Journal of Psychoanalysis, 87*(4), 1103–1120.

Wagner, R. (1865). *Tristan und Isolde.* Retrieved from www.rwagner.net/libretti/tristan/e-tristan-a3s1.html (Translator's name is not provided on the website) (accessed September 5 2013).

Wagner, R. (1868). *Die Meistersinger von Nürnberg.* Retrieved from www.rwagner.net/libretti/meisters/e-meisters-a2s3.html

Wampold, B. (2001). *The great psychotherapy debate. Models, methods and findings.* Mahwah, NJ: Lawrence Erlbaum Associates, Inc.

Watillon, A. (1993). The dynamics of psychoanalytic therapies of the early parent–child relationship. *International Journal of Psychoanalysis, 74,* 1037–1048.

Weber, M. (1904). *Die "Objektivität" sozialwissenschaftlicher sozialpolitischer Erkentnisse ("Objectivity" in social science and social politics).* Gesammelte Aufsätze zur Wissenschaftslehre. Tübingen: Mohr.

Werker, J. F. and Tees, R. C. (2002). Cross-language speech perception: Evidence for perceptual reorganization during the first year of life. *Infant Behavior and Development, 25*(1), 121–133.

Wickberg, B. and Hwang, C. P. (1997). Screening for postnatal depression in a population-based Swedish sample. *Acta Psychiatrica Scandinavica, 95*(1), 62–66.

Widlöcher, D. (2002). Primary love and infantile sexuality: An eternal debate. In D. Widlöcher (Ed.), *Infantile sexuality and attachment* (pp. 1–36). New York: Other Press.

Widström, A.-M., Ransjö-Arvidsson, A.-B. and Christensson, K. (2007). *DVD: Breastfeeding: Baby's choice.* Sweden: Liber Utbildning.

Widström, A., Lilja, G., Aaltomaa-Michalias, P., Dahllöf, A., Lintula, M. and Nissen, E. (2011). Newborn behaviour to locate the breast when skin-to-skin: A possible method for enabling early self-regulation. *Acta Paediatrica, 100*(1), 79–85.

Wikipedia. (2012). *Ideal type.* Retrieved from http://en.wikipedia.org/wiki/Ideal_type

Winberg Salomonsson, M. (1997). Transference in child analysis: A comparative reading of Anna Freud and Melanie Klein. *Scandinavian Psychoanalytic Review, 20*(1), 1–19.

Winnicott, D. W. (1941). The observation of infants in a set situation. *Through paediatrics to psycho-analysis* (pp. 52–69). London: Hogarth Press.

Winnicott, D. W. (1953). Transitional objects and transitional phenomena: A study of the first not-me possession. *International Journal of Psychoanalysis, 34,* 89–97.

Winnicott, D. W. (1955). Metapsychological and clinical aspects of regression within the psycho-analytical set-up. *International Journal of Psychoanalysis, 36,* 16–26.

Winnicott, D. W. (1956). Primary maternal preoccupation. In *Through paediatrics to psycho-analysis* (pp. 300–305). London (1982): Hogarth Press.

Winnicott, D. W. (1960). The theory of the parent–infant relationship. *International Journal of Psychoanalysis, 41*, 585–595.

Winnicott, D. W. (1965). *The maturational processes and the facilitating environment: Studies in the theory of emotional development.* London: Hogarth Press.

Winnicott, D. W. (1971). *Playing and reality.* London: Tavistock Publications.

Winnicott, D. W. (1971). *Therapeutic consultations in child psychiatry.* London: The Hogarth Press.

Winnicott, D. W. (1975). *Through paediatrics to psycho-analysis.* London: The Hogarth Press and the Institute of Psycho-Analysis.

Zeanah, C., Benoit, D. and Barton, M. (1986). *Working model of the child interview.* Unpublished interview. New Orleans: Tulane University.

ZERO-TO-THREE. (2005). *Diagnostic classification of mental health and developmental disorders of infancy and early childhood* (DC 0–3:R). Washington: DC: ZERO TO THREE Press.

Zeuthen, K. and Gammelgaard, J. (2010). Infantile sexuality: The concept, its history and place in contemporary psychoanalysis. *Scandinavian Psychoanalytic Review, 33*(1), 3–12.

Zuckerman, E. (1964). *The first hundred years of Wagner's Tristan.* New York: Columbia University Press.

# Index

Introductory Note
When the text is within a table, the number span is in **bold**.
For example – MIP (mother–infant psychoanalytic treatment): RCT comparison results **174, 175**
When the text is within a figure, the number span is in *italics*.
For example: ghosts and monsters *86, 87*

To find a certain case, please go to the entry "vignettes"